MW00756228

PREFACE

SINCE our first book, *Quinoa 365: The Everyday Superfood*, was released in early 2010, people have been sharing their quinoa stories with us, writing to tell us how quinoa is transforming their lives. Parents. Spouses. Whole families. Athletes. Weight-loss dieters. Vegetarians. Cancer survivors. Diabetics. Heart patients. People with food allergies. Those who are gluten-intolerant. Everyone seems to have a story about how they first learned about quinoa, how they're now eating it, what they love about quinoa and how it is revolutionizing their life.

Many of you wrote to share your experiences—"I've lost 15 pounds"... "I've now got energy to exercise"... "I don't feel the need to snack like I used to"... "Gluten-intolerance has prevented me from eating great-tasting foods for years. Now I can't believe I can even eat delicious chocolate cake!"... "I've improved my personal best triathlon time!" And we've heard funny stories too, such as, "The quinoa baking tasted so good my husband snatched it to take to poker night."

Today it seems quinoa is talked about everywhere. Television talk shows, radio, blogs, celebrities. Oprah recommends quinoa. Martha Stewart cooks with quinoa. Dr. Oz says to cleanse with quinoa. It is a common subject in books such as *The 150 Healthiest Foods on Earth: The Surprising, Unbiased Truth about What You Should Eat and Why*; *Food Synergy: Unleash Hundreds of Powerful Healing Food Combinations to Fight Disease and Live Well*; *Power Aging*; *101 Foods That Could Save Your Life!*; *Conscious Health: A Complete Guide to Wellness through Natural Means*; *What Your Doctor May Not Tell You about Diabetes*; and *Get Balanced: The Natural Way to Better Health with Superfoods*.

More than ever, people are being watchful of unwanted processing of and chemicals in their food, choosing to be consciously aware of everything they are putting into their mouths. Increasing numbers of people are keeping close track of their nutrition to ensure they're being calorie-smart and their bodies are getting the minerals and vitamins they need to stay healthy and prevent illness and disease. (With closer attention being paid to calories and nutritional content, we have added those values to each recipe in this book.)

The rising sales of quinoa have also brought attention to ensuring that nobody suffers any negative consequences from the increased demand. Sustainable, fair-trade growing programs now exist, and we have seen first-hand in Bolivia the positive results of quinoa farming. There, quinoa farming has given many farm families a sense of pride, allowing them to support each other as well as their communities.

Amid environmental concerns, quinoa has re-emerged as a practical alternative to other popular crops that can't be successfully grown in difficult conditions. It can be grown in adverse conditions with relatively little water, such as the high, rocky plateaus of Bolivia. Crops are rotated to maintain the integrity of the soil, and llamas are used to feed on quinoa stalks and further fertilize the soil.

So whether we consume quinoa for weight loss, gluten-intolerance, a vegetarian diet, allergy control, disease prevention, overall great health or any of its other numerous advantages, the positive outcomes of using this powerhouse superfood are extensive and far reaching. With even more recipes, we hope to bring the benefits of quinoa nutrition to your table and inspire you to find many delicious ways to revolutionize your health. As always, we're open to hearing your feedback, ideas and great stories of your quinoa adventures.

INTRODUCTION

Revolutionizing Health & Fitness with Quinoa

By Laurie A. Scanlin, Ph.D., & Claire Burnett, MS

QUINOA boasts the highest nutrition profile of all grains (because it's not a grain!) and is the fastest to cook, a prerequisite for almost everyone these days. Most important, whether nutritious food is eaten for boosting health, preventing illness, reaching top athletic performance or for pure pleasure, it should taste good. This book takes a step further into the full advantages of quinoa with recipes for delicious, easy-to-make dishes that nourish. Carolyn and Patricia combine quinoa's appealing taste, versatility and light texture with a variety of fresh vegetables, fruits, legumes, nuts, healthy oils and lean proteins in over 150 tasty recipes, all under 500 calories per serving.

Quinoa's long list of distinguishing traits means there are many benefits to incorporating it into any lifestyle. Dedicated athletes are using it pre and post workout, vegetarians eat it as a source of non-animal protein, those with celiac disease benefit from its being gluten-free, those looking to detoxify or lose weight eat it because of its antioxidants, rich fiber, lean protein and complex carbohydrates. Diabetics, heart patients, those healing from cancer and those who simply choose quinoa as a dietary staple for overall improved health all benefit from quinoa. There is no question quinoa has the power to help many on a large scale and to completely revolutionize what we eat.

Unlike most of today's highly refined crops that have been genetically engineered or selectively bred and monocropped, quinoa does not require this. It is naturally genetically complex. One advantage of its genetic complexity is its ability to withstand harsh climates, where other crops fail to grow at all. The extreme mountain terrain where quinoa thrives is as rugged and hardy as quinoa is—which translates into superior nutrition. And that nutritional powerhouse explains why quinoa started to gain attention and began to be exported from South America over thirty years ago.

Awareness of this superfood continues, and in 2011 alone, the market for quinoa rose 40 percent, as everyone from health-conscious consumers to athletes added quinoa to their diets.

QUINOA'S STRUCTURE

In order to better understand this superfood, it's helpful to know what quinoa *is* rather than what it is not. Although it looks like a cereal grain, quinoa is not a grain. True cereal grains, such as wheat, corn, barley and rice, are seeds of the single-leaf grass family (or monocotyledons). Quinoa is a seed of the double-leaf vegetable family (or dicotyledons). Specifically it is the seed of a broad-leaf plant in the family Chenopodiaceae, which also includes spinach and beets. Quinoa's difference from cereal grains is significant when it comes to superior nutrition and hypoallergenic proteins. Quinoa seeds consist of three basic parts: an outer pericarp, or bran layer; an internal perisperm, a mass of storage tissue that provides carbohydrates and energy; and a large embryo, or germ (the equivalent of an egg yolk). Quinoa germ is high in albumin protein. Similar to the way egg albumin whitens, during cooking the germ "sprouts" from the seed and becomes visible as a white spiral around each cooked seed. These three basic components give quinoa its distinguishing nutritional traits that fit the special dietary needs of so many consumers.

ULTRAMETABOLISM, DETOXIFICATION, VEGAN DIETS & WEIGHT LOSS

Listening to your body's needs, in combination with being educated about food, can go a long way in reaching an optimal body weight and maintaining energy balance. A fundamental step in weight loss is detoxification, eliminating foods that prevent weight loss (empty calories from sugars and refined grains that are stripped of vitamins and minerals, processed foods and foods that we tend to eat in excess). Removing foods from the diet even for a short time, such as favorite foods eaten too often, can detoxify the system and reboot the metabolism. Foods that make us feel bloated or sluggish (such as wheat- or soy-based foods that may be hard to digest or cause inflammation, saturated fat from rich meats and dairy, and fried foods) can negatively affect our metabolism and contribute to chronic health problems. The focus of detox is replacing foods that prevent weight loss with those that cleanse, renew energy and optimize the metabolism so it works as it was originally designed to.

Quinoa is on the list of foods to enjoy for ultrametabolism in Dr. Mark Hyman's series of *UltraMetabolism* books, and in his book *The Conscious Cook*, Tal Ronnen, who once prepared vegan meals for Oprah, makes it a top choice as part of a vegan cleanse. Quinoa is a good source of vegan protein, calcium, B vitamins and iron for renewed energy. It contains both types of dietary fiber: insoluble fiber that helps to curb appetite, and soluble fiber, prebiotic nutrients that fuel the healthy microflora in the intestinal tract, resulting in increased nutrient absorption and improved gut and immune health. High-protein diets have proven to be more effective in promoting weight loss than conventional high-carbohydrate, low-fat diets. The essential amino acid profile, digestibility and bioavailability of quinoa protein are noteworthy. Quinoa protein is the nutritional equivalent of whole milk protein, which is rare for a plant source of protein. For example, rice is limited in lysine, making its protein quality inferior, whereas quinoa has 65 percent more lysine than white rice and 56 percent more than brown rice. Quinoa can restart your metabolism to help you achieve your weight-loss goals and, as part of a sound diet, can improve your long-term health.

QUINOA & EXERCISE

There are many reasons to choose quinoa as an energy source, whether you are just beginning a workout routine or you are an elite competitor. Today, top athletes, from runners and swimmers to road cyclists and triathletes, are consuming quinoa as a daily staple or as a gluten-free option to wheat-based foods. Wheat-based foods such as pasta have been a traditional energy source for athletes, but many of today's top athletes are finding they perform better without wheat. Specifically, some are experiencing increased mental clarity, a reduced bloated or heavy feeling and fewer stomach problems. In people who are sensitive to gluten, the body's defenses end up attacking the nutrient-absorbing cells in the intestine, causing inflammation and a bloated feeling. In a vicious cycle, this inflammation contributes to a reduction in nutrient absorption and may lead to serious malnourishment. This is, of course, of heightened concern for athletes.

Gluten is not the only culprit to blame for inflammation in the intestinal tract and reduced nutrient absorption. Inflammation can be caused by food allergens, sensitivities to food or hard-to-digest food proteins. For those with a food allergy, milk and soy are among the top eight allergens, and some soy-based foods may contain inhibitors (such as trypsin) that actually block protein from being fully digested. Similarly, cereal grains contain anti-nutrients, which are known to impair nutrient absorption (which is why they are avoided in some diets, such as the paleo diet). As quinoa is the seed of a vegetable and not a cereal grain, it does not contain gluten proteins and so does not ignite an inflammatory response. Furthermore, although quinoa is primarily recognized for its balanced amino acid composition (rare for plant-based proteins), it contains proteins that are easy to digest.

Whether for everyday workouts or for bodybuilding or endurance athletics, adding quinoa to a sound diet aimed at avoiding foods that may increase inflammation and reduce nutrient absorption can be extremely effective in enhancing performance.

Exercise & Meal Timing: When to Eat Quinoa
Depending upon your workout goals, quinoa can be a key staple both before and after exercise.

Before your workout
Finding the right pre-exercise meal relies on timing, easy digestibility, balancing calorie intake and managing hunger. A pre-workout meal consumed three hours before competition or two hours before training has been found to work well. Insulin levels can spike an hour or so after eating, causing a dip in blood

sugar and leading to a hypoglycemic state known to athletes as "bonking." Proper meal timing combined with choosing foods with higher protein and healthy fat and a lower glycemic index is ideal. Foods with a glycemic index of 55 or lower (ranked on a scale of 1 to 100) help to stabilize blood sugar while providing slow-release energy to maintain a steady state through exercise. A cup (250 mL) of cooked quinoa has a glycemic index of 53. In addition, "glycemic load" is used to assess the quality of carbohydrates in a food (as indicated by its effect on blood sugar) as well as the quantity of carbohydrates per serving. A cup of cooked quinoa contains 25 grams of carbohydrates and a medium glycemic load of 13. The balance between the quality and quantity of carbohydrates in quinoa makes it an effective energy source that won't cause dramatic fluctuations in blood sugar and will provide consistent slow-release energy. This superior advantage of quinoa stems from the internal perisperm of the seed, which contains microscopic starch granules (fifty times smaller than potato starch!). Finally, a bowl of cooked quinoa is easy to digest before competition or training.

After your workout

The right post-exercise meal contains foods that promote quick recovery. Quinoa has four benefits that are critical to quick recovery after exercise.

Stimulates building and repairing muscle. Quinoa contains the branched-chain amino acids valine, leucine and isoleucine, which stimulate building and repairing muscle. One cup of cooked quinoa has 29 percent more branched-chain amino acids than 1 cup of cooked white rice, and 17 percent more than brown rice. Quinoa is a better choice to complement lean meats (also an excellent source of branched-chain amino acids) following an intense workout.

Prevents muscle and bone loss. Foods that contribute to a net blood alkalinity prevent muscle and bone loss. Quinoa's protein and mineral content give it a net alkaline enhancing effect, sparing bone and muscle loss.

Maintains muscle energy reserves. Starches and sugars maintain muscle glycogen, which is essential for high-level performance. A cup of cooked quinoa offers 30 grams of carbohydrates, both complex and simple, that replenish muscle glycogen stores.

Optimizes immune system function. Micronutrients, including antioxidants, vitamins, minerals and phytochemicals, all promote optimal immune-system functioning. The increased ability to fight off illness improves consistency of training and ultimate performance. Quinoa is a good source of vitamins and minerals (vitamins E, B_2, B_6, folic acid and biotin, calcium, phosphorus, magnesium, potassium, iron, copper, manganese and zinc). Quinoa also contains betalain pigments, which are phytochemicals with antioxidant and anti-inflammatory properties. In addition, quinoa germ contains histidine, an amino acid that plays a significant role in the growth and repair of tissues and is needed for the production of both red and white blood cells. Both types of blood cells are important to athletes in particular, because red blood cells carry oxygen to muscles and other tissues, and white blood cells boost immune health. Rice has previously been recognized as a natural source of histidine, but quinoa is a much better source, containing 57 percent more histidine than white rice and 45 percent more than brown rice.

Quinoa as it pertains to health and wellness fits perfectly with our core competence in quinoa research, food science and human nutrition, as well as our personal lifestyles dedicated to fitness. Try something different from the usual wheat pasta, corn or rice. We encourage you to consider protein-rich quinoa. Because this superfood is so mildly flavored and versatile, you'll find that these nutrient-rich, easy-to-make quinoa recipes will suit your taste and help you achieve your dietary goals whether for health, fitness or overall wellness.

QUINOA REVOLUTION

Quinoa is becoming increasingly popular as an everyday food on the dining tables of all kinds of modern families in a variety of cultural settings. No longer limited to a few similar recipes, it can be found in more than just basic breakfast cereals and side salads. In the last few years we have seen quinoa in everything from our lunch salads, dinner entrées, double-layer cakes, pasta, muffins, soups, bakery bread and smoothies—even our shampoo. "Made with quinoa" is a phrase we are seeing more often as this ancient grain becomes mainstream.

This tiny seed, more than five thousand years old, was once hidden away in the high Andes Mountains of South America, but today it is being included in an increasing number of North American meals, not only pushing aside rice and couscous but sometimes even replacing meat. In 2011, imports of quinoa to the United States increased by an astonishing 39 percent from the previous year. This popularity is the result both of quinoa's versatility in cooking and of the incredible health properties of this superfood.

As a superfood, quinoa boasts an array of exceptional properties even beyond a stellar nutritional profile. For starters, it is vegetarian-friendly, gluten-free and a complete protein. It can help prevent disease, encourage the body to heal and provide vitamins and minerals that nourish. While other superfoods exist, even some with tremendous qualities that may seem comparable, none offers a similar nutritional profile. As well, quinoa is by far the most versatile. It can be used in almost any dish, whereas other superfoods may find a place in only a select number of recipes. Not all superfoods are as adaptable to everyday menus and lifestyles.

VITAMIN & MINERAL CONTENT

Quinoa is a good source of minerals such as iron, phosphorus, magnesium, calcium and potassium. It is also rich in vitamins such as vitamin E, riboflavin and folic acid.

1 cup (185 g) All cooked	CALORIES (KCAL)	FAT	PROTEIN	CARBOHYDRATES	FIBER	MINERALS (MG)						VITAMINS						
						CALCIUM	IRON	MAGNESIUM	PHOSPHORUS	POTASSIUM	SODIUM	THIAMINE B_1 (MG)	RIBOFLAVIN B_2 (MG)	NIACIN B_3 (MG)	VITAMIN B_6 (MG)	FOLATE (MCG)	VITAMIN A (IU)	VITAMIN E (MG)
QUINOA	222	3.6	8.1	3.9	5.2	31	2.8	118	281	318	13	0.2	0.2	0.76	0.23	78	9	1.17
AMARANTH	189	2.92	7	35	3.9	87	3.89	120	274	250	11	0.03	0.04	0.44	0.21	41	0	0.3
BARLEY, PEARLED	228	0.81	4	52	7	20	2.5	41	100	172	6	0.15	0.12	3.82	0.21	30	13	0.02
CHIA SEEDS, DRIED	899	56.9	30.6	78	64	1167	14	620	1591	753	30	1.1	0.3	16.3	—	—	100	0.9
COUSCOUS	207	0.3	7	43	2.6	15	0.7	15	41	107	9	0.12	0.05	1.82	0.09	28	0	0.24
ROLLED OATS	131	2.81	4.7	22	3.1	17	1.66	50	142	130	7	0.14	0.03	0.42	0.01	11	0	15
RICE, BROWN LONG GRAIN	205	1.7	4.8	42	3.3	18	0.78	80	154	80	9	0.18	0.05	2.83	0.27	7	0	0.06
RICE, WHITE LONG GRAIN	240	0.52	4.9	52	0.7	18	2.22	22	80	65	2	0.30	0.02	2.73	0.17	179	0	0.07
TEFF	187	1.2	7.2	37	5.2	91	3.8	92	222	198	15	0.34	0.06	1.68	0.18	33	4	—
WHITE POTATO	174	0.28	3.9	39	3.9	18	1.18	50	139	1006	13	0.09	0.08	2.83	0.39	70	18	0.07

USDA National Nutrient Database for Standard Reference, 2011

VEGETARIAN-FRIENDLY

An ideal non-animal protein source for vegetarians, 1 cup (250 mL) of cooked quinoa provides approximately the same amount of protein as a whole egg. Plus, quinoa's versatility in the kitchen means that vegetarians can find many creative ways to enjoy this protein-rich food.

GLUTEN-FREE

Since quinoa is not a grain, it is not related to wheat and does not contain gluten. For the increasing number of people who are affected by wheat-related allergies, celiac disease, colitis or Crohn's disease, quinoa is an ideal food to eat every day. Gluten has also been thought to be a source of problems for children with autism and attention deficit hyperactivity disorder (ADHD). Quinoa is a reasonable solution for a gluten-restricted diet.

COMPLETE PROTEIN

Quinoa is a complete protein—in other words, it contains all eight essential amino acids. Nothing else needs to be combined with quinoa in order for the body to digest and efficiently use quinoa's energy, vitamins and minerals. Hence, quinoa's high digestibility and protein content allow the muscles to effectively make use of available protein and quickly rebuild lean muscle.

WEIGHT LOSS, HEALTH & FITNESS

Quinoa can assist with weight loss. A complex carbohydrate, quinoa does not quickly convert sugars to fats, thus providing an effective long-term energy source. Lower glycemic index foods such as quinoa take longer to digest and as a result do not promote the spike of insulin levels in the blood that triggers the body to store fat. The complete chemistry was not likely known by the ancient Incas, who worshipped quinoa, but we now know that quinoa can help make us healthy, make us strong and help us reach and maintain personal health and nutritional goals.

BUYING QUINOA

Since the release of *Quinoa 365: The Everyday Superfood* in 2010, quinoa has become more readily available in most major supermarkets in North America. It is no longer restricted to health-food stores or specialty or organic aisles in the grocery store. It can usually be found in the same aisle as rice or couscous, and the growing excitement over this superfood means it can often be found featured on display. It can be purchased in bulk, in boxes or in bags, in a variety of brands. Quinoa seeds are available in white (also known as golden), red and black and are also sold as flakes and flour. Quinoa is often a featured ingredient in many processed foods such as commercial breads, pastas and crackers and even in household cleaning products and soaps.

Increasing demand has meant the cost of quinoa has risen slightly. In 2010 it was $3 to $4 a pound ($6 to $8/kg), and as of the time of writing this book it is almost one dollar more. Yet we now benefit from more brands than ever before, better selection and increased availability of quinoa in stores. Also worth considering is that quinoa expands in cooking to three times or more its original volume, so you are getting more for your money than you would with similar foods that only double in volume at best. Therefore, with quinoa, the nutrition you get for your dollar is more than you would get from, say, rice or pasta. Remember that global food prices are on the rise in general, so quinoa is not alone. Even the cost of rice will likely continue to rise.

USING QUINOA

Quinoa is incredibly versatile in the kitchen. Cooked, it makes a great key ingredient in soups, salads, entrées, baked goods, desserts, breakfast cereal and even baby food. Used raw, quinoa seeds can be ground or sprouted and used in salads, sandwiches or breakfast smoothies, making it especially popular with people who follow a raw-food diet.

Quinoa flour is a smart alternative to many flours that contain gluten or have inferior nutritional profiles. It can be used to improve moistness and can be used alongside other flours. A blend of quinoa flour (or cooked seeds) and a wheat flour, for example, will absorb and hold liquid. This is especially useful in baked goods, where the increased moisture helps to produce a fluffy, soft texture. Various combinations of quinoa flour with other flours such as rice, tapioca, almond, coconut and potato starch allow you to create impressive recipes that meet your specific nutritional requirements and invent new fusions of delightfully complex flavors. Quinoa's easily adaptable flavor is also what adds to its versatility. It is complemented by an endless range of flavors, from vegetables, fruits and meats to simple foods such as butter or toasted ingredients. For example, toasted quinoa flour has an incredible affinity with butter in baked shortbread.

Quinoa seeds and flour can also be used as a thickener. In soups, quinoa seeds added whole to the stock or cooked and then puréed with the stock produce a thick soup that could be mistaken for a heavy cream soup in texture, and without the added fat and calories. Quinoa seeds can also improve the texture of otherwise ordinary dishes, adding dimension and character. See page 3 for basic recipes for using quinoa as a thickener. Good examples of recipes that use it as a thickener include Chipotle Corn Chowder (page 90) and Simple Chicken Pot Pie Stew (page 109).

Quinoa flakes are widely available and can be used as a breakfast cereal, a coating for meats and vegetables, and in baking or as a dessert ingredient. Basic instructions for cooking quinoa flakes are on page 4. Examples of flake recipes are Thai Chicken Fingers (page 78) and Lemon Ginger Blueberry Crisp (page 200).

BABY QUINOA

Less common than regular quinoa but growing in popularity is baby quinoa. Also known as kaniwa or kañawa, baby quinoa is an even smaller seed closely related to quinoa. In South America it grows around Lake Titicaca, in both Peru and Bolivia. Baby quinoa contains no saponin, a break for those who are sensitive to any bitter saponin flavor and dedicated to rinsing their quinoa. This tiny red seed tastes milder and sweeter than regular quinoa, but contains even more protein and fiber. It is great sprouted or cooked together with regular white quinoa. Baby quinoa and regular quinoa cook just the same, 2 cups (500 mL) of water to 1 cup (250 mL) of seeds.

Rinsing Quinoa

Some people prefer to rinse quinoa seeds before cooking. This may help eliminate any bitter flavor that might remain on the quinoa. A slightly bitter taste may occasionally persist, however. The bitterness is caused by saponin, the protective coating of the quinoa seed that works as a natural insecticide and pesticide. Most packaged quinoa has been repeatedly rinsed during processing and does not require further rinsing. However, if you purchase quinoa in bulk, or direct from growers, it may require some rinsing. If you prefer to rinse your quinoa before cooking, see page 6 for complete instructions.

Cooking Quinoa

People new to cooking quinoa often ask us what recipe they should begin with. First recipes usually include simple salad dishes and breakfasts such as Spiced Carrot & Raisin Cereal (page 23) and Greek Quinoa Salad (page 58). But there are really no overly complicated quinoa dishes! The recipes in this book will show you how easy it is to cook with quinoa. We encourage cooks of all levels to be inspired and find even more ways to incorporate quinoa into their daily meals.

Quinoa may more than triple its original volume when cooked. Cooking proportions are the same as those for rice, 2 cups (500 mL) of water for every 1 cup (250 mL) of quinoa seeds. It can be cooked in a variety of liquids, from water to soup stock, fruit juices, various types of milk and more. Our simple method for cooking quinoa in water can be found on page 5. Methods for cooking quinoa in other liquids can be found on pages 7 to 9. Cooked quinoa can be conveniently stored in the refrigerator for up to five days and used in many different and easy meals during the week.

Quinoa can be cooked on the stovetop, in a rice cooker or in a slow cooker. Since quinoa can more than triple in volume when cooked, be sure you use exactly the amount of liquid specified in the recipe you are using. Do not guess! Many people write us to tell us their quinoa didn't cook completely, and it's usually because they didn't add enough liquid. Ratios of uncooked quinoa to water and cooked yields can be found on page 5.

When cooking quinoa with oils, it's best not to use unrefined oils that have a low smoke point (the temperature at which they begin to break down). Oils such as extra virgin olive oil, flaxseed, hemp and walnut are better used in marinades or salads, because the heat of cooking degrades their nutrients and eliminates their essential fatty acids, such as omega-3s, that are so beneficial in the first place.

SUSTAINABILITY & FAIR TRADE

Although grown in various locations around the world, quinoa is primarily produced where it originated, in South America, mainly in Bolivia, Peru and Ecuador. The increasing global demand for quinoa means that these countries are once again producing quinoa much like their ancestors did more than five thousand years ago—and because of it, are able to improve their standard of living.

More and more consumers today want to understand where their food comes from and how it is grown, and they want reassurance that foods are grown in healthy and sustainable environments in which the growers are treated well and trading is fair. Quinoa is no exception. Not only is quinoa healthful and enriching

A NOTE ON NUTRITIONAL VALUES

Nutritional values in this book are always based on the first option provided in the recipe. For instance, if the ingredient option is "vegetable or chicken stock," the nutritional values provided are based on vegetable stock. Also, optional ingredients are not included in the nutritional values. For lower-cholesterol diets, we have provided reduced-cholesterol options for eggs in the recipes along with the normal egg count. For example, a recipe may call for "2 large eggs + 4 large egg whites (or 4 eggs total)," meaning that if you are not on a low-cholesterol diet, you may simply use 4 whole eggs.

for those who eat it, but it is also beginning to have a positive impact on the people who grow it, their communities and the overall environment where it grows.

Quinoa-farming communities throughout South America are continuing to improve their practices for sustainability as they now have increased access to technology and training. In 2011, of all the quinoa grown in Bolivia, Peru and Ecuador, 42 percent was exported to other countries such as the United States and Canada, and 58 percent was consumed locally. This means that many South American farm communities are consuming even more quinoa than they were before, as what was once viewed as a peasant food is now being valued because of its desirability and demand in the North American marketplace, and the world.

In this cookbook you will find simple recipe ideas for quick meal preparation such as breakfasts and salads, along with family meals and ideas for more formal settings. With each recipe we have provided nutritional breakdowns that will help you meet the requirements of your medical, health or fitness goals. Whatever your family's tastes or your personal health demands, we are confident you'll find something to enjoy.

NEED GLUTEN-FREE?

All the recipes in this book can be made gluten-free. If you require your recipes to be gluten-free, always make sure that all the ingredients you use are consistently gluten-free. Each region will have different products available that meet gluten-free standards, including products such as Worcestershire sauce, tamari, oats, buns, sour cream and more.

You Asked Us!

We receive many questions about quinoa, from cooking tips to nutrition. Here are some of the most commonly asked questions and their answers.

Where can I buy quinoa?

You should be able to find quinoa in most major supermarkets across North America. It is usually found near the rice or couscous. Different colors (red, white, black) and types (flakes, flour, seeds) are occasionally kept in the specialty section of the grocery store. If you can't find it, be sure to ask because it may be hiding. Quinoa can also be found in most natural food stores and bulk food stores. It is generally easier to find than you might think.

I have just started using quinoa. What type of recipe should I start with?

The best choice for starting out cooking with quinoa is to use quinoa seeds (rather than flakes or flour). Quinoa seeds are generally the least expensive and will introduce you to the flavor of quinoa. The seeds have the longest shelf life and have the best nutrition, as they have not been processed. The type of recipe to start with is truly up to you, but you will find that soups and stews are easy, along with basic breakfasts and salads. Most people start by using cooked quinoa in recipes where they have traditionally used rice. Quinoa puffs or quinoa sprouts are good options as introductions to quinoa, as their flavor is very mild. Many people find that quinoa flour has a stronger flavor, so we suggest trying it after you have tried a few of the other forms first.

Should you always eat quinoa cooked? Are there any advantages to eating it uncooked?

If you are consuming uncooked quinoa seeds, you can certainly benefit from all of the nutrients, provided that the seeds are cracked or partially ground. This is because the uncooked seed has a shell, or pericarp, that protects it. (During cooking, this shell will soften and break open.) If this shell is still intact when you swallow it, the quinoa seed will simply pass through your body without being digested and without providing you with any of its fabulous nutritional benefits. (The same applies to flaxseeds.) Therefore, we recommend slightly grinding or soaking the seeds before you consume them uncooked.

When you add quinoa to a recipe, should you cook it first?
Not necessarily. If the recipe has sufficient liquid and cooking time, such as chili, then you would add raw (uncooked) quinoa. If the dish requires the quinoa to be cooked separately first, the recipes in this book will tell you so in the instructions.

I already have cooked quinoa in the refrigerator and want to use it in my recipe. How do I know how much cooked quinoa to use in place of the uncooked amount the recipe calls for?
Refer to the cooked yields chart (table 2 on page 5). For instance, if the recipe calls for ⅔ cup (150 mL) uncooked quinoa, that would produce approximately 2 cups (500 mL) of cooked quinoa. Keep in mind, however, that many recipes in this book require the quinoa to be uncooked at first, as it will cook along with the rest of the dish. Timing can also be an important factor in many recipes. For instance, in preparing a soup, you would add *uncooked* quinoa much earlier in the method than you would add *cooked* quinoa. Also, sometimes cooking times of quinoa vary and can be critical in recipe preparation. Some recipes require the quinoa to be cooked extremely fluffy, almost overcooked. Plump or very fluffy quinoa is essential, for example, in purées, soups, baking, puddings, baby foods and sauces. If the quinoa is not cooked enough, you will end up with a purée full of tiny, crunchy seeds rather than a smooth, flawless end result.

Quinoa seeds can sometimes taste bitter. How can I fix this?
If you are noticing bitterness, thoroughly rinse your quinoa before you cook it. For complete instructions, see page 6. Also, if you are

extremely sensitive to bitterness caused by the saponin of regular quinoa, you may want to try baby quinoa instead. It is saponin-free. Learn more on page xxiii.

Do I have to rinse quinoa seeds?

No, quinoa seeds do not require rinsing. Any saponin that remains on the seeds has no negative effects on the body. In fact, we do not rinse our quinoa at all. To rinse or not to rinse depends on how sensitive you are to the bitterness. Usually, most traces of bitterness are already rinsed off after the seeds are cultivated and processed or washed. Most of the quinoa that is processed and in the market today requires minimal rinsing, if any (it's already been rinsed so much). If you prefer to rinse, instructions are on page 6. If you are extremely sensitive to bitterness caused by the saponin of regular quinoa, you may want to try "baby quinoa" instead. Learn more on page xxiii.

I like the flavor of cooked quinoa but my kids do not like it. How can I get them to eat it?

Some people don't like the slight bitter flavor in some quinoa, so try rinsing your quinoa thoroughly before cooking with it. For complete instructions, see page 6. Soups, stews , puddings and especially recipes where quinoa is puréed are good ways to introduce quinoa to children. Try the Individual Mighty Meat Loaves on page 143 and Creamy Banana Breakfast Cereal on page 25.

I tried your recipe for sprouting quinoa but nothing happened. Why not?

Occasionally, quinoa seeds just won't sprout. This may be because they have not been soaked long enough, possibly they are old or because of the way they have been handled. We suggest you try again, ensuring all steps are followed closely, or buy a different brand or purchase seeds from a different store.

I cooked the quinoa according to your instructions, but there was still some water left in the bottom of the pot and the quinoa looked partially cooked. What did I do wrong?

Occasionally, quinoa can sometimes cook that way. If the water is still warm, just cover the saucepan and let it sit for another 5 to 10 minutes. If the saucepan has cooled, return it to the burner and bring it to a boil. Then turn the heat off, cover and leave it for another 5 minutes. Check to see if the water has absorbed. If water still remains, replace the cover again and the quinoa should absorb the remaining water.

What is the quickest way to cool cooked quinoa for something like a salad?

Place the saucepan or bowl of hot or warm quinoa in the sink or in a larger bowl with water and ice. It will cool within about 15 minutes. Another option is to spread the cooked quinoa on a baking sheet. This is useful when you are cooking large amounts of quinoa. You can also place the saucepan in the freezer briefly.

I made one of your salad recipes and it tasted great, but I noticed after an hour it tasted as though there was hardly any dressing. What happened?

Most likely the quinoa that you used was still warm. Freshly cooked quinoa, even when only slightly warm, will continue to absorb liquid, including salad dressing. To prevent this, ensure that your cooked quinoa cools before you add sauces or dressings.

The salad I made was great the first day but lost some flavor by the second day. How can I fix it?

If you cooled the quinoa completely before making the salad, it is probably just a matter of making some more dressing. Keep in mind that our recipes are designed to have the most flavor without unnecessary additional calories.

I overcooked my quinoa. What can I do with it?

Don't toss it out! Overcooked or extra-fluffy quinoa is perfect for many recipes. It works great in this book's blender recipes, added to smoothies or cake batters, in scrambled eggs or added to meat loaves, burgers, breakfast cereals or salads during the week. It is fantastic blended into a thick and creamy texture, where it is useful in baby foods, as a soup thickener or as a custard or pudding dessert. Some recipes that can use overcooked quinoa are the Baked Roasted Red Pepper Dip on page 71, Blackberry Brûlée on page 193, and Chocolate Hazelnut Cream on page 196. Examples of recipes that require extra-fluffy cooked quinoa are Choco-late Cream Mini Cupcakes with Avocado Icing on page 179 and Healthy Baked Quinoa Falafels on page 138.

Can I freeze leftover cooked quinoa or cook it and then freeze it for future meals?

Yes, you can. We suggest measuring the cooked quinoa into reseal-able freezer bags in amounts you would normally use. For best freshness and flavor, we recommend quinoa be frozen for no more than one month.

I don't have the pan size called for in the recipe. Can I use another pan size?

Unless alternative pan sizes are given in the recipe, we don't recommend changing pan sizes. Different pan sizes may dramatically affect the results of your baking. This is especially true in recipes that contain little or no gluten. If you must use a different-sized pan, carefully monitor your baking and adjust cooking times as needed to ensure it cooks properly, as using a different pan size affects rising, and may result in underbaking or overbaking a recipe.

Does quinoa flour have the same nutritional benefits as quinoa seeds?

Yes, quinoa flour has the same nutritional breakdown as regular white quinoa. Nutrition labels on packaged quinoa do not include much of the vitamin and mineral values, so refer to the complete nutritional breakdown on page xx. Keep in mind that over time, flours of all kinds lose nutritional value because they are not whole. Quinoa *seeds*, being whole, retain their nutrients and have a much longer shelf life.

You often use cooked quinoa seeds instead of flour in baking. Can I replace regular flour with cooked quinoa seeds in other recipes?

We do not have a simple formula for using cooked quinoa in baking. It is difficult to find a consistent formula for replacing flour with cooked quinoa because baking chemistry is so recipe-specific. If you are determined to figure it out, the best way is through trial and error for each recipe—as tiresome as that may be.

Quinoa flour can be expensive. Are there any alternatives?

You can certainly grind your own flour to reduce the cost of buying it. We recommend that you test this first in whatever appliance you are using to grind, as different appliances will provide coarse or fine flours. Consider the desired texture when using home-ground flour in recipes, as it may especially affect baking results. Also, some grinding methods can be problematic—for instance, we do not recommend using a standard wheat-flour grinder, because the natural oil in quinoa seeds may permanently damage the grinder. Instructions for how to best grind your own flour can be found on page 3.

If you are looking for quinoa flour at a better price, try to find stores that sell it in bulk and possibly offer it cheaper. If you are not on a gluten-restricted diet, you may also bake with half quinoa flour and half whole wheat or all-purpose flour.

I have purchased both white and red quinoa. Do I cook them both in the same manner and can they be used interchangeably?

You can certainly cook both the white (golden) quinoa and the red quinoa using the same method. Some people prefer to cook red quinoa slightly longer, with a bit more water, to soften the seeds even further. Depending on the recipe, and how the quinoa is to be used, you may choose to cook one color rather than the other. The only difference after cooking is that red quinoa has a slightly different texture, similar to that of wild rice. Deciding whether to use red or white often depends on your personal preference. For example, if you wish to accent a particular dish with color, you may opt for red or black quinoa. If you plan to serve the dish to fussy eaters such as children, you may choose white quinoa.

When I cooked colored quinoa, there was some water left in the bottom of the pot. What should I do?

Sometimes when you cook black or red quinoa, you may find that not all the water in the saucepan has absorbed at the end of the recommended cooking time. If the quinoa has cooked to the desired level, you can drain the water off. If you want to cook the quinoa a little more, while it is still warm simply leave the lid on for 5 more minutes. The quinoa will continue to absorb the remaining water and expand.

What types of recipes work best with black quinoa?

Black quinoa is much the same as white and red quinoa when it comes to taste and flavor. The texture of black quinoa is slightly different from that of white quinoa—it is similar to the texture of wild rice. Choosing a recipe to use with black quinoa is mostly a personal preference. Some people use black quinoa when they want dishes to look different or to add some drama to a dish. It's really up to you when you use black quinoa instead of the other color varieties. Experiment and have fun!

Is it possible, or practical, to cook quinoa in a microwave oven?

Of all the ways to cook quinoa, we don't recommend cooking it in a microwave oven. We've tested cooking it this way, and it just doesn't turn out well or consistently enough. However, feel free to experiment with cooking quinoa in your microwave oven; you may find that with a certain cooking time, power level and amount of water, it works in your microwave.

Reheating quinoa in a microwave is a personal preference. You may even discover that reheating quinoa leftovers is completely unnecessary. Many cooked quinoa dishes do not require reheating and are delicious for lunches. Quinoa salads are a great option to carry with you and eat during your day.

Keep in mind that microwave ovens are suspected of contributing to ill health, as they significantly deplete or modify nutrients in food and are said to create cancer-causing free radicals.

Can you cook quinoa in a rice cooker?

Absolutely! Simply follow the manufacturer's instructions for cooking white rice. However, since quinoa triples or more in volume as it cooks (whereas rice only doubles), make sure there's enough room in your cooker.

Is quinoa good for those with gluten-intolerance?

Yes! Quinoa does not contain gluten. Combined with other gluten-free ingredients, you can make some fantastic gluten-free meals. Every recipe in this book can be made gluten-free. Readers are constantly telling us how these recipes have improved their quality of life and allow them to enjoy their food more than ever before. In some cases those affected by gluten-intolerance have previously felt restricted to less flavorful foods, and have not been able to eat delicious foods for a long time. We have had many people tell us that eating quinoa has put pleasure back into their daily gluten-free menus. If you want extra tips and information, see pages xiii–xviii, where quinoa scientist Laurie Scanlin outlines some of the key benefits of quinoa and reasons to avoid gluten.

I am gluten-intolerant, so if one of your recipes calls for regular all-purpose or whole wheat flour, can I use a gluten-free substitute?

Yes. Many of our recipes work with a variety of gluten-free flours and blends. One type or several types are often used together to achieve a desired result, such as ability to rise, bond and stick together, particular texture and so on. However, this is not stated in each recipe because whether you use all-purpose gluten-free or brown rice flour—or any of the others—may change the flavor and overall outcome of the dish. So experiment with your preferred replacement flour and see how you like the flavor and final result.

I am a vegetarian. Can I benefit from eating quinoa?

Vegetarians can definitely benefit from eating quinoa. Quinoa is a terrific non-animal protein source and provides all eight essential amino acids. Highly digestible and extremely versatile, quinoa allows vegetarians to increase their meal options with healthful nutrients.

Can I eat quinoa if I am on diet?

Yes! Quinoa is a complex carbohydrate, so it provides energy throughout the day, digesting slowly and not causing insulin levels to spike, which is believed to cause fat storage in the body. In the popular points-based weight-loss programs, a serving of 1 cup (250 mL) of cooked quinoa is equal to 3 points. If you want extra tips and information, see pages xiii–xviii, where quinoa scientist Laurie Scanlin outlines some of the key reasons quinoa makes an ideal food for dieting, health and fitness.

Is quinoa good for diabetics?

Quinoa is a great food for diabetics. It has a low glycemic index and is a complex carbohydrate, so sugars digest slowly, maintaining proper blood sugar levels. The complete nutrition of quinoa will also provide many of your daily vitamins and minerals. Ensure you ask your doctor any questions you have about maintaining proper blood sugar levels. If you want extra tips and information, see pages xiii–xviii, where quinoa scientist Laurie Scanlin outlines some of the key reasons quinoa makes an ideal food for dieting, health and fitness.

*I'm on a raw-food diet. How can I still benefit from
eating quinoa?*

You can still enjoy quinoa if you eat raw foods. One option is
sprouted quinoa and another is raw, cracked quinoa or quinoa
soaked for a short period of time. Sprouted and raw quinoa each
contain similar nutrition to cooked quinoa seeds. Quinoa sprouts
can be used in shakes and smoothies, salads and sandwiches.
(See the quinoa sprout recipe on pages 10 and 11 and recipes that
use sprouts such as Carrot & Raisin Sprout Salad on page 52 and
Apple Cabbage Sprout Salad on page 46.) (For raw-food recipes, do
not toast nuts.) Other alternatives include cracking the raw seeds
(see the basic method for cracked quinoa on page 11), grinding
them or cooking the seeds for only a few quick minutes. Simply
cook the quinoa just long enough to split the outer pericarp (shell),
quickly halt the cooking process and cool the quinoa. Then it is
ready to add to your meals and recipes.

*How does quinoa compare with products that are "enriched"
with the same minerals and vitamins?*

When products are "enriched," it means that minerals or vitamins
are added during the product's processing and either are not natural to the product or were depleted during processing. Quinoa is a
complete protein (it contains all eight essential amino acids) and
is naturally chock-full of vitamins and minerals—meaning nothing needs to be added! It is simply one of nature's perfectly created
nutrient-rich foods.

Can quinoa be grown in North America?

Quinoa prefers a growing climate that is dry, and it grows best
where it originated, in South America. Some farmers do grow it in
North America, and some do so quite successfully, but not without
tackling challenges caused by the differences in climate. There
are several commercial growers in Canada and the United States;
however, the majority of quinoa comes from South America, where
it has been cultivated since the 1500s. Today it is best grown in
fair-trade, sustainable programs.

EASY QUINOA
BASICS

EASY QUINOA BASICS

WHETHER you're just starting to cook with quinoa or are experienced with quinoa in the kitchen, this chapter will provide you with a quick reference to all of the quinoa basics—everything from how to use the flour, how to use flakes, different cooking methods, grinding your own flour, sprouting quinoa, to how to cook quinoa in various liquids (which can sometimes be tricky). With plenty of simple solutions, best practices and tips, we've got everything to get you started cooking quinoa and on your way to becoming a polished pro. Soon your friends and family will be asking you for quinoa advice.

THICKENING LIQUIDS WITH QUINOA FLOUR

Quinoa flour is a great option for thickening liquids. It adds a hint of nutty flavor to your dish and holds up well to cooking and freezing. It may separate ever so slightly after sitting in the refrigerator for a few days, but this is solved with a quick stir.

Soup or stew

- Whisk in 2 Tbsp (30 mL) flour for every 1 cup (250 mL) liquid.

Gravy, cheese sauce or pudding

- Whisk in 3 Tbsp (45 mL) flour for every 1 cup (250 mL) liquid.

Cold liquid: To thicken a cold liquid, whisk in the flour until evenly dispersed. Bring the liquid to a boil. Reduce to medium heat and simmer for approximately 3 minutes, stirring constantly until thickened.

Hot liquid: To thicken a hot liquid (which may or may not also contain solids such as meat and vegetables), in a small bowl, whisk the flour into an equal amount of cold liquid (such as water, stock or wine). Stir the mixture into the hot liquid and simmer for approximately 3 minutes, stirring constantly until thickened.

MAKING QUINOA FLOUR

You can easily make your own quinoa flour using a household coffee grinder. If you don't mind a coarser, more rustic grind of flour, this is the best method we've found so far. Use a coffee grinder or mill to grind ¼ cup (60 mL) of quinoa seeds at a time. This type of grinding will result in a consistency slightly smaller than cornmeal. This size of grind is best used in a soup or stew, as a thickener or in any recipe where the ground seeds are able to absorb liquid. Be cautious when using it in baking, as it may make recipes such as cookies or pastry a bit crunchy. We do not suggest using a traditional flour mill to grind quinoa, as the natural oils in the quinoa may permanently damage your expensive grinder.

QUINOA FLAKES

Quinoa flakes are very quick to hydrate and are generally used for breakfast cereals, for baking and as a batter or coating for poultry, fish and other meats. Flakes can also be used as a thickener in a soup or stew or ground into a flour. Flakes may have a bit more nutty flavor to them than seeds, but the taste can complement other flavors quite nicely. If you are adding dried fruit to your recipe, add a couple more tablespoons of boiling water so there is enough liquid available to be absorbed by both the fruit and the quinoa.

BASIC QUINOA FLAKES

½ cup (125 mL) water

¼ cup (60 mL) quinoa flakes

Bring the water to a boil in a small saucepan (or appropriate-sized saucepan if you're making a larger amount). Stir in the flakes and reduce to medium heat. Continue to stir for 2 to 3 minutes, until the flakes have thickened and are tender.

PER SERVING: Energy 110 calories; Protein 4 g; Carbohydrates 21 g; Dietary Fiber 2 g; Fat 2 g; Sugar 0 g; Cholesterol 0 mg; Sodium 260 mg

QUICK & EASY QUINOA FLAKES

No saucepan required! This method is great if you want a quick way to prepare flakes at home, at work or any time you want a portable meal. Perfect for when you go camping!

⅓ cup (75 mL) quinoa flakes

½ cup (125 mL) boiling water

Place the quinoa flakes in a bowl. Pour the boiling water over the flakes. Stir quickly and cover with a plate or piece of foil. Let sit for 8 minutes without removing the cover. Fully cooked quinoa flakes should be tender.

PER SERVING: Energy 140 calories; Protein 5 g; Carbohydrates 28 g; Dietary Fiber 2 g; Fat 2 g; Sugar 0 g; Cholesterol 0 mg; Sodium 340 mg

COOKING QUINOA (SEEDS)
Simmer method

Generally, quinoa cooks in water at a ratio of 2:1, that is, 2 cups (500 mL) of water for every 1 cup (250 mL) of quinoa. Combine the water and quinoa in an appropriate-sized saucepan (for amounts, see table 2 below). Bring to a boil. Reduce heat to a simmer, cover and cook for 15 minutes. Check to see if the quinoa is tender. The quinoa is cooked when the center of the seed is no longer white and is translucent. If the quinoa still has a distinctly white center or if water remains in the bottom of the saucepan (when cooking any color), cover the saucepan and allow the quinoa to sit, off the heat, for 5 more minutes or until all the remaining liquid has been absorbed. Remove the lid and fluff with a fork.

TABLE 2: Amounts to Use for Cooking

SERVING	COOKED YIELD (APPROXIMATELY)	AMOUNT OF UNCOOKED QUINOA & WATER	
		QUINOA	WATER
1	½ cup (125 mL)	2 Tbsp + 2 tsp (40 mL)	⅓ cup (75 mL)
2	1 cup (250 mL)	⅓ cup (75 mL)	⅔ cup (150 mL)
3	1½ cups (375 mL)	½ cup (125 mL)	1 cup (250 mL)
4	2 cups (500 mL)	⅔ cup (150 mL)	1⅓ cups (325 mL)
6	3 cups (750 mL)	1 cup (250 mL)	2 cups (500 mL)

TOASTING QUINOA SEEDS OR FLOUR

Toasting quinoa releases and deepens its flavor, giving it a mild, fragrant aroma that adds another dimension to any dish. (If you are sensitive to any bitter flavor quinoa sometimes has, toasting the seeds first can help to mellow any bitterness.) This technique can be used in almost any recipe in which you might want a toasted flavor. There are two basic methods for toasting quinoa.

Oven method

Preheat the oven to 350°F (180°C). Place the seeds or flour on a baking sheet and bake for 5 to 7 minutes, until fragrant and you smell a "toasted" aroma. Watch closely as it can burn quickly. Toasted flour will be light golden brown, but seeds will not change color much, even when completely toasted.

Stovetop method

Place the quinoa seeds or flour in a large saucepan on medium heat. Stir for 3 to 5 minutes, until fragrant and you smell a "toasted" aroma. Watch closely as both seeds and flour will not change color much and can burn quickly.

RINSING QUINOA

Although generally unnecessary, some people prefer to rinse quinoa before using it. This will remove any remaining bitter flavor that is sometimes present. This bitter taste comes from saponin, a natural protective coating on the seed. Most of this bitterness is removed during commercial processing, when the seeds are thoroughly washed. Still, if you prefer to rinse, these are some of the best methods.

Strainer method

Rinse the quinoa in a fine-mesh strainer under running water or immerse the quinoa in water while in the strainer and use your hand to swish the quinoa around, then rinse. Continue immersing and rinsing until you've satisfied yourself that the bitter flavor is gone.

Soak-and-rinse method

Rinse the quinoa in a fine-mesh strainer under running water. Place the quinoa in a glass bowl or jar, cover with water and put in the refrigerator for at least 1 hour or overnight. (Be sure to use glass. Plastic can harbor micro-organisms that affect sprouting; metal can affect chemistry.) Remove from the refrigerator and rub the quinoa seeds together in the water. Rinse under running water in the mesh strainer once more. (Note: If your seeds are left overnight to soak, there is a chance that they may sprout slightly. However, small sprouts should not affect your cooking too much. In fact, your living quinoa sprouts are even more nutritious than you may have expected!)

Stocking method

Place the quinoa in a new piece of pantyhose or a knee-high stocking and tie the open end securely. Immerse in a bowl of water and soak for 5 to 20 minutes—the shorter time if you're not as concerned about the bitter flavor, and the longer time if you are sensitive to the bitter flavor. Rub the quinoa seeds together in the stocking. Rinse the stocking under cold running water. Repeat until you've satisfied yourself that the bitter flavor is gone.

COOKING QUINOA IN LIQUIDS

This section accommodates those who have dietary restrictions or are creating or adapting their own quinoa recipes. These basic recipes can easily be doubled, tripled or more. When using colored quinoa in these recipes, note that it may require a few extra minutes of cooking time to absorb all the liquid after being removed from the heat.

STOCK (VEGETABLE, CHICKEN OR BEEF)

MAKES 1½ CUPS (375 ML) OR 2 SERVINGS

1 cup (250 mL) vegetable, chicken or beef stock

½ cup (125 mL) quinoa

Combine the stock and quinoa in a medium saucepan. Bring to a boil, then reduce to a simmer. Cover and cook for 17 minutes. Remove from the heat. Check to see if the quinoa is cooked (the center of the seed should be translucent and all the water should have been absorbed). If it needs a few more minutes, just replace the lid and let it rest for another 5 minutes, until all remaining liquid is absorbed. Fluff with a fork and serve.

PER SERVING (sodium-reduced vegetable stock): Energy 160 calories; Protein 6 g; Carbohydrates 29 g; Dietary Fiber 3 g; Fat 2 g; Sugar 1 g; Cholesterol 0 mg; Sodium 70 mg

TOMATO JUICE

MAKES 1 ¾ CUPS (400 ML) OR 2 SERVINGS

1 cup (250 mL) tomato juice

½ cup (125 mL) water

½ cup (125 mL) quinoa

Combine the tomato juice, water and quinoa in a medium saucepan. Bring to a boil, then reduce to a simmer. Cover and cook for 15 minutes. Stir quinoa, cover again and cook for another 15 minutes. Remove from the heat and check to see if the quinoa is cooked (the center of the seed should be translucent and all the water should have been absorbed). If not, replace the lid and let sit for another 5 minutes. Fluff with a fork and serve.

PER SERVING (sodium-reduced tomato juice): Energy 180 calories; Protein 7 g; Carbohydrates 32 g; Dietary Fiber 3 g; Fat 2 g; Sugar 4 g; Cholesterol 0 mg; Sodium 15 mg

APPLE, ORANGE OR PINEAPPLE JUICE

MAKES 1 ½ CUPS (375 ML) OR 2 SERVINGS

1 cup (250 mL) apple, orange or pineapple juice

⅓ cup (75 mL) water

½ cup (125 mL) quinoa

Combine the juice, water and quinoa in a medium saucepan. Bring to a boil, then reduce to a simmer. Cover and cook for 25 minutes. Remove from the heat and let sit, covered, for another 5 minutes. Fluff with a fork and serve.

PER SERVING (unsweetened apple juice): Energy 210 calories; Protein 6 g; Carbohydrates 41 g; Dietary Fiber 3 g; Fat 2 g; Sugar 12 g; Cholesterol 0 mg; Sodium 10 mg

ALMOND MILK (SWEETENED OR UNSWEETENED)

MAKES 1½ CUPS (375 ML) OR 2 SERVINGS

1 cup (250 mL) almond milk

½ cup (125 mL) water

½ cup (125 mL) quinoa

Combine the milk, water and quinoa in a medium saucepan. Bring to a boil, then reduce to a simmer. Cover and cook for 20 minutes, stirring occasionally. Remove from the heat and let sit, covered, for another 5 minutes. Fluff with a fork and serve.

PER SERVING (unsweetened): Energy 180 calories; Protein 7 g; Carbohydrates 28 g; Dietary Fiber 3 g; Fat 4 g; Sugar 0 g; Cholesterol 0 mg; Sodium 95 mg

SOY MILK (SWEETENED OR UNSWEETENED)

MAKES 1½ CUPS (375 ML) OR 2 SERVINGS

1 cup (250 mL) soy milk

½ cup (125 mL) quinoa

Combine the milk and quinoa in a medium saucepan. Bring to a boil, then reduce to a simmer. Cover and cook for 25 minutes, stirring occasionally. Remove from the heat and let sit, covered, for 5 minutes. Fluff with a fork and serve.

PER SERVING (unsweetened): Energy 200 calories; Protein 10 g; Carbohydrates 29 g; Dietary Fiber 3 g; Fat 4 g; Sugar 0 g; Cholesterol 0 mg; Sodium 45 mg

LIGHT COCONUT MILK

MAKES 1½ CUPS (375 ML) OR 2 SERVINGS

1 cup (250 mL) light coconut milk

½ cup (125 mL) quinoa

Combine the milk and quinoa in a medium saucepan. Bring to a boil, then reduce to a simmer. Cover and cook for 15 minutes. Remove from the heat and let sit, covered, for another 5 minutes. Fluff with a fork and serve.

PER SERVING: Energy 240 calories; Protein 6 g; Carbohydrates 29 g; Dietary Fiber 3 g; Fat 11 g; Sugar 0 g; Cholesterol 0 mg; Sodium 20 mg

TABLE 3: Cooking Quinoa in Various Liquids—Yields

	WATER	STOCK	TOMATO JUICE	FRUIT JUICE	ALMOND MILK	SOY MILK	COCONUT MILK
COOKING TIME (MINUTES)	15	22	35	30	25	30	20
½ CUP (125 ML) UNCOOKED	makes 1½ cups (375 mL)	makes 1½ cups (375 mL)	makes 1¾ cups (400 mL)	makes 1½ cups (375 mL)	makes 1½ cups (375 mL)	makes 1½ cups (375 mL)	makes 1½ cups (375 mL)

QUINOA IN A RAW-FOOD DIET

People who eat raw foods have several options for incorporating quinoa into their diets. Sprouting is extremely popular with raw-food eaters, and it certainly provides a good dose of nutrition. There are extraordinary benefits to eating the enzyme-rich, super nutrition of sprouted quinoa. Eating quinoa uncooked or raw increases the ways you can add it to your daily meals, and in the raw form it is extremely portable because it does not require refrigeration. Sprouted and raw quinoa both contain the same great foundation of nutrition found in cooked quinoa seeds.

Sprouting Quinoa

Quinoa sprouts are a great way to grow your own local produce at any time of the year. It is becoming increasingly popular to eat raw, sprouted foods that are full of enzymes and rich in vitamins and minerals. Quinoa sprouts can be eaten as a nutritious snack all on their own, used in cold recipes such as salads or used as a sandwich topping. Recipes that feature sprouted quinoa are Blueberry Sprout Smoothie on page 31, Green Veggie Super Shake on page 32, Apple Cabbage Sprout Salad on page 46, and Carrot & Raisin Sprout Salad on page 52.

For sprouts, use organic quinoa when possible, as it has been handled in a manner that reduces the risk of contamination. Cleanliness when sprouting is important in eliminating any chance of contamination, which may occur with any kind of sprout. Quinoa is one of the quickest-sprouting seeds, rapidly germinating in two to 4 hours. Quinoa sprouts are best when eaten small because they have more crunch and stay fresh longer. Sprouts that are grown for a longer time are larger, softer in texture and deteriorate more quickly.

Distilled water

½ cup (125 mL) quinoa

Wash your hands thoroughly. Place the quinoa in a clean glass or ceramic casserole dish with a lid (do not use plastic, which can harbor residual bacteria that may contaminate your sprouts). (You can also use a sterilized mason jar, with the opening covered with cheesecloth and an elastic band.) Pour in enough distilled water to cover the quinoa, stir with a clean spoon and soak for 40 minutes at room temperature.

Using a fine-mesh strainer, drain the seeds. While the seeds are in the strainer, rinse them with more distilled water. Rinse the casserole dish with distilled water. Return the wet quinoa to the casserole dish and cover with the lid, leaving a slight opening for air circulation. Place in the refrigerator or a cool, dark location. Repeat rinsing every 8 to 10 hours until the quinoa has sprouted to the desired length; it will be ready to eat anytime after about 8 hours.

Store the sprouts in a glass or ceramic (not plastic or metal) container in the refrigerator with the lid open slightly to allow for air circulation. Use sprouts within 3 days. Do not eat them if they have any odor or visible mold, which can result from lack of air, not enough rinsing or being sprouted in too warm an environment. The final quantity of sprouts will depend on the duration the sprouts are grown: the longer they're grown, the bigger they'll be.

Cracked or Raw Quinoa

Similar to flaxseeds, uncooked quinoa is protected by a pericarp. If this shell is still intact when you swallow it, the quinoa seed will simply pass through your body without being digested. However, raw quinoa seeds can still provide fantastic nutrition if cracked or partially ground before you ingest them.

Quinoa can be ground slightly in a blender, food processor or coffee grinder. It is then ready to be added to your recipes. Even easier, you can place raw quinoa seeds in a resealable plastic bag and gently crack them by rolling over them with a rolling pin. You can add ground or cracked quinoa seeds to breakfast cereals, shakes, salads, desserts and more.

REVOLUTIONIZE
BREAKFAST

REVOLUTIONIZE BREAKFAST

WE seem to have less time than ever these days, but now you can start loving your mornings again! This chapter is sure to bring you back to life with quinoa recipes so enticing and energizing you will start to look forward to breakfast. With solutions for busy schedules and restricted diets, we have uncomplicated recipes you can make often and grab when you're heading out the door. When you're getting your family ready for the day, breakfast needs to be quick and easy, yet nutritious and delicious enough to make breakfast worth eating! Extra-quick recipes include Grab & Go Breakfast Cereal (page 24) and Anytime Breakfast Bars (page 34).

Quinoa will give you that extra boost you need to get through a busy morning, whatever it is you do. It's hard enough to get the required amount of daily vegetables, so why not start in the morning? With quinoa you can load up on extra antioxidants, energy, fiber, nutrients and protein, even before noon. Try Green Veggie Super Shake (page 32) and Orange Ginger Quinoa Breakfast Cereal (page 29).

For those mornings where peace and relaxation are in the plans, and you're up for something extra tasty, several recipes are delicious enough for dessert, like Red Velvet Waffles (page 18) and Apple Pie Pancakes (page 16). For an extra-special breakfast, try Vanilla Crème Crêpes with Fresh Strawberries (page 20).

Whether you're feeding a family, entertaining or cooking for one, quinoa breakfasts offer something a bit different, with the complete nutritional elements to feed the body. Now that is worth getting out of bed for!

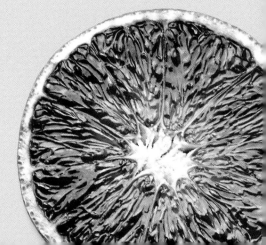

Apple Pie Pancakes 16

Carrot Cake Pancakes 17

Red Velvet Waffles 18

Vanilla Crème Crêpes
with Fresh Strawberries 20

Apricot Matcha Breakfast Porridge 21

Baked Vanilla Bean Quinoa 22

Spiced Carrot & Raisin Cereal 23

Coconut Omega-3 Cereal 23

Creamy Chocolate Breakfast Cereal 24

Grab & Go Breakfast Cereal 24

Creamy Banana Breakfast Cereal 25

Hot Pistachio Cereal with
Greek Yogurt & Honey 27

Hot Cinnamon Zucchini Breakfast 28

Orange Ginger Quinoa Breakfast Cereal 29

Strawberry Rhubarb Breakfast 30

Blueberry Sprout Smoothie 31

Sunshine Sprout Smoothie 31

Green Veggie Super Shake 32

Chocolate Hazelnut Bars 34

Cranberry Coconut Bars 34

Dark Chocolate Cherry Bars 35

Date and Walnut Bars 35

Maple Pecan Granola 36

Peanut Butter & Tomato Sprout Toast 37

Quinoa Mushroom Omelet 38

Smoked Gouda & Onion Omelet 39

Sunday Brunch Casserole 40

Traditional Breakfast Sausage Rounds 41

APPLE PIE PANCAKES

MAKES 18 PANCAKES, SERVING 6

2 ⅔ cups (650 mL) quinoa flour

¼ cup (60 mL) organic
    cane sugar or white sugar

2 Tbsp (30 mL) baking powder

½ tsp (2 mL) salt

1 tsp (5 mL) cinnamon

½ tsp (2 mL) nutmeg

2 ½ cups (625 mL) buttermilk

2 large eggs

2 Tbsp (30 mL) vegetable oil

1 tsp (5 mL) pure vanilla extract

1 ½ cups (375 mL) peeled
    and diced apples

A nutritious breakfast that could easily double as dessert. Warm, spicy apples fill these velvety soft buttermilk pancakes, with every serving containing 25 percent of your daily value of iron and 40 percent of your calcium. Top these pancakes with caramel sauce and pecans for an extra-special treat.

Combine the flour, sugar, baking powder, salt, cinnamon and nutmeg in a large bowl. In a medium bowl, whisk together the buttermilk, eggs, oil and vanilla; stir in the apples. Add the buttermilk mixture to the flour mixture and combine well.

Lightly grease a large skillet or spray with cooking oil and place on medium-high heat. When the skillet is hot, spoon the batter into the pan to make 4-inch (10 cm) rounds. When a few bubbles form on the top, flip the pancakes and cook for 30 seconds more or until the center springs back when gently pressed. Serve hot with butter and maple syrup.

PER SERVING: Energy 390 calories; Protein 14 g; Carbohydrates 58 g; Dietary Fiber 8 g; Fat 12 g; Sugar 17 g; Cholesterol 70 mg; Sodium 320 mg

Want something different? Try birch syrup. It has a slightly spicy caramel flavor that is unique and delicious. It is a little more expensive than maple syrup, at an average of $22 per ½ cup (125 mL), but this is because producing it is a bit trickier. It is made in Canada, Alaska, Russia, Ukraine and Scandinavian countries. It is worth the treat!

CARROT CAKE PANCAKES

Breakfast that tastes like dessert! These golden pancakes are packed with carrots, raisins and pineapple along with the goodness of quinoa. Tasty topped with maple syrup, or step it up with freshly whipped cream.

Measure the flour, sugar, baking powder, salt, cinnamon and nutmeg into a large bowl. Mix well. In a medium bowl, whisk together the milk, eggs and applesauce. Stir in the carrots, pineapple, raisins and pecans. Add the milk mixture to the flour mixture and stir just until blended.

Grease a large skillet or spray with cooking oil and place on medium heat. When hot, pour scant ¼-cup (60 mL) portions of batter into the pan. The pancakes will be ready to flip when you first see bubbles and the underside is lightly golden brown. Watch them carefully, as they brown quickly. Flip and cook the pancakes for another 30 seconds, until the center springs back when pressed. If the pancakes buckle when you slide the spatula under them, lightly oil the pan again for the next batch. Serve with maple syrup.

PER SERVING: Energy 250 calories; Protein 9 g; Carbohydrates 38 g; Dietary Fiber 6 g; Fat 8 g; Sugar 12 g; Cholesterol 65 mg; Sodium 240 mg

SERVES 6

1½ cups (375 mL) quinoa flour

1 Tbsp (15 mL) organic cane sugar or white sugar

3½ tsp (17 mL) baking powder

½ tsp (2 mL) salt

1½ tsp (7 mL) cinnamon

½ tsp (2 mL) nutmeg

1 cup (250 mL) 1% or 2% milk, buttermilk or soy milk

2 large eggs, beaten

¼ cup (60 mL) applesauce

1 cup (250 mL) shredded carrots

⅓ cup (75 mL) crushed pineapple, drained well

⅓ cup (75 mL) seedless raisins

¼ cup (60 mL) chopped toasted pecans

To toast nuts, preheat the oven to 350°F (180°C). Spread the nuts on a baking sheet and toast in the oven, stirring once if necessary, for 5 to 7 minutes, until fragrant and lightly toasted.

RED VELVET WAFFLES

SERVES 5

WAFFLES

2 to 3 small red beets, unpeeled

2 cups (500 mL) water

2 cups (500 mL) quinoa flour

¼ cup (60 mL) unsweetened
    cocoa powder

3 Tbsp (45 mL) organic
    cane sugar or white sugar

4 tsp (20 mL) baking powder

¼ tsp (1 mL) salt

2 large eggs, beaten

1¼ cups (300 mL) 1% or 2% milk

¼ cup (60 mL) vegetable oil

1 tsp (5 mL) pure vanilla extract

LEMON CREAM CHEESE TOPPING
(OPTIONAL)

½ cup (125 mL) light cream cheese

½ cup (125 mL) low-fat plain yogurt

1 Tbsp (15 mL) pure maple syrup

½ tsp (2 mL) grated lemon zest

¼ tsp (1 mL) pure vanilla extract

Shhh. No one will guess these velvety waffles are sweetened with nutritious puréed red beets. Extra-delicious served with the optional Lemon Cream Cheese Topping.

For the waffles, in a medium saucepan, bring the beets and water to a boil. Lower heat to medium and simmer the beets until tender. Remove beets from the pot, reserving the red cooking water. Rinse beets under cool water and gently remove the skin with your fingers. (You may want to wear rubber gloves!) Chop beets into large chunks and place in a food processor. Process until smooth. Set aside to cool.

Combine the flour, cocoa, sugar, baking powder and salt in a large bowl. In a medium bowl, whisk together the eggs, milk, oil, vanilla, ¼ cup (60 mL) of the puréed beets and 1 cup (250 mL) of the reserved beet cooking water. Add the beet mixture to the flour mixture. Blend well and set aside.

For the lemon cream cheese topping, in a medium bowl, whip the cream cheese, yogurt, maple syrup, lemon zest and vanilla until smooth. Set aside.

Grease or lightly spray a waffle iron with cooking oil and preheat it. Pour the batter onto the waffle iron according to the manufacturer's instructions and close. Remove the waffles when the lid lifts open easily, after 5 to 6 minutes. Serve waffles with lemon cream cheese topping (if using) or butter and maple syrup.

Waffles will keep in the refrigerator for up to 2 days in a sealed container. Reheat in a toaster or toaster oven.

PER SERVING: Energy 390 calories; Protein 12 g; Carbohydrates 49 g; Dietary Fiber 8 g; Fat 17 g; Sugar 11 g; Cholesterol 75 mg; Sodium 200 mg

VANILLA CRÈME CRÊPES WITH FRESH STRAWBERRIES

MAKES 12 (6-INCH/15 CM) CRÊPES, SERVING 6

CRÊPES

⅓ cup (75 mL) quinoa flour

¼ cup (60 mL) brown rice flour or whole wheat flour

2 tsp (10 mL) cornstarch

2 large eggs

2 large egg whites

1 cup (250 mL) 1% or 2% milk

FILLING

3 cups (750 mL) low-fat plain thick Greek yogurt

⅓ cup (75 mL) pure maple syrup or honey

1½ tsp (7 mL) pure vanilla extract

3 cups (750 mL) sliced fresh strawberries

Easy to make and even easier to eat, this nutritious breakfast will satisfy breakfast eaters of any age. Vanilla crème, made with thick Greek yogurt, is wrapped in a lightly sweetened crêpe with fresh strawberries.

For the crêpes, stir together the quinoa flour, rice flour and cornstarch in a medium bowl. Add the eggs, egg whites and milk. Whisk until smooth.

Heat a lightly oiled 6-inch (15 cm) skillet on medium-high heat. Pour 2 Tbsp (30 mL) of batter into the center of the pan; quickly tilt the pan in a circular motion to spread the batter over the bottom. Flip the crêpe when the edges begin to curl, after about 30 to 45 seconds. Cook the other side for another 30 seconds, then remove from the pan. Place the hot crêpe on a plate and cover with foil. Repeat with the remaining batter.

For the filling, mix together the yogurt, maple syrup and vanilla.

Place a crêpe on a plate and spoon ¼ cup (60 mL) each of filling and strawberries in the center. Fold sides over. Serve garnished with additional strawberries, if desired.

PER SERVING: Energy 250 calories; Protein 16 g; Carbohydrates 36 g; Dietary Fiber 3 g; Fat 5 g; Sugar 22 g; Cholesterol 70 mg; Sodium 105 mg

APRICOT MATCHA
BREAKFAST PORRIDGE

Matcha is a finely ground superior green tea from Japan. It is said to be rich in phytonutrients and antioxidants that can be easily absorbed because the powdered leaves are ingested rather than removed after steeping, as with traditional teas. If you are a matcha fan, you will enjoy this delicious combination with apricots and coconut milk.

Bring the water, quinoa, apricots and matcha to a boil in a medium saucepan. Reduce to a simmer, then cover and cook for 20 minutes. Pour in the coconut milk and continue to cook only until heated through. Remove from the heat and stir in the maple syrup and vanilla. Serve.

PER SERVING: Energy 260 calories; Protein 6 g; Carbohydrates 43 g; Dietary Fiber 4 g; Fat 7 g; Sugar 13 g; Cholesterol 0 mg; Sodium 15 mg

SERVES 2

1½ cups (375 mL) water

½ cup (125 mL) quinoa

3 Tbsp (45 mL) diced dried apricots

¾ tsp (4 mL) matcha
green tea powder

½ cup (125 mL) light coconut milk

1 Tbsp (15 mL) pure maple syrup

¾ tsp (4 mL) pure vanilla extract

Leftover coconut milk? Measure easy-to-use portions in sealed freezer bags and store in the freezer for up to 3 months.

BAKED VANILLA
BEAN QUINOA

SERVES 4

1 cup (250 mL) water

½ cup (125 mL) quinoa

1 vanilla bean

½ cup (125 mL) whole milk

2 Tbsp (30 mL) unsalted
    butter, melted

¼ cup (60 mL) organic
    cane sugar or white sugar

1 large egg

½ tsp (2 mL) baking powder

½ tsp (2 mL) salt

Fluffy quinoa is baked with whole milk and the natural aromatic goodness of vanilla beans. A superb way to spice up a traditional hot baked breakfast cereal and an impressive brunch dish to serve guests.

Preheat the oven to 350°F (180°C).

Combine the water and quinoa in a medium saucepan. Split the vanilla bean lengthwise, and use the end of a butter knife or small spoon to scrape out the sandy black seeds. Add the seeds and the pod to the pot. Bring to a boil, then reduce to a simmer. Cover and simmer for 15 minutes. Remove from the heat and discard the vanilla pod. Fluff quinoa with a fork and set aside.

In a medium bowl, whisk together the milk, butter, sugar, egg, baking powder and salt. Add the cooked quinoa and stir well. Pour the mixture into an 8-inch (2 L) square baking dish. Bake for 25 to 30 minutes, until the center is firm to the touch. Serve warm, scooped into individual serving dishes. Serve with fresh fruit and cream if desired.

PER SERVING: Energy 210 calories; Protein 6 g; Carbohydrates 28 g; Dietary Fiber 1 g; Fat 9 g; Sugar 14 g; Cholesterol 65 mg; Sodium 380 mg

> If you don't have a vanilla bean, use 2 tsp (10 mL) pure vanilla extract.

SPICED CARROT & RAISIN CEREAL

Nothing satisfies like a hot home-cooked breakfast. This will become one of your favorite breakfast recipes with its ever-popular combination of carrots, raisins and cinnamon.

Combine the water, apple juice and quinoa in a medium saucepan. Bring to a boil, reduce to a simmer, cover and cook for 15 minutes. Stir in the carrots, raisins and cinnamon. Continue to simmer, covered, for another 7 minutes. Remove from the heat and stir in the vanilla and the walnuts and maple syrup (if using). Serve hot.

PER SERVING: Energy 210 calories; Protein 7 g; Carbohydrates 41 g; Dietary Fiber 4 g; Fat 2.5 g; Sugar 10 g; Cholesterol 0 mg; Sodium 25 mg

SERVES 2

¾ cup (175 mL) water

¼ cup (60 mL) unsweetened
   apple juice

½ cup (125 mL) quinoa

½ cup (125 mL) grated carrots

2 Tbsp (30 mL) seedless raisins

¼ tsp (1 mL) cinnamon

¾ tsp (4 mL) pure vanilla extract

1 Tbsp (15 mL) chopped
   walnuts (optional)

1 Tbsp (15 mL) pure maple syrup
   or honey (optional)

COCONUT OMEGA-3 CEREAL

Rich in omega-3 fatty acids and fiber, this quinoa cereal is a super dose of superfoods. We don't need to tell you why fiber is great, and omega-3 oil supports healthy brain development and functioning. Literally, it's great food for thought.

Combine the coconut milk, water, quinoa and raisins in a medium saucepan. Bring to a boil, reduce to a simmer, cover and cook for 17 minutes. Remove from the heat and stir in the chia and flaxseeds. Serve.

PER SERVING: Energy 390 calories; Protein 11 g; Carbohydrates 51 g; Dietary Fiber 9 g; Fat 16 g; Sugar 5 g; Cholesterol 0 mg; Sodium 30 mg

SERVES 2

1 cup (250 mL) light coconut milk

⅔ cup (150 mL) water

⅔ cup (150 mL) quinoa

2 Tbsp (30 mL) seedless raisins or
   chopped pitted prunes or dates

2 Tbsp (30 mL) chia seeds

1 Tbsp (15 mL) ground flaxseeds

CREAMY CHOCOLATE
BREAKFAST CEREAL

SERVES 2

1½ cups (375 mL) 1% milk

½ cup (125 mL) quinoa

1 Tbsp (15 mL) unsweetened
    cocoa powder

2 large egg whites

½ tsp (2 mL) pure vanilla extract

1 Tbsp (15 mL) pure maple syrup

Who says you can't have chocolate for breakfast? Sprinkle some toasted nuts on top for added crunch, if you like.

Combine the milk, quinoa and cocoa in a medium saucepan. Bring to a boil on medium heat, then reduce to a simmer. Cover and cook for 18 minutes.

Whisk together the egg whites and vanilla in a small bowl. Temper the egg whites by whisking in a spoonful of the hot quinoa mixture. Repeat, whisking in spoonfuls of quinoa mixture 4 more times. Stir the egg mixture into the hot quinoa mixture and cook for another 2 to 3 minutes, until thickened. Stir in the maple syrup. Serve.

PER SERVING: Energy 300 calories; Protein 16 g; Carbohydrates 45 g; Dietary Fiber 4 g; Fat 5 g; Sugar 15 g; Cholesterol 10 mg; Sodium 140 mg

GRAB & GO
BREAKFAST CEREAL

SERVES 1

¼ cup (60 mL) quinoa flakes

1 Tbsp (15 mL) dried blueberries
    (or fruit of your choice)

1 Tbsp (15 mL) chopped walnuts
    (or nut of your choice)

1 tsp (5 mL) chia seeds

Pinch of cinnamon

½ cup (125 mL) boiling water

This is a great cereal for when you are on the go and need to take a hot, nutritious breakfast with you. Multiply this recipe and premeasure the dry mix into resealable plastic bags ahead of time, then simply grab one on your way out the door. Add your choice of sweetener and milk, if you like. Don't forget to take along a bowl and cover (such as foil), if needed.

Put the quinoa flakes, fruit, nuts, chia seeds and cinnamon into a resealable plastic bag or other container.

When ready to prepare, pour the contents into a bowl and add the boiling water. Give it one quick stir. Cover with a plate or foil and let sit for 9 to 10 minutes. Make sure all the water has been absorbed before eating. Serve with a sweetener, such as honey, syrup or sugar, as well as milk, if desired.

PER SERVING: Energy 210 calories; Protein 6 g; Carbohydrates 30 g; Dietary Fiber 5 g; Fat 8 g; Sugar 3 g; Cholesterol 0 mg; Sodium 260 mg

CREAMY BANANA
BREAKFAST CEREAL

This breakfast cereal is creamy and smooth, and naturally sweetened with banana. It makes a delicious morning meal for both adults and children and is a cereal babies are sure to gobble up. (If using as a baby food, purée the banana together with the quinoa mixture.)

Bring the water and quinoa to a boil in a medium saucepan. Reduce to a simmer, cover and cook for 10 to 17 minutes. The quinoa should be overcooked and extra-plump. Fluff with a fork and set aside to cool slightly.

While still warm (but not hot), process the cooked quinoa in a food processor or blender until completely smooth and creamy. It should be the consistency of thick pudding. Add the milk, cinnamon and nutmeg. Blend well. Remove from the food processor and fold in the banana. Serve warm.

PER SERVING: Energy 250 calories; Protein 9 g; Carbohydrates 45 g; Dietary Fiber 5 g; Fat 5 g; Sugar 10 g; Cholesterol 5 mg; Sodium 35 mg

SERVES 2

1 cup (250 mL) water

½ cup (125 mL) quinoa

½ cup (125 mL) whole milk

1 tsp (5 mL) cinnamon

½ tsp (2 mL) nutmeg

½ cup (125 mL) chopped
　ripe banana

- Need a quick breakfast ready to go every day during the work week? Cook and purée the quinoa and store it in the refrigerator in an airtight container. Every morning, place a serving of the puréed quinoa in a small saucepan on low to medium heat. Add milk, cinnamon, nutmeg and mashed banana. Heat and stir until the mixture is smooth. This same method can be used daily for baby food.

- If you want to switch up the flavors, replace the banana with 4 or 5 stewed and chopped (or mashed for baby food) pitted prunes or apricots.

HOT PISTACHIO CEREAL WITH GREEK YOGURT & HONEY

Something a bit different. Quinoa and the buttery taste of pistachios are more than enough to provide a great-tasting, wholesome breakfast.

Combine the water and quinoa in a medium saucepan and bring to a boil. Reduce to a simmer, cover and cook for 17 minutes. Remove from the heat and stir in the pistachios and vanilla. Divide between 2 dishes and top each with ¼ cup (60 mL) yogurt and 1 tsp (5 mL) honey. Serve.

PER SERVING: Energy 260 calories; Protein 11 g; Carbohydrates 39 g; Dietary Fiber 4 g; Fat 7 g; Sugar 10 g; Cholesterol 5 mg; Sodium 50 mg

SERVES 2

1 cup (250 mL) water

½ cup (125 mL) quinoa

2 Tbsp (30 mL) chopped unsalted pistachios

¼ tsp (1 mL) pure vanilla extract

½ cup (125 mL) low-fat plain thick Greek yogurt

2 tsp (10 mL) liquid honey

Cooked quinoa already on hand? Reheat or use cold 1½ cups (375 mL) cooked quinoa instead of cooking the quinoa in this recipe.

HOT CINNAMON ZUCCHINI BREAKFAST

SERVES 2

1 ½ cups (375 mL) water

½ cup (125 mL) quinoa

1 cup (250 mL) grated zucchini

1 Tbsp (15 mL) pure maple
    syrup or honey

½ tsp (2 mL) cinnamon

½ tsp (2 mL) pure vanilla extract

1 Tbsp (15 mL) chopped pecans

Zucchini is a versatile vegetable, having a plain flavor that works as a blank slate in many different applications. This tasty hot breakfast gives you yet another way to use all that zucchini you have in your garden.

Combine the water and quinoa in a medium saucepan. Bring to a boil, reduce to a simmer, cover and cook for 12 minutes. Stir in the zucchini. Return to a boil, cover, reduce to a simmer and cook for another 8 minutes or until the quinoa is cooked and fluffy. Remove from the heat and stir in the maple syrup, cinnamon and vanilla. Divide the cereal between 2 bowls and sprinkle with pecans. Serve.

PER SERVING: Energy 220 calories; Protein 7 g; Carbohydrates 37 g; Dietary Fiber 4 g; Fat 5 g; Sugar 8 g; Cholesterol 0 mg; Sodium 15 mg

- Young zucchini are best as they have not developed large seeds in the center.

- Measure easy-to-use portions of grated zucchini in sealed freezer bags and store in the freezer for up to 2 months.

ORANGE GINGER QUINOA BREAKFAST CEREAL

The mixture of orange, ginger, apricots, dates and toasted almonds is sure to perk up your morning—and you just might want to have it again for lunch! Combine all the ingredients in one saucepan and serve warm or cold. If you're feeling indulgent, serve with cream.

Bring the water and quinoa to a boil in a medium saucepan. Reduce to a simmer, cover and cook for 15 minutes. Fluff with a fork. Add the dates, apricots, ginger and cinnamon; stir well to combine. Add the orange juice and zest and mix well. Sprinkle with the almonds and serve.

PER SERVING: Energy 170 calories; Protein 5 g; Carbohydrates 32 g; Dietary Fiber 4 g; Fat 4 g; Sugar 13 g; Cholesterol 0 mg; Sodium 10 mg

SERVES 4

1 cup (250 mL) water

½ cup (125 mL) quinoa

⅓ cup (75 mL) chopped pitted dates

¼ cup (60 mL) chopped dried apricots

1 tsp (5 mL) grated fresh ginger

½ tsp (2 mL) cinnamon

¼ cup (60 mL) freshly squeezed orange juice

½ tsp (2 mL) grated orange zest

¼ cup (60 mL) toasted sliced almonds

> To toast nuts, preheat the oven to 350°F (180°C). Spread the nuts on a baking sheet and toast in the oven, stirring once if necessary, for 5 to 7 minutes, until fragrant and lightly toasted.

STRAWBERRY RHUBARB BREAKFAST

SERVES 2

1⅓ cups (325 mL) water

⅔ cup (150 mL) quinoa

½ tsp (2 mL) cinnamon

1 cup (250 mL) fresh or frozen chopped rhubarb

1 cup (250 mL) quartered strawberries

1 Tbsp (15 mL) honey or pure maple syrup (optional)

2 Tbsp (30 mL) toasted sliced almonds (optional)

Why not bring a delicious dessert combination to the breakfast table? A hot and healthy breakfast made with comfort foods is a great way to positively kick-start your day.

Bring the water, quinoa and cinnamon to a boil in a medium saucepan. Reduce to a simmer, cover and cook for 10 minutes. Stir in the rhubarb and strawberries. Again bring to a boil. Cover, reduce to a simmer and cook for another 10 minutes. Remove from the heat when the rhubarb is tender. Stir in the honey (if using). Serve topped with toasted almonds (if using) and milk or vanilla yogurt, if desired.

PER SERVING: Energy 250 calories; Protein 9 g; Carbohydrates 45 g; Dietary Fiber 7 g; Fat 4 g; Sugar 4 g; Cholesterol 0 mg; Sodium 5 mg

To toast nuts, preheat the oven to 350°F (180°C). Spread the nuts on a baking sheet and toast in the oven, stirring once if necessary, for 5 to 7 minutes, until fragrant and lightly toasted.

BLUEBERRY SPROUT SMOOTHIE

This is a favorite smoothie of ours—and breakfast is the perfect time for veggies! The taste of spinach is completely unnoticeable in this recipe. A fabulously refreshing breakfast (or even lunch) that is great any morning, especially in hot weather.

Combine all the ingredients in a blender and purée. Serve immediately.

PER SERVING: Energy 120 calories; Protein 7 g; Carbohydrates 22 g; Dietary Fiber 2 g; Fat 1 g; Sugar 15 g; Cholesterol 0 mg; Sodium 80 mg

SERVES 2

1 cup (250 mL) fresh or
    frozen blueberries

¼ cup (60 mL) quinoa sprouts
    (pages 10 and 11)

½ cup (125 mL) fresh spinach

½ cup (125 mL) low-fat plain yogurt

½ cup (125 mL) skim milk

....

SUNSHINE SPROUT SMOOTHIE

A sprout smoothie is a great thing to wake up to, or if you need some extra energy before or after a tough workout. The sprouts and orange juice blend delightfully together for a fresh and healthful breakfast.

Combine all the ingredients in a blender and blend until smooth. Serve immediately.

PER SERVING: Energy 160 calories; Protein 6 g; Carbohydrates 29 g; Dietary Fiber 2 g; Fat 2 g; Sugar 16 g; Cholesterol 5 mg; Sodium 45 mg

SERVES 2

1 cup (250 mL) unsweetened
    orange juice

⅓ cup (75 mL) quinoa sprouts
    (pages 10 and 11)

½ cup (125 mL) low-fat
    vanilla yogurt

½ medium banana

Make your own vanilla yogurt by combining ½ cup (125 mL) plain yogurt, 1 tsp (5 mL) honey and ¼ tsp (1 mL) pure vanilla extract.

GREEN VEGGIE SUPER SHAKE

SERVES 2

½ cup (125 mL) unsweetened
apple juice

½ cup (125 mL) water

½ to ⅔ cup (125 to 150 mL)
quinoa sprouts (pages 10 and 11)

⅔ cup (150 mL) peeled and sliced
English cucumber

⅔ cup (150 mL) baby spinach

Getting all the vegetables you need can be difficult in a busy day. Consuming vegetables in the morning will get you off on the right foot, give you energy and help you feel fantastic. These flavors complement each other well and go down smooth. It is up to you how much sprouts you use.

Place the apple juice, water and quinoa sprouts in a blender. Blend until sprouts are puréed or are very small pieces. Add the cucumber and spinach. Blend again until the shake is as smooth as possible. Serve immediately.

PER SERVING: Energy 110 calories; Protein 4 g; Carbohydrates 22 g;
Dietary Fiber 2 g; Fat 1.5 g; Sugar 7 g; Cholesterol 0 mg; Sodium 15 mg

Don't have apple juice on hand? Use ½ cup (125 mL) of diced apple or applesauce.

ANYTIME BREAKFAST BARS

CHOCOLATE HAZELNUT BARS
MAKES 10 BARS

1½ cups (375 mL) quinoa flakes

1½ cups (375 mL) quick-cooking
    rolled oats (gluten-free if
    required)

1 cup (250 mL) mashed ripe bananas

¾ cup (175 mL) hazelnuts,
    coarsely chopped

½ cup (125 mL) unsweetened
    applesauce

⅓ cup (75 mL) unsweetened
    cocoa powder

2 Tbsp (30 mL) chia seeds (optional)

2 Tbsp (30 mL) liquid honey

1½ tsp (7 mL) pure vanilla extract

CRANBERRY COCONUT BARS
MAKES 12 BARS

1½ cups (375 mL) quinoa flakes

1½ cups (375 mL) quick-cooking
    rolled oats (gluten-free if
    required)

1 cup (250 mL) mashed ripe bananas

⅔ cup (150 mL) sweetened
    dried cranberries

½ cup (125 mL) unsweetened
    applesauce

½ cup (125 mL) unsweetened
    shredded coconut

2 Tbsp (30 mL) chia seeds (optional)

2 Tbsp (30 mL) liquid honey

2 tsp (10 mL) cinnamon

1½ tsp (7 mL) pure vanilla extract

When you are short on time and need to get out the door, these yummy, filling bars are great to grab on the run or to tuck into your pocket for later. And they're great pre- or post-workout fuel! Choose your favorite lightly sweetened combination! You can freeze these bars for up to 1 month.

Preheat the oven to 350°F (180°C). Lightly grease a baking sheet or line with parchment.

Mix together all the ingredients in a medium bowl. (The dough will be sticky.) Using a ¼-cup (60 mL) measure, place scoops of dough on the baking sheet. Dampen your hands with water and use the palm of your hand to flatten each scoop until ¾ inch (2 cm) thick. Form dough into circles or rectangles, arranging them 1½ inches (4 cm) apart.

Bake for 12 minutes. These bars do not brown much, so be careful not to overbake. Let cool on the baking sheet before storing in an airtight container.

CHOCOLATE HAZELNUT BARS

PER SERVING: Energy 180 calories; Protein 5 g; Carbohydrates 29 g; Dietary Fiber 4 g; Fat 6 g; Sugar 7 g; Cholesterol 0 mg; Sodium 125 mg

CRANBERRY COCONUT BARS

PER SERVING: Energy 170 calories; Protein 4 g; Carbohydrates 33 g; Dietary Fiber 4 g; Fat 4 g; Sugar 12 g; Cholesterol 0 mg; Sodium 130 mg

MORE ANYTIME BREAKFAST BARS

A busy schedule requires quality fuel at hand. These two types of naturally sweet, naturally nourishing bars will power you through your day. You can freeze these bars for up to 1 month.

Preheat the oven to 350°F (180°C). Lightly grease a baking sheet or line with parchment.

Mix together all the ingredients in a medium bowl. (The dough will be sticky.) Using a ¼-cup (60 mL) measure, place scoops of dough on the baking sheet. Dampen your hands with water and use the palm of your hand to flatten each scoop until ¾ inch (2 cm) thick. Form dough into circles or rectangles, arranging them 1½ inches (4 cm) apart.

Bake for 12 minutes. These bars do not brown much, so be careful not to overbake. Let cool on the baking sheet before storing in an airtight container.

DARK CHOCOLATE CHERRY BARS

PER SERVING: Energy 170 calories; Protein 4 g; Carbohydrates 33 g; Dietary Fiber 5 g; Fat 3 g; Sugar 10 g; Cholesterol 0 mg; Sodium 125 mg

DATE AND WALNUT BARS

PER SERVING: Energy 180 calories; Protein 5 g; Carbohydrates 32 g; Dietary Fiber 4 g; Fat 5 g; Sugar 11 g; Cholesterol 0 mg; Sodium 125 mg

DARK CHOCOLATE CHERRY BARS
MAKES 12 BARS

1½ cups (375 mL) quinoa flakes

1½ cups (375 mL) quick-cooking rolled oats (gluten-free if required)

1 cup (250 mL) mashed ripe bananas

¾ cup (175 mL) coarsely chopped dried sour cherries

½ cup (125 mL) unsweetened applesauce

⅓ cup (75 mL) semisweet mini chocolate chips or carob chips

2 Tbsp (30 mL) chia seeds (optional)

2 Tbsp (30 mL) liquid honey (optional)

2 tsp (10 mL) cinnamon

2 tsp (10 mL) pure vanilla extract

DATE AND WALNUT BARS
MAKES 12 BARS

1½ cups (375 mL) quinoa flakes

1½ cups (375 mL) quick-cooking rolled oats (gluten-free if required)

1 cup (250 mL) mashed ripe bananas

¾ cup (175 mL) coarsely chopped pitted dates

½ cup (125 mL) unsweetened applesauce

½ cup (125 mL) chopped walnuts

2 Tbsp (30 mL) chia seeds (optional)

1 Tbsp (15 mL) liquid honey (optional)

2 tsp (10 mL) cinnamon

1½ tsp (7 mL) pure vanilla extract

Pinch of nutmeg

MAPLE PECAN GRANOLA

SERVES 6

¼ cup (60 mL) quinoa

2 cups (500 mL) large-flake rolled oats (gluten-free if required)

½ cup (125 mL) chopped pecans

2 Tbsp (30 mL) unsweetened flaked coconut

¼ cup (60 mL) pure maple syrup

1 Tbsp (15 mL) liquid honey

1 tsp (5 mL) cinnamon

½ tsp (2 mL) pure vanilla extract

¼ cup (60 mL) seedless raisins

Avoid the high fat and calories often found in store-bought granola by making it yourself. This granola is highly portable and a terrific complement to plain yogurt, so take a serving of each along with you and mix them together when you need a snack.

Preheat the oven to 350°F (180°C). Lightly spray or grease a baking sheet or line with parchment.

Place the quinoa in a small resealable plastic bag. Roll over it with gentle pressure a few times with a rolling pin to crack the seeds. (Why crack the seeds? See page 11.) Pour the quinoa into a medium bowl and stir in the oats, pecans and coconut.

Whisk together the maple syrup, honey, cinnamon and vanilla; pour over the quinoa mixture. Stir until completely coated. Pour onto the baking sheet, spread it out in an even layer and bake for 10 minutes. Stir, then bake for another 5 minutes. Stir again and bake for 3 to 5 minutes. Granola can quickly burn, so watch it closely. It should be golden brown. Remove from the oven, stir in the raisins and let cool. Store in an airtight container for up to 2 months.

PER SERVING: Energy 270 calories; Protein 7 g; Carbohydrates 41 g; Dietary Fiber 5 g; Fat 10 g; Sugar 15 g; Cholesterol 0 mg; Sodium 0 mg

PEANUT BUTTER & TOMATO SPROUT TOAST

Sweet vine-ripened tomatoes paired with the creamy saltiness of peanut butter is a surprisingly delicious combination. Sprinkle on some sprouts and you have a quick, nutritious breakfast. This recipe is perfect if you have leftover sprouts from another recipe

Toast the bread and spread with peanut butter. Sprinkle with quinoa sprouts and top with slices of tomato. Serve.

PER SERVING (whole-grain bread): Energy 190 calories; Protein 7 g; Carbohydrates 20 g; Dietary Fiber 3 g; Fat 9 g; Sugar 3 g; Cholesterol 0 mg; Sodium 210 mg

SERVES 1

1 slice sprouted whole grain or gluten-free bread

1 Tbsp (15 mL) smooth or chunky natural peanut butter

1 Tbsp (15 mL) quinoa sprouts (pages 10 and 11)

2 to 3 slices ripe tomato

> Hit a local farmers' market for fresh produce. Not only do these markets support the local economy, but the food will taste even better than store bought.

QUINOA MUSHROOM OMELET

SERVES 4

½ cup (125 mL) water

¼ cup (60 mL) quinoa

1 tsp (5 mL) grapeseed or vegetable oil

½ cup (125 mL) sliced brown or white mushrooms

1 large egg

4 large egg whites

2 Tbsp (30 mL) shredded reduced-fat aged Cheddar cheese

2 tsp (10 mL) sliced green onions

Fluffy quinoa, eggs and sautéed mushrooms make a delicious high-protein breakfast.

Bring the water and quinoa to a boil in a small saucepan. Reduce to a simmer, cover and cook for 15 minutes. Fluff with a fork and set aside.

Heat the oil in a skillet on medium heat. Add the mushrooms. Cook until tender, 5 to 7 minutes. In a small bowl, whisk together the egg, egg whites and cooked quinoa. Pour the egg mixture over the mushrooms. Cook, covered, for 2 minutes. Using a spatula, fold omelet in half. Cook, covered, for another 2 to 4 minutes, until egg is set. Turn off the heat and sprinkle omelet with cheese and green onions. Cover for another minute or two, until the cheese is melted. Cut into quarters and serve.

PER SERVING: Energy 140 calories; Protein 10 g; Carbohydrates 15 g; Dietary Fiber 2 g; Fat 4 g; Sugar 1 g; Cholesterol 50 mg; Sodium 115 mg

Cooked quinoa already on hand? Add ¾ cup (175 mL) to the eggs in this recipe.

SMOKED GOUDA & ONION OMELET

Reconnect with your better half over breakfast, lunch or supper by sharing a delicious omelet for two. Add as much or as little mustard as you prefer. Colored quinoa looks best in this recipe, but white will work. Increase the nutrition even more by using ½ cup (125 mL) of sprouted quinoa instead of regular cooked quinoa.

Combine the water and quinoa in a small saucepan and bring to a boil. Reduce to a simmer, cover and cook for 15 minutes. Remove from the heat, fluff with a fork and set aside.

Heat a 10-inch (25 cm) nonstick skillet on medium-low heat. Add 1 tsp (5 mL) of the oil. Add the onions and a spoonful of water. Cover and cook, stirring occasionally, for 10 minutes or until the onions are soft and transparent. Transfer to a bowl and stir in the mustard. Set aside.

Rinse out the skillet and wipe dry. Heat the skillet again on medium-low. Add the remaining 1 tsp (5 mL) oil. Whisk together the egg, egg whites and milk. Pour the egg mixture into the pan and cook until firm enough to flip, 3 to 4 minutes. Flip the omelet over. Cook until set. Sprinkle the cooked quinoa and onions on one half of the omelet. Fold in half, cut in half and place on plates. Sprinkle with cheese and serve.

PER SERVING: Energy 210 calories; Protein 14 g; Carbohydrates 18 g; Dietary Fiber 2 g; Fat 8 g; Sugar 4 g; Cholesterol 95 mg; Sodium 220 mg

SERVES 2

⅓ cup (75 mL) water

2 Tbsp + 2 tsp (40 mL) quinoa

2 tsp (10 mL) grapeseed
    or vegetable oil

1 cup (250 mL) onions
    sliced ½ inch (1 cm) thick

1 to 2 tsp (5 to 10 mL) of your
    favorite Dijon or grainy mustard

1 large egg

4 large egg whites

2 tsp (10 mL) 1% or 2% milk

3 Tbsp (45 mL) shredded smoked
    Gouda or Cheddar cheese

Cooked quinoa already on hand? Sprinkle ⅓ to ½ cup (75 to 125 mL) over the omelet in this recipe.

SUNDAY BRUNCH CASSEROLE

SERVES 12

1 lb (450 g) ground turkey, chicken or pork

1 tsp (5 mL) minced fresh sage

1 tsp (5 mL) minced fresh parsley (optional)

1 tsp (5 mL) pure maple syrup or honey

¼ tsp (1 mL) minced fresh thyme

¾ tsp (4 mL) salt (optional)

½ tsp (2 mL) black pepper

Pinch of ground cloves

1 cup (250 mL) water

½ cup (125 mL) quinoa

1 Tbsp (15 mL) grapeseed oil or vegetable oil

1 cup (250 mL) chopped red bell pepper

1 cup (250 mL) shredded reduced-fat (or regular) aged Cheddar cheese

½ cup (125 mL) thinly sliced green onion

6 large eggs + 12 large egg whites (or 12 whole, large eggs total)

¼ cup (60 mL) 1% milk

2 tsp (10 mL) minced garlic

2 tsp (10 mL) ground mustard

Prepare the sausage meat and vegetables ahead of time and have them ready in the refrigerator so you can easily make this in the morning.

In a medium bowl, combine the ground turkey, sage, parsley (if using), maple syrup, thyme, ¼ tsp of the salt (if using), ¼ teaspoon of the pepper and the ground cloves. Mix well. Refrigerate until needed.

Bring the water and quinoa to a boil in a medium saucepan. Reduce to a simmer, cover and cook for 15 minutes. Remove from the heat and let sit, covered, for another 5 minutes. Fluff with a fork. Set aside to cool.

Meanwhile, preheat the oven to 375°F (190°C). Lightly grease a 13- × 9-inch (3 L) baking dish.

Heat the oil in a large skillet on medium heat. Add the sausage meat and fry until browned and no pink remains. Spread the sausage mixture evenly in the baking dish. Equally distribute the quinoa and red pepper. Sprinkle with Cheddar and green onions.

In a medium bowl, whisk together the eggs, egg whites, milk, garlic, mustard, remaining salt (if using) and remaining ¼ tsp black pepper. Pour the egg mixture evenly into the casserole dish. Bake for 35 to 45 minutes or until the center is set and the edges have browned. Let sit for 8 minutes, then cut into 12 pieces. Serve.

PER SERVING (including sausage filling): Energy 190 calories; Protein 18 g; Carbohydrates 7 g; Dietary Fiber 1 g; Fat 9 g; Sugar 2 g; Cholesterol 125 mg; Sodium 180 mg

TRADITIONAL BREAKFAST SAUSAGE ROUNDS

Traditional Breakfast Sausage rounds can be used wherever you would normally use regular breakfast sausage. Fry in a small amount of oil or bake for an even lower-fat option. The cooked sausage patties can also be frozen for up to 1 month.

Bring the water and quinoa to a boil in a small saucepan. Reduce to a simmer, cover and cook for 15 minutes. Remove from the heat and keep covered for another 10 minutes. Fluff with a fork. Set aside to cool completely.

In a medium bowl, mix together the cooled quinoa and the ground turkey, sage, parsley (if using), syrup, thyme, salt (if using), pepper and cloves.

PAN-FRY METHOD Heat the oil in a large skillet on medium-low heat. Scoop out ¼-cup (60 mL) servings of sausage mixture and with wet hands shape into rounds 1 inch (2.5 cm) thick. Fry for about 4 minutes on each side, until cooked through and golden brown. Serve.

OVEN METHOD Preheat the oven to 350°F (180°C). Line a baking sheet with parchment. Scoop out ¼-cup (60 mL) servings of sausage mixture and with wet hands shape into rounds 3 inches (8 cm) wide and ½ inch (1 cm) thick. Arrange on the baking sheet about 1½ inches (4 cm) apart. Bake for 10 minutes per side. Serve.

PER SERVING: Energy 200 calories; Protein 19 g; Carbohydrates 8 g; Dietary Fiber 1 g; Fat 9 g; Sugar 1 g; Cholesterol 65 mg; Sodium 55 mg

MAKES 10 ROUNDS, SERVING 5

⅔ cup (150 mL) water

⅓ cup (75 mL) quinoa

1 lb (450 g) ground turkey, chicken or pork

1 tsp (5 mL) minced fresh sage

1 tsp (5 mL) minced fresh parsley (optional)

1 tsp (5 mL) pure maple syrup or honey

¼ tsp (1 mL) minced fresh thyme

¼ tsp (1 mL) salt (optional)

¼ tsp (1 mL) black pepper

Pinch of cloves

2 tsp (10 mL) grapeseed or vegetable oil (pan-fry method only)

REVOLUTIONIZE
SALADS,
SIDES & SNACKS

REVOLUTIONIZE SALADS, SIDES & SNACKS

QUINOA is all about versatility and simplicity, so it is often used in side dishes and salads, yet sometimes it's so good it ends up putting the rest of the meal to shame. These recipes may do just that—but we hope instead that they'll complement the other foods you're serving.

The versatility of quinoa means that many times quinoa side dishes work equally great as a lunch or a snack. Most of the recipes in this chapter serve multiple duty, as they're terrific for any occasion and work well as a side dish, a lunch salad or an after-school snack and for entertaining. Just be warned that your guests may ask you for the recipe! Want something new and interesting? Try Crisp Lemon Snap Pea Salad (page 56) and Basil Watermelon Salad (page 49).

With quinoa you can feel okay about snacking between meals. Actually, eating small snacks throughout the day can keep you alert and keep your metabolism in check. Portability is really the key to eating well with our busy lifestyles. Having something within reach that's healthful and ready to eat when you need it helps you avoid having to opt for nutritionally inferior convenience foods. Salads that can be prepared in advance and are ready to grab from the refrigerator on your way out the door, and sides that are balanced and filling enough all on their own, are ideal solutions. For convenient, simple foods that are fresh and exciting, try Berry Cucumber Salad with White Balsamic Dressing (page 51) and Red Cabbage & Sprout Slaw (page 64). For a stunning and delicious recipe that is great for guests, try the Pear, Walnut & Blue Cheese Salad with Thyme Dressing in Radicchio Cups (page 61).

APPLE CABBAGE SPROUT SALAD

SERVES 6

2 cups (500 mL) quinoa
    sprouts (pages 10 and 11)

1 cup (250 mL) thinly sliced or
    shredded red cabbage

1 cup (250 mL) grated carrots

½ cup (125 mL) sliced green onions

1 cup (250 mL) grated apple

½ cup (125 mL) toasted
    slivered almonds

3 Tbsp (45 mL) olive or
    flaxseed oil

2 Tbsp (30 mL) apple cider vinegar

2 tsp (10 mL) pure maple syrup
    or honey

¼ tsp (1 mL) salt (optional)

High in vitamin A, this salad is versatile enough for any season. This fresh and tasty slaw will be a great addition to any casual lunch or supper. Consider using flaxseed oil in your salads to meet your omega-3 requirements.

Combine the sprouts, cabbage, carrots, green onions, apple and almonds in a medium bowl. In a separate bowl, whisk together the oil, vinegar, maple syrup and salt (if using). Toss veggie mixture with the dressing and serve.

PER SERVING: Energy 220 calories; Protein 5 g; Carbohydrates 23 g; Dietary Fiber 4 g; Fat 13 g; Sugar 5 g; Cholesterol 0 mg; Sodium 20 mg

> To toast nuts, preheat the oven to 350°F (180°C). Spread the nuts on a baking sheet and toast in the oven, stirring once if necessary, for 5 to 7 minutes, until fragrant and lightly toasted.

AVOCADO BASIL
PESTO SALAD

SERVES 10

3 cups (750 mL) water

1 ½ cups (375 mL) quinoa

1 avocado, peeled and diced

½ cup (125 mL) fresh basil leaves

⅓ cup (75 mL) grated
Parmesan cheese

2 Tbsp (30 mL) water

2 Tbsp (30 mL) extra virgin olive oil

1 tsp (5 mL) minced garlic

¼ tsp (1 mL) each salt and freshly
ground black pepper

¼ tsp (1 mL) cayenne pepper

The robust tastes of basil and garlic are blended with creamy avocado for a smooth, luxurious side dish worthy of taking its place alongside a barbecued chicken or steak and a glass of red wine.

Bring the water and quinoa to a boil in a large saucepan. Reduce to a simmer, cover and cook for 15 minutes. Fluff with a fork and set aside to cool completely.

In a food processor, purée the avocado, basil, Parmesan, water, olive oil, garlic, salt, black pepper and cayenne. Pour mixture over cooked quinoa. Mix well and serve immediately or chilled.

PER SERVING: Energy 160 calories; Protein 5 g; Carbohydrates 18 g; Dietary Fiber 3 g; Fat 8 g; Sugar 0 g; Cholesterol 0 mg; Sodium 100 mg

> Cooked quinoa already on hand? Add the avocado mixture to 4 ½ cups (1.125 L) cooked quinoa.

BASIL WATERMELON SALAD

Treat your guests (or yourself!) to something a bit different—sweet watermelon and basil are a delicious match. Watermelon not only always makes eating fun and joyful, but it also has many surprising health benefits. It contains a good dose of antioxidants and is thought to help reduce inflammation in the body.

Bring the water and quinoa to a boil in a medium saucepan. Reduce to a simmer, cover and cook for 15 minutes. Fluff with a fork and set aside to cool completely.

Combine the quinoa, watermelon, feta, olives, basil and red onion in a medium bowl. Add the lime juice and olive oil. Gently toss until well combined. Serve chilled.

PER SERVING: Energy 200 calories; Protein 6 g; Carbohydrates 24 g; Dietary Fiber 2 g; Fat 10 g; Sugar 8 g; Cholesterol 15 mg; Sodium 260 mg

SERVES 4

1 cup (250 mL) water

½ cup (125 mL) quinoa

3 cups (750 mL) diced seedless watermelon

½ cup (125 mL) crumbled feta cheese

3 Tbsp (45 mL) chopped pitted black olives

1 Tbsp (15 mL) chopped fresh basil

1 Tbsp (15 mL) finely chopped red onion

2 Tbsp (30 mL) lime juice

1 Tbsp (15 mL) extra virgin olive oil

Cooked quinoa already on hand? Add 1 ½ cups (375 mL) cooked quinoa to the other ingredients.

BERRY CUCUMBER SALAD WITH WHITE BALSAMIC DRESSING

Consider this dynamic combination of berries, cucumber, onion and almonds an adventure for your taste buds. This salad is an impressive dish to serve for a brunch or a lunch.

Combine the water and quinoa in a medium saucepan and bring to a boil. Reduce to a simmer, cover and cook for 15 minutes. Transfer to a salad bowl to cool completely.

Whisk together the vinegar, maple syrup and olive oil; stir into the quinoa. Gently toss in the blueberries, strawberries, cucumber and red onion. Just before serving, sprinkle with almonds (if using).

PER SERVING: Energy 170 calories; Protein 5 g; Carbohydrates 30 g; Dietary Fiber 3 g; Fat 4 g; Sugar 8 g; Cholesterol 0 mg; Sodium 10 mg

To toast nuts, preheat the oven to 350°F (180°C). Spread the nuts on a baking sheet and toast in the oven, stirring once if necessary, for 5 to 7 minutes, until fragrant and lightly toasted.

SERVES 6

2 cups (500 mL) water

1 cup (250 mL) quinoa

¼ cup (60 mL) white balsamic vinegar

1 Tbsp (15 mL) pure maple syrup or honey

1 Tbsp (15 mL) extra virgin olive oil

1 cup (250 mL) fresh blueberries

1 cup (250 mL) quartered fresh strawberries

1 cup (250 mL) diced English cucumber

¼ cup (60 mL) thinly sliced red onion cut into ¾-inch (2 cm) lengths

¼ cup (60 mL) toasted slivered or sliced almonds (optional)

CARROT & RAISIN SPROUT SALAD

SERVES 6

1½ cups (375 mL) grated carrots

1⅓ cups (325 mL) quinoa sprouts
    (pages 10 and 11)

½ cup (125 mL) sliced green onions

⅓ cup (75 mL) toasted cashews

⅓ cup (75 mL) seedless raisins

¼ cup (60 mL) lemon juice

3 Tbsp (45 mL) olive oil

1 to 2 Tbsp (15 to 30 mL)
    pure maple syrup

¼ tsp (1 mL) curry powder

A lively salad with the fresh, crunchy snap of quinoa sprouts and grated carrot, blended with the natural sweetness of raisins and creamy toasted cashews.

Combine the carrots, sprouts, green onions, cashews and raisins in a medium bowl. Whisk together the lemon juice, olive oil, maple syrup and curry powder. Toss with sprout mixture and serve.

PER SERVING: Energy 220 calories; Protein 4 g; Carbohydrates 27 g; Dietary Fiber 3 g; Fat 12 g; Sugar 9 g; Cholesterol 0 mg; Sodium 25 mg

To toast nuts, preheat the oven to 350°F (180°C). Spread the nuts on a baking sheet and toast in the oven, stirring once if necessary, for 5 to 7 minutes, until fragrant and lightly toasted.

CHERRY, FETA & THYME SALAD

Quinoa tossed with fresh thyme, cherries, feta cheese and honey makes this slightly sweet side dish an instant favorite as part of a quick lunch or as a snack with your favorite cup of tea.

Bring the water and quinoa to a boil in a medium saucepan. Reduce to a simmer, cover and cook for 15 minutes. Fluff with a fork and set aside to cool completely.

Add the cherries, cheese and thyme. Whisk together the olive oil, lemon juice, honey and salt and pepper. Pour over the quinoa mixture and stir until well combined. Chill for at least 1 hour before serving.

PER SERVING: Energy 260 calories; Protein 7 g; Carbohydrates 32 g; Dietary Fiber 3 g; Fat 12 g; Sugar 10 g; Cholesterol 10 mg; Sodium 260 mg

SERVES 2

⅔ cup (150 mL) water

⅓ cup (75 mL) quinoa

½ cup (125 mL) quartered
   pitted fresh cherries

¼ cup (60 mL) crumbled feta cheese

2 tsp (10 mL) minced fresh thyme

1 Tbsp (15 mL) extra virgin olive oil

1 Tbsp (15 mL) lemon juice

1 Tbsp (15 mL) liquid honey

Pinch each of salt and
   freshly ground black pepper

Cooked quinoa already on hand? Combine 1 cup (250 mL) cooked quinoa with the cherries, cheese and thyme.

CHIPOTLE BLACK BEAN SALAD

SERVES 6

2 cups (500 mL) water

1 cup (250 mL) quinoa

1 can (14 oz/398 mL) black beans, drained and rinsed (or 1½ cups/ 375 mL cooked black beans)

1 cup (250 mL) thawed frozen corn

¼ cup (60 mL) finely chopped red onion

¼ cup (60 mL) chopped fresh cilantro

¼ cup (60 mL) extra virgin olive oil or flaxseed oil

¼ cup (60 mL) lime juice (from about 1½ limes)

2 tsp (10 mL) finely chopped chipotle pepper in adobo sauce, with seeds

½ tsp (2 mL) minced garlic

A chipotle pepper is a smoked jalapeño pepper that is known for its spicy, smoky flavor. It is a superb option when you want to add a lot of flavor to a dish without using ingredients that may add unnecessary fat. Chipotle peppers can be found in small cans in adobo sauce in the Mexican section of most grocery stores. Leftover canned peppers can be frozen.

Bring the water and quinoa to a boil in a medium saucepan. Reduce to a simmer, cover and cook for 15 minutes. Fluff with a fork and set aside to cool completely.

Combine the cooled quinoa, black beans, corn, red onion and cilantro in a medium bowl. Whisk together the oil, lime juice, chipotle pepper and garlic. Toss with the quinoa mixture and serve.

PER SERVING: Energy 280 calories; Protein 9 g; Carbohydrates 36 g; Dietary Fiber 6 g; Fat 11 g; Sugar 1 g; Cholesterol 0 mg; Sodium 25 mg

> Dried beans are lower in sodium than canned beans—and half the cost. Cook up a batch ahead of time, then freeze in pre-measured servings in freezer bags for easy use.

GRAPE & CUCUMBER SALAD WITH CHEDDAR

Herbes de Provence give this cheery salad a delectable earthy flavor. Sharp Cheddar, fresh cucumbers and sweet grapes add to the rich combination.

Bring the water and quinoa to a boil in a medium saucepan. Reduce to a simmer, cover and cook for 15 minutes. Fluff with a fork and set aside to cool completely.

Combine the quinoa, tomatoes, cucumber, yellow pepper, grapes and green onions in a medium bowl. Whisk together the olive oil, vinegar, herbes de Provence and salt (if using). Pour over the quinoa mixture and add the cheese. Gently toss until well combined. Serve chilled.

PER SERVING: Energy 240 calories; Protein 11 g; Carbohydrates 22 g; Dietary Fiber 6 g; Fat 11 g; Sugar 5 g; Cholesterol 20 mg; Sodium 251 mg

> Cooked quinoa already on hand? Add 1½ cups (375 mL) cooked quinoa to the vegetables in this recipe.

SERVES 4

1 cup (250 mL) water

½ cup (125 mL) quinoa

½ cup (125 mL) halved cherry tomatoes

½ cup (125 mL) diced seeded cucumber

½ cup (125 mL) diced yellow bell pepper

½ cup (125 mL) halved green grapes

2 Tbsp (30 mL) chopped green onions

2 Tbsp (30 mL) extra virgin olive oil

2 Tbsp (30 mL) apple cider vinegar

1 tsp (5 mL) herbes de Provence

Pinch of salt (optional)

½ cup (125 mL) diced reduced-fat aged Cheddar cheese

CRISP LEMON SNAP PEA SALAD

SERVES 6

2 cups (500 mL) water

1 cup (250 mL) quinoa

2 cups (500 mL) fresh sweet snap peas cut diagonally into thirds

1½ cups (375 mL) button mushrooms, cut into quarters or eighths if large

⅓ cup (75 mL) thinly sliced red onion cut into 1-inch (2.5 cm) lengths

1 Tbsp (15 mL) chopped fresh dill

⅓ cup (75 mL) white balsamic vinegar

¼ cup (60 mL) olive oil or flaxseed oil

1 tsp (5 mL) grated lemon zest

1 Tbsp (15 mL) lemon juice

1 tsp (5 mL) pure maple syrup

Crisp, sweet snap peas are blended with the fresh fragrance of lemon. This salad is even better the next day, after the dressing has completely soaked into the mushrooms.

Combine the water and quinoa in a medium saucepan and bring to a boil. Reduce to a simmer, cover and cook for 15 minutes. Fluff with a fork and set aside to cool completely.

Combine the peas, mushrooms, red onion and dill in a medium bowl. Whisk together the vinegar, oil, lemon zest, lemon juice and maple syrup. Pour over the cooled quinoa in the saucepan and stir until evenly dispersed. Add to the vegetable mixture, toss and serve.

PER SERVING: Energy 230 calories; Protein 6 g; Carbohydrates 28 g; Dietary Fiber 3 g; Fat 11 g; Sugar 5 g; Cholesterol 0 mg; Sodium 10 mg

Unable to find fresh sweet snap peas? Use crisp snow peas instead.

GREEK QUINOA SALAD

SERVES 6

1⅓ cups (325 mL) water

⅔ cup (150 mL) quinoa

1 cup (250 mL) diced English cucumber

½ cup (125 mL) diced red bell pepper

½ cup (125 mL) sliced or chopped pitted black olives

½ cup (125 mL) crumbled reduced-fat feta cheese

¼ cup (60 mL) diced red onion (optional)

3 Tbsp (45 mL) olive oil

3 Tbsp (45 mL) red wine vinegar

1 tsp (5 mL) dried oregano

Cracked black pepper to taste

This full-flavored quinoa salad with a light dressing and healthful vegetables will instantly have you feeling like a god or goddess. Plus, it's so quick and easy, you won't even break a sweat!

Bring the water and quinoa to a boil in a medium saucepan. Reduce to a simmer, cover and cook for 15 minutes. Fluff with a fork and set aside to cool completely.

Combine the cucumber, red pepper, olives, feta and red onion (if using) in a medium bowl. Add the cooled quinoa. Whisk together the olive oil, vinegar and oregano. Pour the dressing over the quinoa mixture and gently toss until evenly distributed. Add cracked black pepper to taste.

PER SERVING: Energy 180 calories; Protein 5 g; Carbohydrates 15 g; Dietary Fiber 2 g; Fat 12 g; Sugar 1 g; Cholesterol 5 mg; Sodium 160 mg

> Cooked quinoa already on hand? Add 2 cups (500 mL) cooked quinoa to the vegetables and feta in this recipe.

MINTED CUCUMBER SPROUT SALAD WITH TOASTED PEANUTS

Cucumber, mint, lime and toasted peanuts are a terrific, fresh-tasting blend that will pleasantly surprise you. When you are tired of your other salad recipes, try this one!

Combine the quinoa sprouts, cucumber, red onion, mint and peanuts in a medium bowl. Whisk together the lime juice, oil and salt (if using). Pour over the quinoa mixture and gently toss until coated. Serve immediately.

Salad can be stored in the refrigerator for up to 1 day. (Sprouts deteriorate quickly once they're combined in a salad.)

PER SERVING: Energy 290 calories; Protein 8 g; Carbohydrates 32 g; Dietary Fiber 4 g; Fat 11 g; Sugar 2 g; Cholesterol 0 mg; Sodium 0 mg

SERVES 6

3 cups (750 mL) quinoa sprouts (pages 10 and 11)

1½ cups (375 mL) diced English cucumber

⅓ cup (75 mL) thinly sliced red onion cut into 1-inch (2.5 cm) pieces

¼ cup (60 mL) chopped fresh mint

¼ cup (60 mL) chopped toasted peanuts

¼ cup (60 mL) lime juice (from about 1½ limes)

¼ cup (60 mL) olive oil or flaxseed oil

Pinch of salt (optional)

To toast nuts, preheat the oven to 350°F (180°C). Spread the nuts on a baking sheet and toast in the oven, stirring once if necessary, for 5 to 7 minutes, until fragrant and lightly toasted.

PEAR, WALNUT & BLUE CHEESE SALAD WITH THYME DRESSING IN RADICCHIO CUPS

Even though this stunningly delicious salad is perfect for a late-summer or early-fall dinner party, it can be enjoyed at any time of the year. All white quinoa looks great, but to maximize the dramatic colors in this dish use half black and half white quinoa. Do not separate the radicchio leaves until just before serving to prevent wilting.

Combine the water and quinoa in a medium saucepan and bring to a boil. Reduce to a simmer, cover and cook for 15 minutes. Fluff with a fork and set aside to cool completely.

In a medium bowl, whisk together the apple juice, vinegar, oil, thyme and salt (if using).

Peel the pears if the skin is thick. Core and dice the pears to make 1½ cups (375 mL). Add the pears to the dressing and gently toss to coat completely. Add the cooled quinoa, walnuts, blue cheese and green onions. Toss gently.

Just before serving, separate the radicchio leaves by cutting at the base of the head. Leaves that are 3½ to 4 inches (9 to 10 cm) across are the perfect size. Place one leaf on each plate and divide the salad between the cups. Serve immediately.

PER SERVING: Energy 240 calories; Protein 5 g; Carbohydrates 27 g; Dietary Fiber 4 g; Fat 13 g; Sugar 9 g; Cholesterol 5 mg; Sodium 90 mg

SERVES 4

1⅓ cups (325 mL) water

⅔ cup (150 mL) quinoa

6 Tbsp (90 mL) unsweetened apple juice

¼ cup (60 mL) white wine vinegar

3 Tbsp (45 mL) flaxseed oil or olive oil

1 tsp (5 mL) chopped fresh thyme

Pinch of salt (optional)

2 to 3 ripe pears (Bartlett, Bosc or Anjou)

¼ cup (60 mL) walnuts or pecans, coarsely chopped

¼ cup (60 mL) crumbled blue cheese (gluten-free if required)

¼ cup (60 mL) sliced green onions

1 head radicchio

Always buy pears that are not too soft or bruised. Ripen hard fruit for a few days in a paper bag at room temperature, then store in the refrigerator. Serve at room temperature.

PEACH & CHICKEN QUINOA

SERVES 6

2 cups (500 mL) water

1 cup (250 mL) quinoa

1 Tbsp (15 mL) grapeseed oil

2 boneless, skinless chicken breasts

2 medium peaches,
    coarsely chopped

⅓ cup (75 mL) chopped
    toasted pecans

¼ cup (60 mL) low-fat plain yogurt

¼ tsp (1 mL) each black pepper,
    onion powder and paprika

Pinch each of dried thyme,
    garlic powder, ground cumin
    and cayenne pepper

Delightfully fresh peaches, gently spiced up and tossed with chicken and creamy yogurt, make this delicious dish unusual and refreshing.

Bring the water and quinoa to a boil in a large saucepan. Reduce to a simmer, cover and cook for 15 minutes. Fluff with a fork and set aside.

In a medium skillet on medium heat, heat the oil. Cook the chicken, turning once, for 6 minutes per side, or until it is no longer pink inside. Chop into bite-size pieces and set aside to cool completely.

In a medium bowl, mix together the peaches, toasted pecans and yogurt. Add the pepper, onion powder, paprika, thyme, garlic powder, cumin and cayenne; mix thoroughly. Add the quinoa and chicken pieces. Mix well and serve immediately or chilled.

PER SERVING: Energy 230 calories; Protein 14 g; Carbohydrates 24 g; Dietary Fiber 3 g; Fat 10 g; Sugar 4 g; Cholesterol 25 mg; Sodium 55 mg

- Cooked quinoa already on hand? Add 3 cups (750 mL) cooked quinoa along with the chicken pieces in this recipe.

- To toast nuts, preheat the oven to 350°F (180°C). Spread the nuts on a baking sheet and toast in the oven, stirring once if necessary, for 5 to 7 minutes, until fragrant and lightly toasted.

PINE NUT & ROASTED RED PEPPER SALAD

A no-fuss, throw-together salad that is a little different than many of the salads you've had before. This looks great with any color of quinoa. You may replace the roasted red pepper with fresh bell pepper, if desired.

Bring the water and quinoa to a boil in a medium saucepan. Reduce to a simmer, cover and cook for 15 minutes. Fluff with a fork and set aside to cool completely.

In a medium bowl, combine the cooled quinoa, roasted peppers, feta, green onions and pine nuts. Whisk together the lemon juice, oil and black pepper. Fold dressing into the quinoa mixture. Serve.

PER SERVING: Energy 210 calories; Protein 7 g; Carbohydrates 23 g; Dietary Fiber 4 g; Fat 10 g; Sugar 2 g; Cholesterol 5 mg; Sodium 80 mg

SERVES 6

2 cups (500 mL) water

1 cup (250 mL) quinoa

1¼ cups (300 mL) chopped roasted red peppers (homemade or store-bought)

½ cup (125 mL) crumbled reduced-fat feta cheese

⅓ cup (75 mL) thinly sliced green onions

¼ cup (60 mL) pine nuts

2 Tbsp (30 mL) lemon juice

2 Tbsp (30 mL) olive oil or flaxseed oil

Pinch of freshly ground black pepper

ROASTED RED PEPPERS
It's easy to make your own roasted red peppers. Once you roast them yourself, you'll experience a flavor that cannot be beat. They can be used wherever you like, including on sandwiches and burgers and in salads, omelets and quiches. For this recipe, broil 2 red bell peppers in the oven on a baking sheet. The skin of the peppers will turn black and char. Turn the peppers gradually until the whole pepper has charred. Place the peppers in a covered bowl or closed paper bag. Allow to sit for 15 to 20 minutes for easy removal of the skin. Slice peppers in half and remove the seeds and skin. Peppers will keep in the refrigerator for up to 5 days.

RED CABBAGE & SPROUT SLAW

2 cups (500 mL) quinoa sprouts
(pages 10 and 11)

2 cups (500 mL) shredded red
cabbage

2 cups (500 mL) grated carrots

½ cup (125 mL) sliced green onions

¾ cup (175 mL) reduced-fat or
regular sour cream
(gluten-free if required)

¼ cup (60 mL) liquid honey

3 Tbsp (45 mL) apple cider vinegar

1 Tbsp (15 mL) flaxseed oil or olive oil

¼ tsp (1 mL) salt (optional)

White pepper to taste

Need a healthy, crisp coleslaw that is creamy but without a heavy dressing? Make this one ahead, then mix with the dressing just before serving. This coleslaw is meant to be served alongside the delectable Smoky Chipotle BBQ Pulled Beef on page 146.

Combine the sprouts, cabbage, carrots and green onions in a large serving bowl. Set aside in the refrigerator if not serving immediately.

Whisk together the sour cream, honey, vinegar, oil, salt (if using) and white pepper. Set aside in the refrigerator if not serving immediately.

Just before serving, gently stir dressing into the vegetable mixture. Adjust seasoning if desired and serve.

PER SERVING: Energy 140 calories; Protein 4 g; Carbohydrates 27 g; Dietary Fiber 2 g; Fat 2.5 g; Sugar 10 g; Cholesterol 0 mg; Sodium 60 mg

> Red cabbage is full of antioxidants that help the body eliminate toxins, prevent disease and illness and boost immunity.

SUMMER
VEGETABLE SALAD

Summer brings wonderful local produce to our tables. This salad features the classic combination of basil, zucchini and tomatoes.

Bring the water and quinoa to a boil in a medium saucepan. Reduce to a simmer, cover and cook for 15 minutes. Fluff with a fork and set aside to cool completely.

In a large salad bowl, mix the zucchini, tomatoes, bocconcini and cooled quinoa. Whisk together the oil, lemon juice, basil, garlic and salt. Pour dressing over the vegetable mixture and toss. Serve.

PER SERVING: Energy 200 calories; Protein 9 g; Carbohydrates 16 g; Dietary Fiber 2 g; Fat 12 g; Sugar 1 g; Cholesterol 10 mg; Sodium 75 mg

> Try something different. Instead of using green zucchini, use young yellow zucchini for a brighter, even more beautiful salad.

SERVES 8

2 cups (500 mL) water

1 cup (250 mL) quinoa

1½ cups (375 mL) diced zucchini

1½ cups (375 mL) halved cherry or grape tomatoes

1 cup (250 mL) halved light small bocconcini cheese (one 200 g container)

¼ cup (60 mL) flaxseed oil or olive oil

¼ cup (60 mL) lemon juice

1 tsp (5 mL) finely chopped fresh basil

1 tsp (5 mL) minced garlic

¼ tsp (1 mL) salt

SWEET POTATO SALAD

SERVES 8

1 ½ cups (375 mL) water

¾ cup (175 mL) black quinoa

2 ½ cups (625 mL) peeled sweet
  potatoes cut into 1-inch
  (2.5 cm) chunks

½ cup (125 mL) thinly sliced
  green onions

½ cup (125 mL) chopped
  fresh parsley

⅓ cup (75 mL) toasted pecans

1 ½ tsp (7 mL) grated lemon zest

¼ cup (60 mL) lemon juice

¼ cup (60 mL) olive oil

¼ tsp (1 mL) ground ginger

¼ tsp (1 mL) salt (optional)

This high-contrast color combination will also delight your taste buds. The flavor combo of sweet potato, toasted pecans, green onions, lemon and quinoa will have you loving every bite. Black quinoa has the most dramatic appearance in this salad, but you can use any color.

Bring the water and quinoa to a boil in a small saucepan. Reduce to a simmer, cover and cook for 15 minutes. Fluff with a fork and set aside to cool.

Meanwhile, place the sweet potatoes in a medium saucepan with just enough water to cover. Bring to a boil, reduce to a simmer, cover and cook until potatoes are just tender (don't overcook). Drain the potatoes and cool completely.

Combine the quinoa and sweet potato with the green onions, parsley and pecans in a medium bowl. Whisk together the lemon zest, lemon juice, olive oil, ginger and salt (if using). Gently toss dressing with potato mixture until evenly distributed. Serve immediately or refrigerate.

PER SERVING: Energy 170 calories; Protein 3 g; Carbohydrates 15 g; Dietary Fiber 2 g; Fat 11 g; Sugar 2 g; Cholesterol 0 mg; Sodium 10 mg

> To toast nuts, preheat the oven to 350°F (180°C). Spread the nuts on a baking sheet and toast in the oven, stirring once if necessary, for 5 to 7 minutes, until fragrant and lightly toasted.

TAHINI TOMATO SALAD

Tahini, a toasted sesame paste, makes a creamy, nutty addition to dressings, salads and even granola bars. Here it adds aromatic flair to a fresh tomato salad. Tahini can be found in the ethnic section of grocery or health-food stores.

Bring 1 cup (250 mL) water and the quinoa to a boil in a medium saucepan. Reduce to a simmer, cover and cook for 15 minutes. Fluff with a fork and set aside to cool.

Whisk together the lukewarm water and tahini in a small bowl. Add the lemon juice, mustard, garlic, pepper and salt (if using). Place the cooled quinoa in a salad bowl and toss with the dressing until evenly coated. Gently stir in the tomatoes, cucumber and red onion. Serve.

PER SERVING: Energy 110 calories; Protein 4 g; Carbohydrates 15 g; Dietary Fiber 2 g; Fat 5 g; Sugar 2 g; Cholesterol 0 mg; Sodium 30 mg

SERVES 6

1 cup (250 mL) water

½ cup (125 mL) quinoa

¼ cup (60 mL) lukewarm water

3 Tbsp (45 mL) tahini

2 Tbsp (30 mL) lemon juice

1 tsp (5 mL) Dijon mustard

½ tsp (2 mL) minced garlic

Pinch of freshly cracked
    black pepper

Pinch of salt (optional)

1½ cups (375 mL) diced
    fresh tomatoes

1½ cups (375 mL) diced
    English cucumber

⅓ cup (75 mL) diced red onion

TANGY LENTIL PEPPER SALAD

SERVES 6

2 cups (500 mL) water

⅔ cup (150 mL) quinoa

⅓ cup (75 mL) dried
    red lentils, rinsed

1 cup (250 mL) cooked chickpeas

1 cup (250 mL) chopped
    red bell pepper

½ cup (125 mL) sliced green onions

⅓ cup (75 mL) chopped
    fresh cilantro

3 Tbsp (45 mL) olive oil

2 Tbsp (30 mL) lemon juice

2 Tbsp (30 mL) apple cider vinegar

1 Tbsp (15 mL) liquid honey

Pinch each of curry powder and
    ground cardamom

¼ tsp (1 mL) salt (optional)

Red lentils cook quickly and make for an easy and different ingredient in this fresh salad along with red pepper, cilantro and green onions.

Combine the water and quinoa in a medium saucepan and bring to a boil. Reduce to a simmer, cover and cook for 10 minutes. Stir in the lentils and bring to a boil again. Reduce to a simmer, cover and cook for 8 more minutes or until the lentils are tender. Fluff with a fork and set aside to cool completely.

In a large bowl, combine the cooled quinoa mixture, chickpeas, red pepper, green onions and cilantro; mix well. Whisk together the olive oil, lemon juice, vinegar, honey, curry powder, cardamom and salt (if using). Pour dressing over the quinoa mixture and toss to coat thoroughly. Serve.

PER SERVING: Energy 230 calories; Protein 8 g; Carbohydrates 30 g; Dietary Fiber 5 g; Fat 9 g; Sugar 5 g; Cholesterol 0 mg; Sodium 100 mg

TUNA & WHITE KIDNEY BEAN SALAD

A fresh and high-protein salad for a wholesome lunch or a light dinner. White kidney beans are sometimes labeled cannellini beans.

Bring the water and quinoa to a boil in a medium saucepan. Reduce to a simmer, cover and cook for 15 minutes. Fluff with a fork and set aside to cool completely.

Combine the beans, celery, red pepper, green onions, tuna and quinoa in a medium bowl. Whisk together the olive oil, vinegar, mustard, basil, black pepper and salt (if using). Pour dressing over the bean mixture and stir until well combined.

Place romaine lettuce in a salad bowl or on a plate and scoop the tuna salad on top. Sprinkle with feta cheese (if using). Serve.

PER SERVING: Energy 260 calories; Protein 21 g; Carbohydrates 25 g; Dietary Fiber 6 g; Fat 8 g; Sugar 3 g; Cholesterol 25 mg; Sodium 135 mg

> Cooked quinoa already on hand? Add 1½ cups (375 mL) cooked quinoa to the bean mixture in this salad.

SERVES 6

1 cup (250 mL) water

½ cup (125 mL) quinoa

1 can (19 oz/540 mL) white kidney beans, drained and rinsed

½ cup (125 mL) chopped celery hearts

½ cup (125 mL) chopped red bell pepper

3 Tbsp (45 mL) chopped green onions

2 cans (6 oz/170 g each) sodium-reduced white albacore tuna, drained

2 Tbsp (30 mL) olive oil

2 Tbsp (30 mL) balsamic vinegar

2 Tbsp (30 mL) Dijon mustard

1 Tbsp (15 mL) chopped fresh basil

¼ tsp (1 mL) black pepper

¼ tsp (1 mL) salt (optional)

4 cups (1 L) romaine lettuce (or other salad greens)

½ cup (125 mL) crumbled feta cheese (optional)

WALDORF SALAD

SERVES 8

2 cups (500 mL) water

1 cup (250 mL) quinoa

¾ cup (175 mL) halved red grapes

⅔ cup (150 mL) thinly sliced celery

½ cup (125 mL) thinly sliced
    green onions

½ cup (125 mL) halved fresh or
    thawed frozen cranberries

½ cup (125 mL) toasted
    walnut pieces

½ cup (125 mL) freshly
    squeezed orange juice

2 Tbsp (30 mL) flaxseed oil

¼ tsp (1 mL) salt (optional)

Pinch of cinnamon

¾ cup (175 mL) cored
    and diced apple

This flavorful recipe is a modern take on the classic Waldorf salad. It can be an everyday salad or it can be served at Christmas, Thanksgiving dinner or brunch. This recipe tastes great and looks even better if you use half white and half black quinoa.

Bring the water and quinoa to a boil in a medium saucepan. Reduce to a simmer, cover and cook for 15 minutes. Fluff with a fork and set aside to cool.

In a medium bowl, combine the cooled quinoa with the grapes, celery, green onions, cranberries and walnut pieces. In a small bowl, whisk together the orange juice, oil, salt (if using) and cinnamon. Toss diced apple in dressing, then toss dressing and apples together with the quinoa mixture. This salad is best served after resting for about 2 hours in the refrigerator but can be served right away.

PER SERVING: Energy 190 calories; Protein 5 g; Carbohydrates 22 g; Dietary Fiber 3 g; Fat 10 g; Sugar 6 g; Cholesterol 0 mg; Sodium 10 mg

- Cooked quinoa already on hand? Add 3 cups (750 mL) to the salad ingredients in this recipe.

- To toast nuts, preheat the oven to 350°F (180°C). Spread the nuts on a baking sheet and toast in the oven, stirring once if necessary, for 5 to 7 minutes, until fragrant and lightly toasted.

BAKED ROASTED
RED PEPPER DIP

Fluffy cooked quinoa puréed with meaty roasted peppers and creamy feta adds plenty of hidden nutrition to this favorite dip. Serve with yummy dippers like cucumber and other vegetables, fresh pita or tortilla chips.

Preheat the oven to 350°F (180°C). Spray or grease an 8-inch (20 cm) square baking dish.

Bring the water and quinoa to a boil in a medium saucepan. Reduce to a simmer, cover and cook for 15 minutes. The quinoa must be extra-fluffy. Fluff with a fork and let cool slightly.

In a food processor or using a hand blender, purée the quinoa with ¾ cup (175 mL) of the feta. Add the red peppers and garlic; process until smooth. Pour mixture into the baking dish and top with the remaining feta.

Bake for 20 to 22 minutes, until the top and edges are beginning to brown. Serve warm with your favorite dipping treats.

PER SERVING: Energy 80 calories; Protein 4 g; Carbohydrates 6 g; Dietary Fiber 1 g; Fat 4 g; Sugar 1 g; Cholesterol 15 mg; Sodium 220 mg

SERVES 8

⅔ cup (150 mL) water

⅓ cup (75 mL) quinoa

1 cup (250 mL) crumbled feta cheese

1¼ cups (300 mL) roasted red peppers (page 63 or store-bought)

1 tsp (5 mL) minced garlic

> Extra-fluffy cooked quinoa already on hand? Purée 1 cup (250 mL) extra-fluffy cooked quinoa with the feta.

BAKED SPINACH
PARMESAN ARANCINI

MAKES 2 DOZEN ARANCINI

1⅓ cups (325 mL) water

⅔ cup (150 mL) white quinoa

½ cup (125 mL) dry white wine

1 cup (250 mL) chopped
fresh spinach

1 tsp (5 mL) minced garlic

1 cup (250 mL) grated
Parmesan cheese

2 Tbsp (30 mL) basil pesto

3 oz (85 g) fresh mozzarella cheese

2 eggs

¾ cup (175 mL) fine rice flour or
whole wheat flour

¾ cup (175 mL) fine dry bread
crumbs (gluten-free if required)

Warm marinara sauce for dipping
(optional)

The arancini balls will
not change much in color
while cooking. Keep an
eye on the balls and take
them out of the oven if
you see any cheese
bubbling out. You don't
want to overcook them.

Traditional arancini are fried rice balls that originate from Italy. Enjoy this baked version. Serve warm dipped in marinara sauce for an appetizer that doesn't stay around long! Prepare them the day before for an oven-ready appetizer.

Bring the water and quinoa to a boil in a medium saucepan. Reduce to a simmer, cover and cook for 15 minutes. Turn off the burner and let quinoa sit, covered, for another 10 minutes (quinoa should be light and fluffy). Fluff with a fork and set aside.

In a medium skillet, bring the wine to a boil. Reduce heat to medium-low and add the quinoa, spinach and garlic, stirring until the wine has evaporated or been absorbed (the quinoa-spinach mixture should be more dry than wet). Remove from the heat and add the Parmesan and pesto; stir until the cheese is melted. Pour the mixture onto a baking sheet and cool completely.

Cut the mozzarella into twenty-four ½-inch (1 cm) cubes. Take 1 Tbsp (15 mL) of the quinoa mixture and shape it into a ball in the palm of your hand. Press a piece of mozzarella cheese into the center and firmly press the quinoa around it to seal. Repeat and then refrigerate the balls for at least 1 hour.

Preheat the oven to 400°F (200°C). Line a baking sheet with parchment.

In a shallow dish, whisk the eggs. Place the flour and bread crumbs in two separate shallow dishes. Using one hand for wet ingredients and one for dry, roll each ball in the flour, then the egg (letting excess drip off) and finally the bread crumbs, coating thoroughly. Place 1 inch (2.5 cm) apart on the baking sheet.

Bake for 7 to 10 minutes. Serve immediately with warm marinara sauce.

PER SERVING: Energy 80 calories; Protein 4 g; Carbohydrates 8 g; Dietary Fiber 1 g; Fat 3 g; Sugar 0 g; Cholesterol 20 mg; Sodium 85 mg

APPLE CHEDDAR
MUFFINS

Fresh thyme adds a surprising flavor to these apple and Cheddar muffins. They're a great portable food to take for lunch or anywhere on the run. Serve as an anytime snack, for brunch or as a breakfast muffin.

Preheat the oven to 400°F (200°C). Lightly grease a 12-cup muffin pan or line with paper liners.

In a medium bowl, whisk together the quinoa flour, baking powder, baking soda and salt. Add the apples and shredded cheese; stir until well combined. In a large bowl, beat the eggs. Stir in the applesauce, sugar, butter, buttermilk and thyme. Add the applesauce mixture to the flour mixture; gently stir just until blended. Use a large spoon or ice-cream scoop to divide the batter evenly among the muffin cups.

Bake for 18 minutes or until a toothpick inserted into the center of a muffin comes out with only one or two crumbs. Cool in the pan.

PER SERVING: Energy 180 calories; Protein 6 g; Carbohydrates 19 g; Dietary Fiber 2 g; Fat 8 g; Sugar 7 g; Cholesterol 50 mg; Sodium 190 mg

MAKES 12 MUFFINS

1½ cups (375 mL) quinoa flour

1½ tsp (7 mL) baking powder

½ tsp (2 mL) baking soda

¼ tsp (1 mL) salt

1 cup (250 mL) chopped peeled apples

1 cup (250 mL) shredded reduced fat aged Cheddar cheese

2 large eggs

1 cup (250 mL) unsweetened applesauce

¼ cup (60 mL) organic cane sugar or white sugar

¼ cup (60 mL) unsalted butter, softened

¼ cup (60 mL) buttermilk

1 tsp (5 mL) chopped fresh thyme

We highly recommend using fresh thyme, but if you don't have fresh you can always use ½ tsp (2 mL) dried thyme.

BELL PEPPER MUFFINS
WITH CURRANTS

MAKES 12 MUFFINS

1 tsp (5 mL) grapeseed oil
   or vegetable oil

⅓ cup (75 mL) chopped
   red bell pepper

⅓ cup (75 mL) chopped
   yellow bell pepper

¼ cup (60 mL) chopped
   green onions

½ tsp (2 mL) minced garlic

1½ cups (375 mL) quinoa flour

2 Tbsp (30 mL) organic
   cane sugar or white sugar

1½ tsp (7 mL) baking powder

¼ tsp (1 mL) baking soda

¼ tsp (1 mL) salt

¼ cup (60 mL) cold unsalted
   butter, cut into small pieces

⅓ cup (75 mL) dried currants

½ tsp (2 mL) dried basil

2 large eggs

⅔ cup (150 mL) low-fat plain yogurt

¼ cup (60 mL) unsweetened
   applesauce

These savory quinoa muffins are filled with sautéed bell peppers and onions and accented with sweet currants. Warm or cold, they make a great take-out breakfast or mid-morning snack.

Preheat the oven to 350°F (180°C). Lightly grease or spray a 12-cup muffin pan or line with paper liners.

In a medium saucepan on medium heat, heat the oil. Cook the red and yellow peppers, green onions and garlic until the peppers and onions have softened, about 5 minutes. Set aside to cool slightly.

In a large bowl, combine the quinoa flour, sugar, baking powder, baking soda and salt. Using your fingers or a pastry blender, cut in the cold butter until the mixture resembles bread crumbs. Stir in the currants and basil.

In a medium bowl, beat the eggs. Whisk in the yogurt and applesauce. Stir in the pepper mixture. Add the egg mixture to the flour mixture and stir until batter is just moistened.

Use a large spoon or ice-cream scoop to divide the batter evenly among the muffin cups. Bake for 20 minutes or until a toothpick inserted into the center of a muffin comes out clean. Cool in the pan.

PER SERVING: Energy 140 calories; Protein 4 g; Carbohydrates 18 g; Dietary Fiber 2 g; Fat 6 g; Sugar 7 g; Cholesterol 40 mg; Sodium 160 mg

OREGANO, OLIVE & FETA STUFFED TOMATOES

Healthy appetizers needed for a healthy crowd? This recipe doubles easily if required. It is possible to use cherry tomatoes, but because they are slightly smaller, they are more challenging to prepare.

Bring the water and quinoa to a boil in a small saucepan. Reduce to a simmer, cover and cook for 15 minutes. Fluff with a fork and set aside to cool completely.

Slice the tomatoes in half. Using a small spoon, scoop out the insides (see Tip).

In a medium bowl, combine the quinoa, green pepper, feta, olives and red onion. Stir in the oil, vinegar and oregano until evenly mixed. Scoop ½ teaspoon (2 mL) of filling into each tomato half and arrange on a tray. Serve.

PER SERVING (5 pieces): Energy 60 calories; Protein 2 g; Carbohydrates 6 g; Dietary Fiber 1 g; Fat 3 g; Sugar 2 g; Cholesterol 5 mg; Sodium 70 mg

MAKES 42 TOMATOES

⅔ cup (150 mL) water

⅓ cup (75 mL) quinoa

1 lb (450 g) cocktail tomatoes

¼ cup (60 mL) finely diced green bell pepper

¼ cup (60 mL) crumbled feta cheese

¼ cup (60 mL) finely chopped pitted black olives

2 Tbsp (30 mL) finely diced red onion

4 tsp (20 mL) olive oil or flaxseed oil

4 tsp (20 mL) red wine vinegar

1½ tsp (7 mL) finely chopped fresh oregano (or ½ tsp/2 mL dried)

Freeze the tomato insides to use in chili or tomato sauce.

SMOKED WILD PACIFIC SALMON, CUCUMBER & QUINOA SPROUT BITES

MAKES 54 BITES

4 oz (115 g) light or regular
    cream cheese

2 Tbsp (30 mL) reduced-fat
    or regular sour cream
    (gluten-free if required)

1 English cucumber, cut into 54 slices
    each ¼ inch (5 mm) thick

½ cup (125 mL) black quinoa
    sprouts (pages 10 and 11)

4 ½ oz (125 g) smoked wild
    Pacific salmon, torn or
    cut into 54 squares each
    1 inch (2.5 cm) wide

Freshly cracked black pepper
    (optional)

54 small sprigs fresh dill

An entertaining favorite, this combination of cucumber, cream cheese and smoked salmon is always a hit. Sprouted black quinoa makes a dramatic appearance and tastes fantastic on these stunning appetizers.

Whip together the cream cheese and sour cream. Place mixture in a piping bag fitted with a small star tip or in a resealable plastic bag. If using a plastic bag, cut ¼ inch (5 mm) off one corner.

Spread out the cucumber slices on a tray and place ½ tsp (2 mL) of sprouts on each. Place a piece of salmon on top of the quinoa sprouts. Pipe ½ tsp (2 mL) swirl of cream cheese mixture on each and grind some pepper (if using) over the tops. Garnish with a small sprig of dill. Keep refrigerated, and serve in small quantities to keep them cool.

PER SERVING: Energy 15 calories; Protein 1 g; Carbohydrates 1 g; Dietary Fiber 0 g; Fat 1 g; Sugar 0 g; Cholesterol 5 mg; Sodium 25 mg

THAI CHICKEN FINGERS

¾ cup (175 mL) low-fat plain yogurt

1 tsp (5 mL) minced garlic

¾ tsp (4 mL) curry powder

½ tsp (2 mL) salt (optional)

¾ cup (175 mL) quinoa flakes

⅓ cup (75 mL) unsweetened
    shredded coconut

¼ cup (60 mL) chopped
    fresh cilantro

1½ lb (675 g) boneless, skinless
    chicken breasts

These tasty chicken fingers are baked, not fried. They can be eaten as a main dish or as an appetizer. Delicious served with a sweet chili dipping sauce.

Preheat the oven to 450°F (230°C). Line the baking sheet with parchment paper.

Stir together the yogurt, garlic, curry powder and salt (if using) in a shallow dish. In another shallow dish, stir together the quinoa flakes, coconut and cilantro.

Cut chicken breasts crosswise into ½-inch (1 cm) slices. Using one hand for dipping (yogurt mixture) and the other for coating (flake mixture), dip one piece of chicken in the yogurt, coating all sides, then repeat with the flakes. Place on a baking sheet 1½ inches (4 cm) apart. Repeat with the remaining chicken.

Bake for 15 minutes or until the center is no longer pink. Serve immediately with a sweet chili dipping sauce.

PER SERVING: Energy 220 calories; Protein 27 g; Carbohydrates 11 g; Dietary Fiber 1 g; Fat 7 g; Sugar 2 g; Cholesterol 75 mg; Sodium 250 mg

APRICOT, PINE NUT & ROSEMARY DRESSING

Try this stuffing-style dressing with your next chicken dinner. Make the quinoa-onion mixture an hour before and toss with the remaining ingredients just before serving.

Heat the oil in a large saucepan on medium-low heat. Add the onions and cook for 7 minutes or until tender and opaque. Add the stock and quinoa. Bring it to a boil. Reduce to a simmer, cover and cook for 15 minutes or until the quinoa is tender.

If not serving immediately, transfer quinoa to a small baking dish, cover and keep warm in a 200°F (100°C) oven for up to 1 hour.

Just before serving, stir in the apricots, pine nuts, butter, parsley, rosemary, lemon zest, salt (if using) and pepper.

PER SERVING: Energy 170 calories; Protein 5 g; Carbohydrates 26 g; Dietary Fiber 3 g; Fat 6 g; Sugar 4 g; Cholesterol 5 mg; Sodium 55 mg

SERVES 6

1 tsp (5 mL) grapeseed oil
or vegetable oil

½ cup (125 mL) chopped onions

2 cups (500 mL) vegetable or
chicken stock

1 cup (250 mL) quinoa

⅓ cup (75 mL) diced dried apricots

3 Tbsp (45 mL) pine nuts

2 tsp (10 mL) unsalted butter

2 Tbsp (30 mL) chopped fresh
parsley (or 2 tsp/10 mL dried)

¾ tsp (4 mL) minced fresh
rosemary (or ¼ tsp/1 mL dried)

¼ tsp (1 mL) grated lemon zest

¼ tsp (1 mL) salt (if desired)

Pinch of black pepper

CRANBERRY, HAZELNUT & SAUSAGE DRESSING

Tangy cranberries, apple pieces, hazelnuts and Italian sausage blended with seasoned quinoa make a wonderful gluten-free alternative to any traditional turkey stuffing.

SERVES 8

1 Tbsp (15 mL) grapeseed oil
or vegetable oil

½ lb (225 g) Homemade Italian
Ground Sausage (recipe follows)

1 cup (250 mL) chopped celery

1 leek (white part only), halved
lengthwise and sliced

2 cups (500 mL) sodium-reduced
chicken or turkey stock

1 cup (250 mL) quinoa

1 Granny Smith apple,
cored and diced

⅓ cup (75 mL) water

¼ cup (60 mL) sweetened
dried cranberries

½ cup (125 mL) coarsely
chopped hazelnuts

2 Tbsp (30 mL) chopped fresh
parsley (or 1½ tsp/7 mL dried)

1 tsp (5 mL) minced fresh thyme
(or ¼ tsp/1 mL dried)

1 tsp (5 mL) minced fresh sage
(or ¼ tsp/1 mL ground sage)

¼ tsp (1 mL) salt (optional)

Pinch of pepper

Heat the oil in a large saucepan on medium heat. Add the sausage meat and cook until browned and no pink remains. Reduce heat to medium-low and stir in the celery and leek. Cover and cook for another 7 minutes or until the celery is tender (add a spoonful of water if pan is dry). Add the stock, quinoa, apple and ⅓ cup (75 mL) water. Bring to a boil. Reduce to a simmer, cover and cook for 20 minutes. Remove from the heat and let sit, covered, for another 5 minutes. Just before serving, stir in the cranberries, hazelnuts, parsley, thyme, sage, salt (if using) and pepper.

HOMEMADE ITALIAN GROUND SAUSAGE

Freeze any unused portion of
this recipe for up to 3 months.

Makes 1 lb (450 g)

¼ tsp (1 mL) fennel seeds

1 lb (450 g) ground turkey,
chicken or pork

¼ cup (60 mL) finely chopped onions

1 Tbsp (15 mL) chopped fresh
oregano (or 1 tsp/5 mL dried)

1 Tbsp (15 mL) chopped fresh
parsley (or 1 tsp /5 mL dried)

1 tsp (5 mL) minced garlic

½ tsp (2 mL) salt (optional)

¼ tsp (1 mL) ground coriander

¼ tsp (1 mL) black pepper

Pinch of cayenne pepper

Break up the fennel seeds with a mortar and pestle or crush with a rolling pin in a resealable plastic bag. Combine all the ingredients and mix well.

PER SERVING (including sausage filling): Energy 130 calories; Protein 4 g; Carbohydrates 19 g; Dietary Fiber 3 g; Fat 4.5 g; Sugar 3 g; Cholesterol 19 mg; Sodium 45 mg

ITALIAN SAUSAGE ROUNDS

Italian sausage rounds can be used wherever you would normally use regular Italian sausage. Fry in a small amount of oil or bake for an even lower-fat option. The cooked sausage patties can also be frozen for up to 1 month.

Bring the water and quinoa to a boil in a small saucepan. Reduce to a simmer, cover and cook for 15 minutes. Remove from the heat and keep covered for another 10 minutes. Fluff with a fork. Set aside to cool completely.

In a medium bowl, mix together the cooled quinoa and the sausage mixture.

PAN-FRY METHOD Heat the oil in a large skillet on medium-low heat. Scoop out ¼ cup (60 mL) servings of sausage mixture and with wet hands shape into rounds 1 inch (2.5 cm) thick. Fry for about 4 minutes on each side, until cooked through and golden brown. Serve.

OVEN METHOD Preheat the oven to 350°F (180°C). Line a baking sheet with parchment. Scoop out ¼ cup (60 mL) servings of sausage mixture and with wet hands shape into rounds 3 inches (8 cm) wide and ½ inch (1 cm) thick. Arrange on the baking sheet about 1½ inches (4 cm) apart. Bake for 10 minutes per side. Serve.

PER SERVING: Energy 200 calories; Protein 20 g; Carbohydrates 9 g; Dietary Fiber 1 g; Fat 10 g; Sugar 0 g; Cholesterol 65 mg; Sodium 55 mg

MAKES 10 ROUNDS, SERVING 5

⅔ cup (150 mL) water

⅓ cup (75 mL) quinoa

1 lb (450 g) Homemade Italian Ground Sausage (page 80)

2 tsp (10 mL) grapeseed oil

JALAPEÑO CORNBREAD

MAKES 24 PIECES

1 ½ cups (375 mL) quinoa flour

1 ½ cups (375 mL) yellow cornmeal

¼ cup (60 mL) organic
    cane sugar or white sugar

4 tsp (20 mL) baking powder

½ tsp (2 mL) baking soda

1 tsp (5 mL) salt

2 ½ cups (625 mL) buttermilk

3 large eggs

6 Tbsp (90 mL) unsalted
    butter, melted

3 Tbsp (45 mL) finely chopped
    pickled jalapeño peppers

Enhance any feast with this moist cornbread. Serve it warm, either plain or with butter. If you don't like jalapeño peppers, this cornbread is still tasty without them.

Preheat the oven to 400°F (200°C). Grease a 13- × 9-inch (3 L) baking pan.

In a large bowl, combine the flour, cornmeal, sugar, baking powder, baking soda and salt. In a medium bowl, whisk together the buttermilk and eggs until well blended. Add the melted butter and jalapeños to buttermilk mixture. Mix well. Add buttermilk mixture to flour mixture and stir just until mixed.

Pour batter into pan. Bake for 20 to 22 minutes or until edges are golden brown and a toothpick inserted into the center comes out clean. Cut lengthwise into 4 strips and cut each strip into 6 pieces. Serve warm.

PER SERVING: Energy 120 calories; Protein 3 g; Carbohydrates 15 g; Dietary Fiber 2 g; Fat 5 g; Sugar 3 g; Cholesterol 35 mg; Sodium 170 mg

No buttermilk on hand? Add 1 Tbsp (15 mL) of lemon juice or white vinegar to every 1 cup (250 mL) of milk, stir and let stand for 5 minutes. Use as directed.

INDIAN-INFUSED QUINOA

Cardamom and cinnamon flavors make this side a great accompaniment to any Indian main dish. It is paired fabulously with Chicken Masala on page 124.

Melt the butter in a medium saucepan on medium heat. Stir in the cardamom pods and bay leaf; heat for 30 seconds. Add the quinoa and stir to coat all the seeds with the butter. Add the water, carrots, cinnamon and salt. Bring to a boil on high heat, then reduce to a simmer, cover and cook for 15 minutes. Turn the heat off and let sit, covered, for another 10 minutes. Discard the cardamom pods and bay leaf and serve.

PER SERVING: Energy 170 calories; Protein 5 g; Carbohydrates 21 g; Dietary Fiber 3 g; Fat 8 g; Sugar 0 g; Cholesterol 15 mg; Sodium 105 mg

SERVES 4

2 Tbsp (30 mL) butter

4 cardamom pods, cracked but not completely broken (or ¼ tsp/1 mL ground cardamom)

½ bay leaf

¾ cup (175 mL) quinoa

1½ cups (375 mL) water

¼ cup (60 mL) finely diced carrots

Pinch of cinnamon

Pinch of salt

JALAPEÑO & CHILI QUINOA PILAF

SERVES 6

1 Tbsp (15 mL) vegetable oil

¼ cup (60 mL) diced onions

¾ cup (175 mL) quinoa

2 cups (500 mL) sodium-reduced
    chicken or vegetable stock

1 small jalapeño pepper,
    seeded and diced

1 clove garlic, minced

¼ cup (60 mL) chopped canned
    green chili peppers

¼ tsp (1 mL) ground cumin

⅓ cup (75 mL) shredded
    aged white Cheddar or
    mozzarella cheese

½ cup (125 mL) chopped
    fresh cilantro

This pilaf packs serious flavor with only a bit of heat, making it perfect alongside any meat dish, any southwestern-style dish or even all by itself for lunch.

Heat the oil in a large saucepan on medium-low heat. Add the onions and cook until translucent and lightly browned. Add the quinoa and cook for 2 to 3 minutes, until the quinoa is slightly toasted. Pour the stock into the pan, then gently stir in the jalapeño, garlic, chilies and cumin. Bring to a boil. Reduce to a simmer, cover and cook for 15 minutes. Turn the heat off and let sit, covered, for another 5 minutes. Mix in the cheese, stirring slowly until melted and well combined. Stir in the cilantro. Serve immediately. Pilaf keeps, covered and refrigerated, for up to 2 days.

PER SERVING: Energy 130 calories; Protein 6 g; Carbohydrates 16 g; Dietary Fiber 2 g; Fat 4.5 g; Sugar 1 g; Cholesterol 0 mg; Sodium 95 mg

Reduce the amount of cheese you use by using an older, sharper cheese. Aged cheese has more flavor, so you need less.

LEMON QUINOA

The light, buttery lemon taste of this side dish makes it a great partner alongside almost any main course. Subtle flavor, and wonderfully simple to prepare.

Bring the stock and quinoa to a boil in a large saucepan. Add the butter, lemon zest, lemon juice and salt. Reduce to a simmer, cover and cook for 15 minutes. Fluff with a fork. Add the parsley and stir well. Serve immediately.

PER SERVING: Energy 190 calories; Protein 6 g; Carbohydrates 30 g; Dietary Fiber 4 g; Fat 5 g; Sugar 1 g; Cholesterol 10 mg; Sodium 220 mg

SERVES 4

2 cups (500 mL) sodium-reduced vegetable stock

1 cup (250 mL) quinoa

1 Tbsp (15 mL) unsalted butter

2 tsp (10 mL) grated lemon zest

2 Tbsp (30 mL) lemon juice

¼ tsp (1 mL) salt

1 Tbsp (15 mL) chopped fresh parsley

Try Meyer lemons! Increasingly available, this cross between a lemon and mandarin or tangerine results in a less acidic, sweeter version that is such a treat!

REVOLUTIONIZE
SOUPS & STEWS

REVOLUTIONIZE SOUPS & STEWS

QUINOA makes an excellent soup ingredient. The whimsy of curly cooked quinoa seeds adds a fanciful touch to any broth soup. Try Chili, Lime & Kale Soup with Aged White Cheddar (page 95). Puréed quinoa mimics a thick and indulgent consistency you'd mistake for a heavy cream soup. Try Butternut Squash & Pear Soup (page 94) or Lemongrass, Sweet Potato & Coconut Stew (page 106).

One quick trip to the farmer's market or the grocery store and you can make warm and wholesome soups that deliver tremendous nutritional benefit with maximum flavor any time of the year. Prepared in advance and refrigerated or frozen, quinoa soups can be quickly reheated on busy weeknights or lazy weekend afternoons.

ARTICHOKE SOUP

SERVES 6

1 cup (250 mL) quinoa

1 Tbsp (15 mL) grapeseed oil or
  unsalted butter

½ cup (125 mL) chopped onions

1 tsp (5 mL) minced garlic

2 Tbsp (30 mL) lemon juice

4 cups (1 L) sodium-reduced
  chicken or vegetable stock

1 can (14 oz/398 mL) artichoke
  hearts, drained

1 bay leaf

½ cup (125 mL) 1% or 2% milk
  or cream

1 tsp (5 mL) organic cane sugar
  or white sugar

¼ tsp (1 mL) salt (optional)

½ tsp (2 mL) black pepper

The smoky flavor of artichoke hearts and the sweet scent of bay leaf make this soup a warm comfort food that engages all your senses. To add even more flavor, top with fresh bacon bits or browned sausage chunks. Serve with crostini or chewy whole-grain baguette.

Place the quinoa in a large dry saucepan on medium heat. Toast the quinoa, stirring frequently, until fragrant, about 5 minutes. Transfer the quinoa to a bowl and set aside.

Heat the oil in the same saucepan and cook the onions and garlic until the onions are opaque and tender, 7 to 8 minutes. Add the toasted quinoa, lemon juice and stock. Bring to a boil, reduce to a simmer, cover and cook until the quinoa is tender, about 15 minutes.

Add the artichoke hearts and bay leaf; simmer for another 5 minutes. Discard the bay leaf. Purée the soup with a hand blender or cool slightly and purée in two batches in a blender or food processor. Return soup to the saucepan. Add the milk and sugar, stirring thoroughly. Season with salt (if using) and pepper. Serve.

PER SERVING: Energy 190 calories; Protein 10 g; Carbohydrates 27 g; Dietary Fiber 2 g; Fat 5 g; Sugar 3 g; Cholesterol 0 mg; Sodium 200 mg

ASPARAGUS QUINOA SOUP

This vibrant soup's asparagus flavor is complemented by fresh lemon, parsley and creamy Parmesan cheese. Puréed quinoa makes this such a luxuriously thick soup, you can even skip the milk if you choose.

Place the quinoa in a large dry saucepan on medium heat. Toast the quinoa, stirring frequently, until fragrant, about 5 minutes. Transfer the quinoa to a bowl and set aside.

Melt the butter in the same saucepan. Cook the onions and celery until the onions are opaque and tender, 7 to 8 minutes. Add the toasted quinoa, asparagus, stock, parsley, lemon zest and lemon juice. Bring to a boil, reduce to a simmer, cover and cook until the quinoa is tender, 15 to 18 minutes.

Remove 6 to 8 of the cooked asparagus tips and set aside. Purée the soup with a hand blender or cool slightly and purée in two batches in a blender or food processor. Return soup to the saucepan. Stir in the milk, Parmesan and mustard. Season with salt (if using), black pepper and cayenne. Add the reserved asparagus tips and reheat gently before serving.

PER SERVING: Energy 220 calories; Protein 9 g; Carbohydrates 29 g; Dietary Fiber 8 g; Fat 8 g; Sugar 8 g; Cholesterol 20 mg; Sodium 200 mg

SERVES 4

½ cup (125 mL) quinoa

2 Tbsp (30 mL) unsalted butter

½ cup (125 mL) chopped onions

¼ cup (60 mL) diced celery

2 lb (900 g) fresh asparagus, trimmed and cut into 1-inch (2.5 cm) pieces

4 cups (1 L) reduced-sodium vegetable or chicken stock

1 Tbsp (15 mL) chopped fresh parsley

2 tsp (10 mL) grated lemon zest

1 Tbsp (15 mL) lemon juice

⅓ cup (75 mL) 2% milk, whole milk or cream

1 Tbsp (15 mL) grated Parmesan cheese

½ tsp (2 mL) Dijon mustard

¼ tsp (1 mL) salt (optional)

Pinch of black pepper

Pinch of cayenne pepper

BUTTERNUT SQUASH & PEAR SOUP

SERVES 6

1 Tbsp (15 mL) unsalted butter

½ cup (125 mL) chopped onions

1 tsp (5 mL) minced garlic

¼ tsp (1 mL) salt

½ cup (125 mL) quinoa

3 cups (750 mL) diced
    butternut squash

3 ½ cups (875 mL) sodium-reduced
    chicken stock

2 cups (500 mL) chopped
    fresh pears

½ cup (125 mL) whole milk or
    whipping cream

½ tsp (2 mL) ground sage

2 Tbsp (30 mL) crumbled blue
    cheese, such as Stilton
    (gluten-free if required)

Not at all shy, this thick, golden soup of blended butternut squash, pear and quinoa is accented with the sharp gusto of crumbled blue cheese— a splendid flavor combination.

Melt the butter in a large saucepan on medium heat. Add the onions, garlic and salt. Cook until the onions are opaque and tender, 7 to 8 minutes. Add the quinoa, butternut squash and stock. Bring to a boil, reduce to a simmer, cover and cook until the quinoa is tender and the squash is cooked, 15 to 18 minutes. Add the pears.

Purée the soup with a hand blender or cool slightly and purée in two batches in a blender or food processor. Return soup to the saucepan. Stir in the milk and sage. Garnish each bowl of soup with 1 tsp (5 mL) of blue cheese. Serve.

PER SERVING: Energy 180 calories; Protein 7 g; Carbohydrates 30 g; Dietary Fiber 4 g; Fat 5 g; Sugar 9 g; Cholesterol 10 mg; Sodium 190 mg

CHILI, LIME & KALE SOUP
WITH AGED WHITE CHEDDAR

The powerhouse superfood kale is full of vitamin A, vitamin C, calcium and iron and tastes fabulous with lime and aged Cheddar. This quick and easy soup looks dramatic and bold when made with black quinoa.

Heat the oil in a large saucepan on medium-low heat. Stir in the onions and cook, covered, for 7 to 10 minutes, until the onions start to soften. (If the pan gets dry, add a few spoonfuls of water.) Add the garlic and chilies. Cook for another minute. Add the kale, stock, water and quinoa. Bring to a boil, reduce to a simmer, cover and cook for 15 to 20 minutes, until the quinoa is tender. Stir in the lime zest and salt (if using). Serve hot topped with a sprinkle of Cheddar cheese.

PER SERVING: Energy 190 calories; Protein 8 g; Carbohydrates 28 g; Dietary Fiber 5 g; Fat 6 g; Sugar 4 g; Cholesterol 0 mg; Sodium 230 mg

SERVES 4

1 Tbsp (15 mL) grapeseed oil
    or vegetable oil

1 cup (250 mL) chopped onions

1½ tsp (7 mL) minced garlic

1 to 4 tsp (5 to 20 mL) minced
    seeded serrano chili or
    jalapeño pepper

4 cups (1 L) chopped kale,
    center ribs and stems removed
    (1 large bunch)

4 cups (1 L) sodium-reduced
    vegetable or chicken stock

1 cup (250 mL) water

½ cup (125 mL) quinoa

2 tsp (10 mL) grated lime zest

¼ tsp (1 mL) salt (optional)

⅓ cup (75 mL) shredded aged
    white Cheddar cheese

CHIPOTLE CORN CHOWDER

1 Tbsp (15 mL) grapeseed oil
or vegetable oil

1 cup (250 mL) chopped onions

¾ cup (175 mL) chopped celery

2 cups (500 mL) fresh or
thawed frozen corn

1¼ cups (300 mL) peeled
and diced potatoes

½ cup (125 mL) chopped
green bell pepper

¾ cup (175 mL) chopped
red bell pepper

¼ cup (60 mL) tomato paste

¾ tsp (4 mL) minced garlic

½ tsp (2 mL) Worcestershire sauce
(gluten-free if required)

½ tsp (2 mL) paprika

¼ tsp (1 mL) white pepper

¼ tsp (1 mL) ground chipotle pepper

4 cups (1 L) sodium-reduced
vegetable or chicken stock

½ cup (125 mL) whole milk or
10% cream

⅓ cup (75 mL) quinoa flour

Salt (optional) and black
pepper to taste

With more than just corn, this medley of vegetable flavors comes together perfectly with the subtle heat and smokiness of chipotle pepper. This recipe requires only a small amount of chipotle, but a little goes a long way. Look for ground chipotle pepper in the spice section of the grocery store.

Heat a large saucepan on medium-high heat. Add the oil and reduce the heat to medium-low. Add the onions and celery. Cook for 7 minutes or until the onions are opaque and the celery is tender. Add the corn, potatoes, green pepper, red pepper, tomato paste, garlic, Worcestershire sauce, paprika, white pepper, chipotle pepper and stock. Increase the heat to a boil, then reduce to a simmer, cover and cook for 15 minutes or until the potatoes are tender.

Whisk together the milk and flour in a small bowl. Slowly stir the mixture into the hot chowder. Allow about 3 to 5 minutes to thicken. Season with salt (if using) and pepper if necessary. Serve.

PER SERVING: Energy 170 calories; Protein 5 g; Carbohydrates 32 g; Dietary Fiber 5 g; Fat 4 g; Sugar 8 g; Cholesterol 0 mg; Sodium 135 mg

FENNEL CREAM SOUP

SERVES 6

2 cups (500 mL) sodium-reduced
vegetable stock

1 cup (250 mL) whole milk

½ cup (125 mL) quinoa

2 cups (500 mL) chopped fennel
(about 1 medium bulb)

1 Tbsp (15 mL) chopped
fennel fronds

2 tsp (10 mL) minced garlic

½ tsp (5 mL) salt (optional)

Pinch of black pepper

⅓ cup (75 mL) toasted pine nuts

Enjoy the sweet, subtle taste of anise in a creamy soup, thickened with quinoa and topped with toasted pine nuts. If you use vegetable stock that contains sodium, skip the salt in the recipe.

In a large saucepan on high heat, bring the stock, milk, quinoa, fennel, fennel fronds and garlic to a boil. Reduce to a simmer and cook for 15 minutes. Remove from the heat and let cool for 5 to 10 minutes. Purée the soup with a hand blender or in a blender or food processor. Return soup to the saucepan. Season with salt (if using) and pepper. Reheat before serving. Top each bowl with a sprinkle of toasted pine nuts and serve.

PER SERVING: Energy 130 calories; Protein 5 g; Carbohydrates 15 g; Dietary Fiber 3 g; Fat 5 g; Sugar 3 g; Cholesterol 5 mg; Sodium 85 mg

> To toast nuts, preheat the oven to 350°F (180°C). Spread the nuts on a baking sheet and toast in the oven, stirring once if necessary, for 5 to 7 minutes, until fragrant and lightly toasted.

GINGERED CITRUS CARROT SOUP

Carrots shine in this inexpensive but extraordinary soup that is one of our favorites. Ginger, garlic and citrus zest dress it up, and you can make it even more delicious with cream and a final sprinkle of chives. Use a slow cooker if desired.

Heat a large saucepan on medium-low heat. Add the oil and onions. Cover and cook for 7 minutes or until the onions start to soften. (Add a spoonful of water if the pan gets dry.) Stir in the garlic and cook for another minute. Add the carrots, stock, water and quinoa. Cover and simmer for 25 minutes or until the carrots are very tender. Remove from the heat and let cool slightly. Purée in a blender, one half at a time, until smooth or use a hand blender. Return soup to the saucepan and return to a simmer. Add the ginger, zest, salt (if using) and cayenne. Simmer the soup for 2 or 3 minutes. Stir in the cream (if using) or garnish with a drizzle just before serving. Garnish with chives (if using) and serve.

PER SERVING: Energy 130 calories; Protein 3 g; Carbohydrates 22 g; Dietary Fiber 5 g; Fat 3.5 g; Sugar 7 g; Cholesterol 0 mg; Sodium 150 mg

SERVES 6

1 Tbsp (15 mL) grapeseed oil or vegetable oil

1 cup (250 mL) chopped onions

1 tsp (5 mL) minced garlic

4 cups (1 L) sliced carrots

4 cups (1 L) sodium-reduced vegetable or chicken stock

1 cup (250 mL) water

½ cup (125 mL) quinoa

2 tsp (10 mL) grated fresh ginger

1½ tsp (7 mL) grated lemon or lime zest

½ tsp (2 mL) salt (optional)

¼ tsp (1 mL) cayenne pepper or to taste

½ cup (125 mL) 10% cream (optional)

1 Tbsp (15 mL) sliced chives (optional)

If using the slow cooker, add the onions, garlic, carrots, stock, water and quinoa. Cook all ingredients on high for 3 to 3½ hours or on low for 6 to 8 hours. Follow the same instructions to purée and serve the soup.

LEMON GINGER TURKEY SOUP

SERVES 6

1 Tbsp (15 mL) vegetable oil
or grapeseed oil

1 cup (250 mL) diced onions

1 cup (250 mL) chopped celery

1 cup (250 mL) chopped carrots

½ tsp (2 mL) minced garlic

4 cups (1 L) chicken or
vegetable stock

1 cup (250 mL) water

⅓ cup (75 mL) quinoa

½ tsp (2 mL) dried oregano

½ tsp (2 mL) grated fresh ginger

1½ cups (375 mL) diced
cooked turkey or chicken

1 tsp (5 mL) grated lemon zest

Wanting to use up some holiday turkey? Or feeling guilty after indulging during the holiday season? This fresh take on an old favorite will quickly become your family's favored pick-me-up. For a vegetarian option, replace the chicken stock with vegetable stock and the chicken with one can (14 oz/398 mL) drained and rinsed navy or soybeans.

Heat the oil in a large saucepan on medium-low heat. Add the onions, celery and carrots and cook for about 7 minutes, until the onions and celery are tender. (If you find the pan is dry, add a spoonful or two of water and cover with the lid.) Stir in the garlic and cook for another minute. Add the stock, water, quinoa, oregano and ginger. Bring to a boil, reduce to a simmer, cover and cook for 15 minutes or until the quinoa is cooked. Stir in the chicken and lemon zest. Continue to cook until heated through, 3 to 5 minutes.

PER SERVING: Energy 190 calories; Protein 25 g; Carbohydrates 13 g; Dietary Fiber 3 g; Fat 3.5 g; Sugar 4 g; Cholesterol 65 mg; Sodium 170 mg

Want to add another dimension to this soup? Add a thinly sliced stalk of lemongrass to the saucepan at the same time you add the vegetables.

QUINOA CHICKEN SOUP

A favorite standard, chicken soup is not only easy but a go-to meal if you're feeling under the weather. Using sodium-reduced stock means you can salt the soup to your own personal taste.

In a large saucepan on medium-high heat, bring the stock and quinoa to a boil. Reduce to a simmer, cover and cook until the quinoa is tender, 15 to 18 minutes. Add the chicken, carrots, onions, celery, garlic, sage and bay leaf. Continue to simmer for another 20 minutes. Season with salt and pepper. Serve.

PER SERVING: Energy 130 calories; Protein 13 g; Carbohydrates 14 g; Dietary Fiber 2 g; Fat 3 g; Sugar 2 g; Cholesterol 20 mg; Sodium 200 mg

Cayenne pepper contains capsaicin, which naturally warms the body, increases circulation and helps to ease congestion and sore throats.

SERVES 4

4 cups (1 L) sodium-reduced chicken or vegetable stock

¼ cup (60 mL) quinoa

1 cup (250 mL) diced cooked chicken breast

½ cup (125 mL) chopped carrots

½ cup (125 mL) chopped onions

½ cup (125 mL) diced celery

2 tsp (10 mL) minced garlic

¼ tsp (1 mL) ground sage

1 bay leaf

Salt and black pepper to taste

Cayenne pepper to taste

ROASTED GARLIC & MUSHROOM SOUP

Roast the garlic in advance and you can whip up this mushroom soup for a lunch or light supper. Experiment with different types of mushrooms and different stock.

Heat the oil in a large saucepan on medium-low heat. Add the onions and cook, covered, for 8 minutes or until the onions are soft and opaque. (If the pan looks dry, add a few spoonfuls of water.) Add the mushrooms and cook, covered, for another 7 minutes or until they soften. Remove 1 ½ cups (375 mL) of the mushroom mixture and set aside.

Add the stock, water, quinoa, roasted garlic, thyme, salt (if using) and pepper. Bring to a boil, reduce to a simmer, cover and cook for 15 minutes or until the quinoa is tender. Purée soup with a hand blender or in a blender. Return soup to the saucepan. Stir in the spinach and reserved mushrooms. Cook gently until heated through. Adjust seasoning and serve sprinkled with Parmesan (if using).

PER SERVING: Energy 110 calories; Protein 4 g; Carbohydrates 18 g; Dietary Fiber 3 g; Fat 2.5 g; Sugar 4 g; Cholesterol 0 mg; Sodium 105 mg

SERVES 6

2 tsp (10 mL) grapeseed oil or vegetable oil

1 cup (250 mL) chopped onions

1 lb (450 g) cremini mushrooms, sliced

4 cups (1 L) sodium-reduced vegetable, chicken or beef stock

2 cups (500 mL) water

½ cup (125 mL) quinoa

1 Tbsp (15 mL) roasted garlic (see Tip)

2 tsp (10 mL) chopped fresh thyme

¾ tsp (4 mL) salt (optional)

¼ tsp (1 mL) black pepper

1 cup (250 mL) chopped fresh spinach

Freshly grated Parmesan cheese (optional)

HOW TO ROAST GARLIC

Preheat the oven to 400°F (200°C). Take as many heads of garlic as you like, and slice off the top ½ inch (1 cm) to expose the cloves. Tear off pieces of foil large enough to entirely wrap each head of garlic. Place each head of garlic in the center of a piece of foil and pour about 2 tsp (10 mL) of grapeseed oil (or whichever oil you would like) over the top. Sprinkle with fresh herbs, if desired. Wrap snugly and place on a baking sheet. Bake for 30 to 35 minutes or until the garlic cloves can easily be squeezed from the skins. Add roasted garlic to soups, stews, roasts, spreads and dips. Keep refrigerated in an airtight container for a couple of weeks. Or freeze roasted garlic so you can flavor all your fabulous meals in a snap. First freeze it in ice cube trays, and then transfer the cubes to small freezer bags.

SLOW COOKER VEGETABLE BEAN SOUP

SERVES 6

¾ cup (175 mL) dried navy beans, soaked in water overnight

1 can (28 oz/796 mL) unsalted diced tomatoes with juice

1 cup (250 mL) cubed zucchini or red potatoes

1 cup (250 mL) chopped onions

1 cup (250 mL) chopped celery

1 cup (250 mL) sliced carrots

½ cup (125 mL) quinoa

¾ tsp (4 mL) dried oregano

½ tsp (2 mL) minced garlic

¼ tsp (1 mL) dried marjoram

1 bay leaf

3 cups (750 mL) boiling water

2 cups (500 mL) vegetable, chicken or beef stock

Salt and black pepper (optional)

Croutons (optional)

Easy! Soak the beans and cut up the veggies the night before. In the morning, throw all the ingredients into the slow cooker and turn it on. A hot and delicious meal will be waiting for you when you get home.

Drain the navy beans and rinse under running water. Add the beans and all the other ingredients (except the salt, pepper and croutons) to the slow cooker. Cover and cook on high for 3½ to 4 hours or on low for 6 to 8 hours, until the vegetables and beans are tender. Season to taste with salt and pepper (if using) and serve topped with croutons (if using).

PER SERVING (vegetable stock, zucchini): Energy 200 calories; Protein 10 g; Carbohydrates 38 g; Dietary Fiber 10 g; Fat 1.5 g; Sugar 9 g; Cholesterol 0 mg; Sodium 95 mg

---

LIGHT HERB AND GARLIC CROUTONS

4 cups (1 L) of your favorite bread, cut in ¾-inch (2 cm) cubes

2 Tbsp (30 mL) melted salted butter or grapeseed oil

1 tsp (5 mL) minced or pureed garlic

1 tsp (5 mL) each of dried thyme, basil and oregano

¼ tsp (1 mL) salt

Preheat the oven to 400°F (200°C). Heat a small saucepan on medium heat and add the butter and garlic. Cook for 30 seconds and remove from the heat. Toss all ingredients together in a medium bowl until bread cubes are evenly coated. Pour onto an ungreased baking sheet and bake for 7 minutes. Stir and continue to bake for another 7 minutes or until the croutons are lightly golden and dry. Store cooled and dried croutons in a resealable container for up to 1 month.

WEEKNIGHT MEXICAN SOUP

Quick suppers are perfect during the week, and this Mexican-inspired soup is so full of veggies, it's close to being a stew. Customize the heat of this soup with as many jalapeños as you like.

Heat the oil in a large saucepan on medium-low heat. Add the onions and cook for 7 minutes or until they begin to soften. Add the beans, tomatoes, green peppers, corn, quinoa, tomato paste, chili powder, cumin, stock and water. Bring to a boil, reduce to a simmer, cover and cook for 15 minutes or until the quinoa is tender. Stir in the cilantro and lime zest. Season with salt and pepper to taste, if desired. Serve with a tablespoon or two of sour cream. Garnish with crumbled corn tortillas, if desired.

PER SERVING: Energy 240 calories; Protein 10 g; Carbohydrates 39 g; Dietary Fiber 9 g; Fat 6 g; Sugar 6 g; Cholesterol 5 mg; Sodium 220 mg

> Increase the vegetables even more by adding ½ to ¾ cup (125 to 175 mL) of chopped fresh yellow or green zucchini.

SERVES 6

1 Tbsp (15 mL) grapeseed oil or vegetable oil

⅔ cup (150 mL) chopped onions

2 cups (500 mL) unsalted cooked black beans (or one 19 oz/540 mL can, drained and rinsed)

1½ cups (375 mL) diced fresh tomatoes (or one 19 oz/540 mL can with juice)

1 cup (250 mL) chopped green bell peppers

¾ cup (175 mL) fresh or frozen corn

⅔ cup (150 mL) quinoa

¼ cup (60 mL) tomato paste

2 tsp (10 mL) chili powder

½ tsp (2 mL) ground cumin

4 cups (1 L) sodium-reduced vegetable or chicken stock

1 cup (250 mL) water

2 Tbsp (30 mL) chopped fresh cilantro

½ tsp (2 mL) grated lime zest

Salt and black pepper (optional)

½ cup (125 mL) reduced-fat sour cream (gluten-free if required)

Corn tortillas (optional)

WINTER BISON SOUP

SERVES 6

1 Tbsp (15 mL) grapeseed oil
     or vegetable oil

1 lb (450 g) lean ground bison
     or beef

1½ cups (375 mL) chopped onions

1½ cups (375 mL) diced carrots

1½ cups (375 mL) diced celery

2 tsp (10 mL) minced garlic

3 cups (750 mL) diced fresh
     tomatoes (or one 28 oz/
     796 mL can with juice)

½ cup (125 mL) quinoa

4 cups (1 L) sodium-reduced
     beef stock

1 cup (250 mL) water

2 Tbsp (30 mL) Worcestershire
     sauce (gluten-free if required)

Inspired by traditional hamburger soup, this healthier version is sure to become one of your favorites. This is a great recipe during the fall and winter and can be frozen for a quick meal later on.

Heat the oil in a large saucepan on medium-high heat. Add the bison and cook, stirring frequently, until browned and cooked through. Stir in the onions, carrots and celery. Reduce the heat to medium-low and cook until the onions and celery start to soften. Add the garlic and cook for another minute. Add the tomatoes, quinoa, stock, water and Worcestershire sauce. Bring to a boil, reduce to a simmer, cover and cook for 15 minutes. Serve.

PER SERVING: Energy 230 calories; Protein 22 g; Carbohydrates 25 g; Dietary Fiber 4 g; Fat 5 g; Sugar 9 g; Cholesterol 40 mg; Sodium 210 mg

WONTON SOUP
AU NATUREL

Take the great flavors of wonton soup, remove the wrappers, add quinoa and a generous amount of vegetables and you have a filling and nutritious soup, plain and simple. As a bonus, it's wheat- and gluten-free!

In a medium bowl, mix together the ground meat, green onions, egg yolk, ¼ tsp (1 mL) of the ginger, sesame oil, salt (if using) and pepper. Gently roll tablespoons of the meat mixture into balls and place on a plate. Set aside.

In a large saucepan, combine the stock, water, quinoa, remaining 1 tsp (5 mL) of ginger and garlic. Bring to a boil on medium-high heat. Reduce to a simmer, cover and cook for 8 minutes. Add the bok choy and carrots. Bring to a boil on medium-high heat and drop the meatballs into the hot stock. Reduce to a simmer, cover and cook for another 8 minutes or until the quinoa is tender and the meatballs are cooked. Serve.

PER SERVING: Energy 160 calories; Protein 14 g; Carbohydrates 14 g; Dietary Fiber 2 g; Fat 6 g; Sugar 2 g; Cholesterol 65 mg; Sodium 125 mg

> Enjoy shrimp? Add ½ lb (225 g) peeled and deveined raw shrimp 2 to 3 minutes before finishing the soup.

SERVES 6

½ lb (225 g) ground chicken or turkey

3 Tbsp (45 mL) thinly sliced green onions

1 large egg yolk

1¼ tsp (6 mL) grated fresh ginger

¾ tsp (4 mL) sesame oil

¼ tsp (1 mL) salt (optional)

Pinch of black pepper

4 cups (1 L) sodium-reduced or regular chicken stock

1 cup (250 mL) water

½ cup (125 mL) quinoa

¼ tsp (1 mL) minced garlic

2 cups (500 mL) bok choy halved down spine and thinly sliced (or broccoli florets)

1 cup (250 mL) carrots thinly sliced on the diagonal

LEMONGRASS, SWEET POTATO & COCONUT STEW

SERVES 8

2 stalks lemongrass

1 Tbsp (15 mL) grapeseed oil
or vegetable oil

1 medium red onion, halved
lengthwise and cut into ½-inch
(1 cm) thick slices (about
1 cup/250 mL)

2 Tbsp (30 mL) Thai green curry
paste (gluten-free if required)

1½ tsp (7 mL) minced garlic

4 cups (1 L) sodium-reduced
chicken or vegetable stock

1⅔ cups (400 mL) light or regular
coconut milk

1 to 3 tsp (5 to 15 mL) minced fresh
Thai red or green chili or jalapeño
pepper (optional)

2 boneless, skinless chicken breasts
(or 5 or 6 boneless, skinless
thighs), cut crosswise into strips
½ inch (1 cm) thick

1¼ lb (565 g) sweet potatoes, cut
into 1-inch (2.5 cm) cubes (about
3 cups/750 mL)

1 cup (250 mL) fresh or thawed
frozen green beans cut into
1-inch (2.5 cm) pieces

½ cup (125 mL) quinoa

1 cup (250 mL) zucchini cut into
1-inch (2.5 cm) cubes

2 tsp (10 mL) chopped fresh
basil or cilantro

The flavors of Thai green curry (or *gaeng keow wan*) inspired this colorful stew. The complementing flavors of sweet potato, coconut and lemongrass make for a scrumptious home-cooked meal-in-a-bowl. If you want to heat things up, add as many chilies as you like. Thai green curry paste is available in the Asian section of the supermarket. You can make this meal vegetarian by leaving out the chicken and adding 1½ cups (375 mL) of cooked white kidney beans with the zucchini.

Cut off the bottom third of the lemongrass stalks. Peel off the dry outer layers. Slice stalks into paper-thin pieces. Set aside.

Heat the oil in a large saucepan on medium-low heat. Add the red onion, cover and cook, stirring occasionally, for 7 minutes or until the onion starts to soften. (If the pan gets dry, add a spoonful of water.) Add the curry paste and garlic; stir for 1 minute. Add the stock, coconut milk, lemongrass and hot chilies (if using). Bring to a boil.

Add the chicken. Return to a boil. Add the sweet potatoes, green beans and quinoa. Reduce to a simmer, cover and cook for 15 minutes. Stir in the zucchini, cover and simmer for another 10 minutes. Remove the lid and simmer for another 5 minutes, until slightly thickened. Stir in the basil or cilantro and serve.

PER SERVING: Energy 190 calories; Protein 9 g; Carbohydrates 26 g; Dietary Fiber 4 g; Fat 5 g; Sugar 5 g; Cholesterol 20 mg; Sodium 300 mg

LENTIL & KALE STEW

SERVES 6

1 Tbsp (15 mL) grapeseed oil
  or vegetable oil

1 cup (250 mL) chopped onions

1 cup (250 mL) chopped celery

1 cup (250 mL) sliced carrots

2 tsp (10 mL) chopped garlic

1 Tbsp (15 mL) dried oregano

1 tsp (5 mL) dried marjoram

6 cups (1.5 L) water

1 can (19 oz/540 mL) unsalted
  diced tomatoes with juice

1½ cups (375 mL) green lentils

½ cup (125 mL) quinoa

3 cups (575 mL) chopped kale,
  center ribs and stems removed
  (1 large bunch)

½ tsp (2 tsp) grated lemon zest

¼ tsp (1 mL) salt (optional)

¼ tsp (1 mL) black pepper

With a small bunch of kale and a few pantry staples, you can make this healthy and hearty stew with ease.

Heat the oil in a large saucepan on medium-low heat. Add the onions, celery and carrots. Cook, covered, for 7 to 10 minutes, until the onions and celery start to soften. (Add a few spoonfuls of water if the pan is dry.) Stir in the garlic, oregano and marjoram. Cook for another minute. Pour in the water and tomatoes. Stir in the lentils and quinoa. Bring to a boil, reduce to a simmer, cover and cook for 45 minutes or until the lentils are almost tender. Stir in the kale and cook for another 10 minutes. Add the lemon zest, salt (if using) and pepper. Serve.

PER SERVING: Energy 290 calories; Protein 15 g; Carbohydrates 49 g; Dietary Fiber 12 g; Fat 4.5 g; Sugar 7 g; Cholesterol 0 mg; Sodium 60 mg

> Kale is a power-packed superfood! Nutritionally dense, it aids digestion and is detoxifying, strengthens immune and cardio-vascular support, is anti-imflammatory, has cell-building properties and more. Try it! Need we say more?

SIMPLE CHICKEN POT PIE STEW

We took a time-consuming, calorie-loaded old favorite and made it easy and healthful—keeping all the tasty elements, of course! You can simplify this recipe even more by using leftover holiday turkey or rotisserie chicken.

Heat the oil in a large saucepan on low heat. Add the onions, carrots, celery, salt (if using) and black pepper. Cook for 8 to 9 minutes, until the onions start to become opaque and the celery starts to soften. Stir in the mushrooms and cook for another 5 minutes. Add the potatoes, red peppers, stock and poultry seasoning. Bring to a boil, reduce to a simmer, cover and cook for 10 minutes or until the potatoes are tender. Stir in the chicken.

In a small bowl, whisk together the milk and flour. Slowly stir this mixture into the hot stew. Cook for another 5 minutes or until the stew thickens. Adjust seasoning if desired and serve.

PER SERVING: Energy 210 calories; Protein 21 g; Carbohydrates 20 g; Dietary Fiber 3 g; Fat 6 g; Sugar 5 g; Cholesterol 40 mg; Sodium 125 mg

SERVES 6

1 Tbsp (15 mL) grapeseed oil
or vegetable oil

1 cup (250 mL) chopped onions

1 cup (250 mL) sliced carrots

1 cup (250 mL) chopped celery

½ tsp (2 mL) salt (optional)

¼ tsp (1 mL) black pepper

8 oz (225 g) button
mushrooms, sliced

1 cup (250 mL) diced potatoes

½ cup (125 mL) red bell pepper cut
into 1½-inch (4 cm) lengths

4 cups (1 L) sodium-reduced
chicken stock

1 tsp (5 mL) dried poultry seasoning

2 cups (500 mL) shredded cooked
chicken or turkey breast

½ cup (125 mL) 1% milk

⅓ cup (75 mL) quinoa flour

REVOLUTIONIZE
MEALS

REVOLUTIONIZE MEALS

Starving at the end of a busy day, you want to eat something satisfying but quick. Coming up with creative dinner ideas for yourself or an entire family can be agonizing at times. Quinoa makes dinner easy to plan ahead for. Prepare your quinoa in advance so you can simply cook and serve these recipes or slip them in the oven the minute you walk in the door. If you're really pressed for time, try Kale, Red Pepper & Quinoa Toss (page 141) or Cabbage Crockpot Casserole (page 120). Is it possible that quick, nutritious meals will have your family asking for seconds? Yes, you can have it all with quinoa. These uncomplicated, no-fuss dinners will soon become your go-to recipes. If you're looking for something extra-impressive for guests, try Savory Mushroom Spinach Crêpes (page 142), Grilled Tarragon Vegetable Quinoa (page 122) or Kung Pao Chicken Quinoa (page 115). For a recipe bursting with flavor, freshness and a bit of sweet and spicy, try the Spicy Salmon Burgers (page 147).

BABY BOK CHOY, SNOW PEA & RED PEPPER STIR-FRY

2 cups (500 mL) +
    2 Tbsp (30 mL) water

1 cup (250 mL) quinoa

2 Tbsp (30 mL) sesame oil

2 cups (500 mL) broccoli florets

6 baby bok choy, bases trimmed

1 medium red bell pepper,
    cut into strips

8 oz (225 g) white button or
    cremini mushrooms, quartered

6 oz (170 g) snow peas

1 stalk lemongrass, trimmed,
    sliced in half lengthwise and
    cut paper thin (optional)

1½ tsp (7 mL) minced garlic

1 tsp (5 mL) grated fresh ginger

½ tsp (2 mL) cinnamon

3 Tbsp (45 mL) sodium-reduced
    soy sauce or tamari
    (gluten-free if required)

2 tsp (10 mL) cornstarch

2 cups (500 mL) diced cooked
    chicken, beef or pork
    (or 1½ cups/375 mL diced
    fried extra-firm tofu)

½ cup (125 mL) sliced green onions

1 lime, cut into 6 wedges

Whereas a typical stir-fry is fried in hot oil in a wok and stirred continuously, this dish is cooked in a covered pot to allow the flavorful juices to blend and thicken. The result is a tasty sauce that the quinoa soaks up. Use your choice of cooked meat or choose tofu to make it vegetarian. Most of the ingredients are added all at once, to make it super-easy—perfect for a weeknight.

Bring 2 cups (500 mL) water and the quinoa to boil in a medium saucepan. Reduce to a simmer, cover and cook for 15 minutes. Remove from the heat but keep covered.

Meanwhile, heat the oil in a large saucepan on medium-high heat. Add the broccoli, bok choy, red pepper, mushrooms, snow peas, lemongrass (if using), garlic, ginger, cinnamon and 2 Tbsp (30 mL) water. Stir well. Reduce the heat to medium-low, cover and cook for 10 minutes.

Whisk together the soy sauce and cornstarch in a small bowl. Stir into the vegetable mixture. Add the meat or tofu and ¼ cup (60 mL) of the green onions. Cook, covered, for another 4 to 5 minutes, until the sauce has thickened slightly and the meat or tofu is heated through.

Fluff quinoa with a fork. Serve stir-fry over hot quinoa with a squeeze of lime and sprinkled with the remaining ¼ cup (60 mL) of green onions.

PER SERVING: Energy 240 calories; Protein 16 g; Carbohydrates 29 g; Dietary Fiber 4 g; Fat 8 g; Sugar 3 g; Cholesterol 25 mg; Sodium 350 mg

Tamari is similar to soy sauce but is frequently made without wheat. It is still important to read labels if you follow a gluten-free diet. Tamari is a deeper brown and slightly thicker than soy sauce, and is also deeper in flavor. Use it where you would normally use soy sauce. Tamari can be found in health-food stores and larger supermarkets.

KUNG PAO
CHICKEN QUINOA

Quinoa along with buttery peanuts, a hint of spice, sweet pineapple and the crunch of broccoli equals a recipe with a big wow factor. Increase the heat by adding as many red hot chili peppers as you like—or can handle.

Stir together the soy sauce, hot chili sauce, ginger, garlic, chili peppers and black pepper in a bowl; pour into a large, resealable plastic bag. Add the chicken. Place in the refrigerator to marinate for at least 1 hour (and up to 24 hours).

Bring 2 cups (500 mL) water and the quinoa to a boil in a medium saucepan. Reduce to a simmer, cover and cook for 15 minutes. Fluff with a fork and set aside.

Place 1 Tbsp (15 mL) of the vegetable oil in a large, wide saucepan on medium heat. When the oil is hot, add the broccoli and 2 Tbsp (30 mL) water and cover the pan. Cook, stirring frequently, until the broccoli is tender, 8 to 10 minutes. If the pan looks dry, add more water. Transfer to a bowl and set aside, keeping warm.

Remove the chicken from the marinade, reserving the marinade. Heat the remaining 1 Tbsp (15 mL) vegetable oil in the same saucepan, then add the chicken. Increase the heat to medium-high and cook the chicken until it is no longer pink, 7 to 8 minutes. Reduce the heat to medium and add the marinade, pineapple, peanuts, peanut butter, green onions and ¾ cup (175 mL) water. Cook for 3 minutes. Remove 2 Tbsp (30 mL) of the sauce; in a small bowl, whisk in the cornstarch until smooth. Stir cornstarch mixture into the chicken mixture and stir until the mixture thickens slightly, 1 to 2 minutes. Divide the quinoa among serving plates and top with the broccoli. Pour chicken mixture on top. Garnish with green onions.

PER SERVING: Energy 430 calories; Protein 28 g; Carbohydrates 37 g; Dietary Fiber 11 g; Fat 19 g; Sugar 10 g; Cholesterol 50 mg; Sodium 400 mg

SERVES 6

3 Tbsp (45 mL) sodium-reduced soy sauce or tamari (gluten-free if required)

2 Tbsp (30 mL) sriracha hot chili sauce

2 tsp (10 mL) minced fresh ginger

1 tsp (5 mL) minced garlic

1 to 2 small red hot chili peppers, sliced lengthwise

Pinch of black pepper

4 boneless, skinless chicken breasts, diced

2 cups (500 mL) + 2 Tbsp (30 mL) + ¾ cup (175 mL) water

1 cup (250 mL) quinoa

2 Tbsp (30 mL) vegetable oil or grapeseed oil

4 cups (1 L) broccoli florets

1 can (14 oz/398 mL) pineapple tidbits, with juice

½ cup (125 mL) chopped roasted unsalted peanuts

3 Tbsp (45 mL) peanut butter

2 green onions, white and green parts chopped separately, some greens reserved for garnish

2 tsp (10 mL) cornstarch

- Cooked quinoa already on hand? Reheat 3 cups (750 mL) cooked quinoa to serve with the chicken.
- Hot peppers contain capsaicin, which has enzymes that help to detoxify the liver. The hotter the peppers, the more capsaicin.

MIDDLE EASTERN STUFFED ACORN SQUASH

SERVES 4

2 acorn squash (1 ¼ to 1 ½ lb/ 565 to 675 g each)

2 Tbsp (30 mL) salted butter

1 Tbsp (15 mL) olive oil

¼ tsp (1 mL) cinnamon

Pinch of ground cardamom

1 ⅓ cups (325 mL) water

⅔ cup (150 mL) red quinoa

3 Tbsp (45 mL) toasted salted cashew pieces

2 Tbsp (30 mL) diced dried apricots

4 tsp (20 mL) chopped fresh mint

This warm, enticing blend of spices and mint will take you away, and this recipe may just become your new household favorite.

Preheat the oven to 400°F (200°C). Cut the acorn squash in half lengthwise and remove the seeds and strings. Place squash cut side down in a shallow baking dish and fill with ¼ inch (5 mm) of water. Bake for 30 to 35 minutes, until the flesh is easily pierced with a fork.

Meanwhile, melt the butter in a small saucepan on medium heat, whisking constantly. Watch closely as brown flecks begin to appear. As soon as the butter turns a caramel brown color and has a nutty fragrance (this should take between 4 to 6 minutes; do not allow the butter to turn black), remove from the heat and transfer to a medium bowl. Stir in the olive oil, cinnamon and cardamom.

Add the water and quinoa to the same saucepan. Bring to a boil, reduce to a simmer, cover and cook for 17 minutes. Remove from the heat and fluff with a fork. Toss 2 cups (500 mL) of the quinoa with the seasoned brown butter, cashews, apricots and mint. Cover the quinoa mixture to keep it warm if the squash needs more time to finish baking.

Equally divide the quinoa filling among the four squash halves. Serve immediately.

PER SERVING: Energy 340 calories; Protein 7 g; Carbohydrates 50 g; Dietary Fiber 6 g; Fat 14 g; Sugar 3 g; Cholesterol 15 mg; Sodium 100 mg

- No mint? For this recipe, replace it with 2 Tbsp (30 mL) thinly sliced green onions. The onions give a different flavor to the dish and are a great option.

- To toast nuts, preheat the oven to 350°F (180°C). Spread the nuts on a baking sheet and toast in the oven, stirring once if necessary, for 5 to 7 minutes, until fragrant and lightly toasted.

BAKED TOMATO & QUINOA–STUFFED ZUCCHINI WITH MOZZARELLA

Bubbly and golden baked mozzarella tops quinoa-stuffed zucchini. If using dried herbs, add them with the chopped garlic.

Combine the water and quinoa in a medium saucepan. Bring to a boil, reduce to a simmer, cover and cook for 15 minutes. Remove from the heat but leave covered for another 10 minutes. Fluff with a fork and set aside to cool slightly.

Preheat the oven to 375°F (190°C). Lightly spray with cooking oil, grease or line with parchment an 11- x 7 inch (2 L) baking dish.

Use a small spoon to scoop out half the insides of each zucchini half. (Reserve zucchini flesh for another use.) Brush zucchini shells with 1 tsp (5 mL) of the oil and place cut side up in baking dish.

Heat the remaining 1 Tbsp (15 mL) oil in a large skillet on medium-low heat. Add the onions; cook, covered, for 5 minutes, stirring occasionally. Stir in the mushrooms and garlic. Cover and cook for another 7 minutes, until the mushrooms are soft. Turn the heat off and stir in 1 cup (250 mL) of the cooked quinoa, the tomato sauce, Parmesan, oregano, basil and salt (if using).

Scoop ¼ cup (60 mL) to ⅓ cup (75 mL) of the quinoa mixture into each of the zucchini halves. Top each with 1 to 2 Tbsp (15 to 30 mL) of mozzarella cheese. Bake for 30 minutes or until the cheese is golden and bubbling. Serve.

PER SERVING: Energy 320 calories; Protein 19 g; Carbohydrates 33 g; Dietary Fiber 6 g; Fat 13 g; Sugar 15 g; Cholesterol 20 mg; Sodium 150 mg

SERVES 4 (OR 8 AS AN APPETIZER OR SIDE DISH)

⅔ cup (150 mL) water

⅓ cup (75 mL) quinoa

4 zucchini (about 7 oz/200 g each), trimmed and halved lengthwise

1 Tbsp (15 mL) grapeseed oil or vegetable oil + 1 tsp (5 mL) for brushing zucchini

⅓ cup (75 mL) finely chopped onions

8 oz (225 g) mushrooms, sliced

½ tsp (2 mL) chopped garlic

1⅔ cups (400 mL) tomato sauce

⅓ cup (75 mL) freshly grated Parmesan cheese

4½ tsp (22 mL) chopped fresh oregano (or 1½ tsp/7 mL dried)

2 tsp (10 mL) chopped fresh basil (or ½ tsp/2 mL dried)

½ tsp (2 mL) salt (optional)

1 cup (250 mL) shredded reduced-fat mozzarella cheese

CABBAGE CROCKPOT CASSEROLE

SERVES 6

1 lb (450 g) lean ground beef

1½ cups (375 mL) chopped onions

4 slices bacon, cooked and
    chopped (optional)

¾ cup (75 mL) quinoa

1 cup (250 mL) chopped
    green bell peppers

1 tsp (5 mL) minced garlic

¼ tsp (1 mL) black pepper

4 cups (1 L) green cabbage chopped
    into 1-inch (2.5 cm) pieces

1 can (28 oz/796 mL) diced
    tomatoes with juice

3 cups (750 mL) sodium-reduced
    tomato juice

Salt (optional)

Want supper already waiting the moment you get home? This is an easy slow cooker recipe inspired by the Ukrainian cabbage roll dish called holubtsi. Prepare the ingredients the night before and quickly throw them together before you leave for work.

Heat a large skillet on medium-high heat. Add the ground beef and cook until browned. Stir in the onions and reduce the heat to low. Continue to cook until the onions are starting to soften. Remove from the heat.

Transfer the ground beef mixture to a 6-quart (6 L) slow cooker. Place the bacon (if using) and quinoa on top of the beef. Add the green peppers in one layer. Sprinkle with the garlic and black pepper. Add the cabbage in one layer. Top with the diced tomatoes and the tomato juice. Cook on low for 8 to 9 hours or on high for 4 to 4½ hours. The casserole is done when the quinoa is cooked and the cabbage is tender. Add salt to taste (if using). Serve.

Refrigerate leftovers or freeze in a sealed container for up to 2 months.

PER SERVING: Energy 260 calories; Protein 21 g; Carbohydrates 34 g; Dietary Fiber 6 g; Fat 5 g; Sugar 13 g; Cholesterol 40 mg; Sodium 85 mg

CHAMPIONSHIP CHILI

Here's our take on a white chili with quinoa. It's a simple throw-together recipe full of flavor. Some like it hot, so make it as bold as you want with your choice of salsa. To make this chili vegetarian, replace the chicken with 2 cups (500 mL) cooked navy beans or chickpeas (or one 19 oz/ 540 mL can).

In a large saucepan on medium heat, combine the mushrooms and water. Reduce the heat to medium-low, cover and cook until the mushrooms soften, 5 to 7 minutes.

In a shallow bowl, mash half a can of kidney beans. Add the mashed beans, remaining whole beans, chicken, salsa, quinoa, oregano, cumin and stock to the mushrooms. Combine well and bring to a boil. Reduce to a simmer, cover and cook for 20 minutes. Remove the lid and simmer for another 5 to 7 minutes, until the chili thickens slightly. Stir cheese (if using) into the chili until melted. Serve hot, topped with fresh cilantro (if using).

PER SERVING: Energy 200 calories; Protein 15 g; Carbohydrates 29 g; Dietary Fiber 7 g; Fat 2.5 g; Sugar 4 g; Cholesterol 20 mg; Sodium 380 mg

SERVES 8

8 oz (225 g) white mushrooms, sliced

2 Tbsp (30 mL) water

2 cups (500 mL) cooked white kidney beans (or two 19 oz/ 540 mL cans, drained and rinsed)

2 cups (500 mL) cubed chicken

1½ cups (375 mL) chunky salsa (medium or hot)

½ cup (125 mL) quinoa

2 tsp (10 mL) dried oregano

1¼ tsp (6 mL) ground cumin

4 cups (1 L) sodium-reduced chicken or vegetable stock

1 cup (250 mL) shredded jalapeño havarti cheese (optional)

⅓ cup (75 mL) chopped fresh cilantro (optional)

GRILLED TARRAGON
VEGETABLE QUINOA

SERVES 4

8 oz (225 g) white or
    cremini mushrooms

1 cup (250 mL) cherry or
    grape tomatoes

1 cup (250 mL) Spanish onion cut
    into ½-inch (1 cm) rings

8 oz (225 g) asparagus, trimmed

1 Tbsp (15 mL) + 2 tsp (10 mL)
    grapeseed oil or vegetable oil

1⅓ cups (325 mL) water

⅔ cup (150 mL) black or red quinoa

2 Tbsp (30 mL) salted butter

1 tsp (5 mL) fresh tarragon leaves
    cut into thirds

1 tsp (5 mL) minced garlic

½ tsp (2 mL) salt (optional)

⅓ cup (75 mL) soft goat cheese

> There are two ways you can remove the woody ends of asparagus. Simply bend the woody end and it will break off naturally, or use a vegetable peeler to remove the bottom 2 inches (5 cm) of the tough outer layer.

The delicious flavor of this barbecue recipe will have you looking forward to grilling weather.

If using bamboo skewers, soak in water for 1 hour. Place all the mushrooms on skewers. On separate skewers, place the tomatoes. On separate skewers, skewer each section of onion horizontally through the rings so they will lie flat on the grill. Place all skewered vegetables and the asparagus on a baking sheet. Brush lightly with 2 tsp (10 mL) oil. Set aside.

Bring the water and quinoa to a boil in a medium saucepan. Reduce to a simmer, cover and cook for 15 minutes. Fluff with a fork and set aside.

Melt the butter in a large saucepan on medium heat. Stir in the remaining 1 Tbsp (15 mL) oil, the tarragon, garlic and salt (if using). Heat for 30 seconds. Remove from the heat and set aside.

Preheat the barbecue to medium. Lightly grease the grill. Grill the onions first, for 3 minutes. Flip the onions, then add the mushrooms. Grill for 3 minutes. Flip the onions and mushrooms, then add the asparagus. Grill for another 3 minutes. Turn the vegetables once again and add the tomatoes for the last 3 minutes. Remove all the vegetables from the grill. Remove the tomatoes and mushrooms from the skewers and place in the saucepan with the seasoned butter. Cut the asparagus into thirds, then cut the onion into large dice. Add to the other vegetables. Toss gently to coat vegetables in the seasoned butter and vegetable juices.

Preheat the broiler with the oven rack in the middle. Spread the quinoa evenly in a casserole dish and spoon the grilled vegetables on top. Crumble the goat cheese over the vegetables. Broil for 3 to 5 minutes, until the goat cheese is slightly melted. Serve.

PER SERVING: Energy 290 calories; Protein 10 g; Carbohydrates 28 g; Dietary Fiber 4 g; Fat 17 g; Sugar 4 g; Cholesterol 25 mg; Sodium 120 mg

CHICKEN MASALA

SERVES 4

3 Tbsp (45 mL) grapeseed oil
   or vegetable oil

1½ lb (675 g) skinless, boneless
   chicken breasts, cut into
   1-inch (2.5 cm) pieces

1 cup (250 mL) onions cut into
   1-inch (2.5 cm) pieces

1 cup (250 mL) sliced carrots

2 tsp (10 mL) minced garlic

1 tsp (5 mL) ground coriander

½ tsp (2 mL) salt (optional)

½ tsp (2 mL) turmeric

¼ tsp (1 mL) cayenne pepper

1 can (28 oz/796 mL) diced
   tomatoes with juice

½ cup (125 mL) water

1 cup (250 mL) 2-inch (5 cm)
   cauliflower florets

1 cup (250 mL) green beans cut
   into 2-inch (5 cm) lengths

¾ tsp (4 mL) garam masala

This masala recipe is modeled after an authentically flavored curry. It tastes fantastic paired with the Indian-Infused Quinoa on page 83. See our tip below for the vegetarian version.

Heat 1½ Tbsp (20 mL) of the oil in a large saucepan on medium-high heat. Add the chicken and brown on all sides. Remove from the pan and set aside.

Reduce the heat to medium-low and add the remaining oil. Add the onions and carrots; cook until the onions become soft and opaque. Stir in the garlic, coriander, salt (if using), turmeric and cayenne. Heat for 3 minutes, stirring frequently. Add the chicken, tomatoes and water. Bring to a boil, reduce to a simmer and cook for 10 minutes. Stir in the cauliflower and green beans; cover and simmer for another 8 to 10 minutes, until the vegetables are tender and the chicken is no longer pink. Stir in the garam masala and season with more cayenne if desired. Serve over warm Indian-Infused Quinoa (page 83) or plain cooked quinoa.

PER SERVING: Energy 370 calories; Protein 38 g; Carbohydrates 20 g; Dietary Fiber 4 g; Fat 14 g; Sugar 11 g; Cholesterol 95 mg; Sodium 140 mg

For a vegetarian version, leave out the chicken. Use only 1½ Tbsp (20 mL) oil to cook the onions and carrots, and add 1 can (19 oz/540 mL) chickpeas, drained and rinsed, along with the tomatoes.

QUINOA BEEF STROGANOFF

An alternative to pasta, quinoa makes a delicious stroganoff with beef or low-fat bison. And it uses only one saucepan!

In a large saucepan on medium-high heat, cook beef strips until they are completely cooked through and are slightly browned. If the pan is a little dry, add a spoonful or two of water. Transfer beef to a plate and cover with foil to keep warm.

Heat the olive oil in the same saucepan on medium heat. Add the mushrooms and onions; cook until they are tender and opaque. Add the garlic. Increase the heat to high. Add the stock, water and quinoa. Bring to a boil, reduce to simmer, cover and cook for 12 minutes, until the mixture is thick, the quinoa is fluffy and almost no liquid remains. Stir in the yogurt and beef strips. Simmer for 5 minutes to reheat stroganoff. Serve immediately.

PER SERVING: Energy 440 calories; Protein 44 g; Carbohydrates 33 g; Dietary Fiber 3 g; Fat 13 g; Sugar 4 g; Cholesterol 90 mg; Sodium 120 mg

SERVES 4

1 lb (450 g) beef or bison steaks, cut into strips

1 Tbsp (15 mL) extra virgin olive oil

1½ cups (375 mL) sliced white or brown mushrooms

½ cup (125 mL) chopped onions

1 tsp (5 mL) minced garlic

1¼ cups (300 mL) sodium-reduced beef stock

1 cup (250 mL) water

1 cup (250 mL) quinoa

½ cup (125 mL) plain yogurt

NOUVEAU BOEUF BOURGUIGNON

SERVES 6

2 cups (500 mL) water

1 cup (250 mL) quinoa

1 Tbsp (15 mL) grapeseed oil
   or vegetable oil

1 top sirloin steak (1 to 1¼ lb/
   450 to 565 g), cubed

½ tsp (2 mL) salt (optional)

½ tsp (2 mL) black pepper

1 cup (250 mL) chopped onions

2 cups (500 mL) thickly
   sliced carrots

1 lb (450 g) cremini mushrooms,
   quartered

1½ tsp (7 mL) minced garlic

4 cups (1 L) sodium-reduced
   beef stock

2 Tbsp (30 mL) unsalted
   tomato paste

1 Tbsp (15 mL) chopped
   fresh thyme

1 Tbsp (15 mL) brown sugar

½ cup (125 mL) dry red wine

3 Tbsp (45 mL) cornstarch

Boeuf bourguignon reinvented! Have the length of time and the amount of wine needed to make this dish been holding you back? Here is our version over quinoa that you can enjoy any day of the week, it's that easy! To save even more time, prep your meat and vegetables the night before. Delicious and uncomplicated. If you don't have a large pan, brown the beef in batches.

Bring the water and quinoa to a boil in a medium saucepan. Reduce to a simmer, cover and cook for 15 minutes. Fluff with a fork and set aside.

Meanwhile, heat a large Dutch oven or 12-inch (30 cm) saucepan on medium-high heat. Add the oil to the hot pan, place the beef pieces about 1 inch (2.5 cm) apart and sprinkle with salt (if using) and pepper. Brown the beef on all sides but don't cook the meat all the way through. Remove the beef from the pan and set aside.

Reduce the heat to medium-low and add the onions and carrots. Cook for 5 minutes. (If the pan is a little dry, add a spoonful of water.) Add the mushrooms and cook for another 7 minutes or until the onions are opaque and the mushrooms are starting to soften. Stir in the garlic and cook for 1 minute.

Stir in the beef and any juices, stock, tomato paste, thyme and brown sugar. Reduce the heat to low and simmer for 15 minutes or until the carrots are tender and the beef is cooked through.

Whisk together the red wine and cornstarch. Stir into the beef mixture. Simmer until thickened enough to coat the back of a spoon, about 3 minutes. Adjust seasoning if necessary. Serve over hot quinoa.

PER SERVING: Energy 370 calories; Protein 32 g; Carbohydrates 36 g; Dietary Fiber 4 g; Fat 10 g; Sugar 7 g; Cholesterol 60 mg; Sodium 140 mg

MEDITERRANEAN CHICKEN QUINOA

Quinoa comes to life in this easy-to-prepare Mediterranean dish full of flavor with artichoke hearts, tomatoes, lemon and oregano.

Bring the water and quinoa to a boil in a small saucepan. Reduce to a simmer, cover and cook for 15 minutes. Fluff with a fork and set aside.

Heat the oil in a large skillet on medium low heat. Add the shallots; cook until transparent and the edges are starting to brown. Add the chicken; cook until the chicken is no longer pink, 6 to 7 minutes. Reduce the heat to low and stir in the quinoa and the garlic, artichoke hearts, tomatoes, feta, parsley, lemon juice and oregano. Gently reheat and serve.

PER SERVING: Energy 210 calories; Protein 20 g; Carbohydrates 22 g; Dietary Fiber 2 g; Fat 4.5 g; Sugar 3 g; Cholesterol 45 mg; Sodium 360 mg

Cooked quinoa already on hand? Add ¾ cup (175 mL) cooked quinoa to the chicken in this recipe.

SERVES 4

½ cup (125 mL) water

¼ cup (60 mL) quinoa

1 tsp (5 mL) grapeseed oil or vegetable oil

1 cup (250 mL) chopped shallots

2 chicken breasts, diced

1 tsp (5 mL) minced garlic

1 can (14 oz/398 mL) artichoke hearts, drained and chopped

1 cup (250 mL) chopped tomatoes

⅓ cup (75 mL) crumbled feta cheese

2 Tbsp (30 mL) chopped fresh parsley

1 Tbsp (15 mL) lemon juice

1 tsp (5 mL) dried oregano

QUINOA LASAGNA

Use your favorite tomato sauce in this layered dish of vegetables, quinoa, cheese and herbs. This lasagna is packed full of flavor that is reminiscent of comfort food without being too heavy. You'll still have plenty of room for dessert.

Preheat the oven to 350°F (180°C). Lightly grease a 13- × 9-inch (3 L) casserole dish or spray with cooking oil.

Bring the water and quinoa to a boil in a medium saucepan. Reduce to a simmer, cover and cook for 15 minutes. Fluff with a fork. Evenly spread the cooked quinoa in the casserole dish. Set aside.

Wipe clean the saucepan, then heat the oil in it on medium heat. Add the onions; cook until transparent and starting to brown. Add the mushrooms; cook until mushrooms are softened and very little moisture remains in the pan. Add the garlic and tomato sauce. Stir until hot. Set aside.

In a medium bowl, combine the cottage cheese with the egg; mix well. Stir in the Parmesan, basil and oregano.

Spread one-third of the tomato sauce over the quinoa. Make a layer of all the zucchini, then all the cottage cheese mixture, then one-third of the tomato sauce, then all the spinach, ending with the remainder of the tomato sauce. Spread the mozzarella cheese evenly on top.

Bake for about 35 minutes, until the lasagna is hot and the cheese is melted, bubbling and slightly browned around the edges. Serve.

PER SERVING: Energy 260 calories; Protein 16 g; Carbohydrates 25 g; Dietary Fiber 3 g; Fat 10 g; Sugar 6 g; Cholesterol 40 mg; Sodium 190 mg

SERVES 8

2 cups (500 mL) water

1 cup (250 mL) quinoa

2 Tbsp (30 mL) vegetable oil
   or olive oil

1 cup (250 mL) chopped onions

1 cup (250 mL) sliced brown or
   white mushrooms

2 cloves garlic, minced

2 cups (500 mL) tomato sauce
   or your favorite prepared
   pasta sauce

2 cups (500 mL) sodium-reduced
   pressed (dry curd) cottage
   cheese

1 large egg, beaten

¼ cup (60 mL) grated
   Parmesan cheese

2 Tbsp (30 mL) minced fresh basil
   (or ½ tsp/2 mL dried)

1 Tbsp (15 mL) dried oregano

2 cups (500 mL) sliced zucchini
   (2 small or 1 medium zucchini)

2 cups (500 mL) packed
   fresh spinach

1½ cups (375 mL) shredded
   reduced-fat mozzarella cheese

Cooked quinoa already on hand? Use 3 cups (750 mL) cooked quinoa as the base for this lasagna.

ROASTED VEGETABLE QUINOA WITH DILL

1 cup (250 mL) vegetable stock

½ cup (125 mL) quinoa

1 Tbsp (15 mL) grapeseed oil
　　or vegetable oil

4 shallots, finely chopped

3 cloves garlic, minced

2 cups (500 mL) coarsely chopped
　　mushrooms (any kind)

2 cups (500 mL) coarsely
　　chopped zucchini

2 cups (500 mL) coarsely chopped
　　yellow or orange bell peppers

1 cup (250 mL) quartered
　　grape tomatoes

½ cup (125 mL) chopped fresh dill

1 Tbsp (15 mL) dried oregano

½ tsp (2 mL) paprika

Pinch each of salt and
　　black pepper

Zucchini, mushrooms, yellow peppers and tomatoes make this colorful quinoa dish an exquisite side. Oregano, dill and the smoky hint of paprika help bring it to life. This dish makes a fantastic lunch salad.

Preheat the oven to 350°F (180°C). Lightly grease a deep 9-inch (23 cm) round baking dish or spray with cooking oil.

Bring the stock and quinoa to a boil in a medium saucepan. Reduce to a simmer, cover and cook for 15 minutes. Fluff with a fork and set aside.

Heat the oil in a large skillet on medium heat. Add the shallots; cook until transparent and the edges are brown. Add the garlic and mushrooms; cook for 7 to 8 more minutes, until the mushrooms sweat. Add the zucchini and yellow peppers; cook until tender, 3 to 5 more minutes. Turn off the heat and toss in the cooked quinoa and the tomatoes, dill, oregano, paprika, salt and black pepper. Stir well. Pour the mixture into the baking dish and bake for 20 minutes or until hot. Serve.

PER SERVING: Energy 100 calories; Protein 3 g; Carbohydrates 15 g; Dietary Fiber 3 g; Fat 3 g; Sugar 4 g; Cholesterol 0 mg; Sodium 65 mg

> Cooked quinoa already on hand? Add 1 ½ cups (375 mL) cooked quinoa to the cooked vegetables in this recipe.

ROASTED TOMATO & OLIVE BRUSCHETTA OVER BAKED HALIBUT & QUINOA

Tomatoes, black olives, basil and cilantro, with a squeeze of fresh orange juice, taste divine over baked halibut, with all the flavors soaking into a warm bed of quinoa. This is a great dish for using tri-color quinoa.

Preheat the oven to 450°F (230°C).

Bring the water and quinoa to a boil in a medium saucepan. Reduce to a simmer, cover and cook for 15 minutes. Remove from the heat and fluff with a fork. Set aside and keep warm.

Meanwhile, gently stir together the tomatoes, olives, oil, garlic, 1½ tsp (7 mL) basil, salt (if using) and pepper in a medium bowl. Pour the mixture into a 13- × 9-inch (3 L) baking dish. Bake for 10 minutes. Place the halibut, skin side up, on top of the tomato mixture. Bake for another 10 to 14 minutes or until the fish is just cooked through (check the fish after 10 minutes to prevent overcooking).

Spoon the quinoa onto plates and top with the halibut. Stir the cilantro, remaining basil and orange juice to taste into the tomato bruschetta. Spoon the bruschetta over the halibut. Serve.

PER SERVING: Energy 250 calories; Protein 11 g; Carbohydrates 29 g; Dietary Fiber 5 g; Fat 11 g; Sugar 6 g; Cholesterol 15 mg; Sodium 140 mg

SERVES 6

2 cups (500 mL) water

1 cup (250 mL) quinoa

3 lb (1.35 kg) Roma tomatoes, chopped

⅔ cup (150 mL) sliced pitted black olives in brine (not vinegar)

3 Tbsp (45 mL) grapeseed oil or vegetable oil

2 tsp (10 mL) minced garlic

1 Tbsp (15 mL) chopped fresh basil

½ tsp (2 mL) salt (optional)

¼ tsp (1 mL) black pepper

6 halibut fillets (each 8 oz/225 g and about 1 inch/2.5 cm thick)

4 tsp (20 mL) chopped fresh cilantro

1 to 2 Tbsp (15 to 30 mL) freshly squeezed orange juice

Know where your fish is coming from! These days, getting any fish in your diet can be difficult with so many questions about which fish are endangered, caught ethically, and healthy to eat. To help you choose fish from healthy, sustainable sources, visit Monterey Bay Aquarium's Seafood Watch at www.montereybayaquarium.org/cr/seafoodwatch.aspx.

ITALIAN SAUSAGE, FETA & TOMATO OVEN-BAKED FRITTATA

SERVES 6

½ cup (125 mL) water

¼ cup (60 mL) quinoa

1 tsp (5 mL) grapeseed oil
    or vegetable oil

½ lb (225 g) Homemade Italian
    Ground Sausage (page 80)

1 cup (250 mL) halved cherry
    tomatoes

1½ cups (375 mL) baby spinach,
    coarsely chopped

3 Tbsp (45 mL) sliced green onions

3 Tbsp (45 mL) coarsely chopped
    pitted black olives

½ cup (125 mL) crumbled
    reduced-fat or regular
    feta cheese

2 large eggs + 8 large egg whites
    (or 6 whole, large eggs total)

¼ cup (60 mL) 1% milk

Making the Homemade Italian Ground Sausage filling ahead makes for an easy and satisfying weeknight dish that is great served with a simple salad. Save even more time by cooking the sausage, tomatoes and quinoa in advance. For a vegetarian alternative, add 1 cup (250 mL) drained, rinsed cannellini beans along with the spinach.

Bring the water and quinoa to a boil in a small saucepan. Reduce to a simmer, cover and cook for 15 minutes. Fluff with a fork and set aside to cool.

Preheat the oven to 350°F (180°C). Lightly grease a 9-inch (2.5 L) square baking dish or a 9-inch (23 cm) pie plate.

Heat the oil in a medium skillet on medium-low heat. Add the sausage mixture and fry until browned completely. Stir in the tomatoes; cook for another 5 minutes, until the tomatoes have softened and released their juices. Remove from the heat and let cool slightly. Stir in the cooled quinoa, spinach, green onions and olives. Pour the mixture into the baking dish and sprinkle with the feta cheese. Whisk together the eggs and milk and pour over the vegetable mixture. (The egg mixture may not cover all the vegetable mixture but it will cook together perfectly.)

Bake for 40 to 50 minutes, until the top is golden and the center of the frittata has set. Let cool for 5 to 10 minutes. Cut into 6 pieces and serve hot or at room temperature.

PER SERVING: Energy 240 calories; Protein 26 g; Carbohydrates 8 g; Dietary Fiber 2 g; Fat 14 g; Sugar 2 g; Cholesterol 120 mg; Sodium 320 mg

LEEK PARMESAN QUICHE

A delicious quinoa crust is topped with sautéed leeks, fresh tarragon, Parmesan cheese and a hint of nutmeg.

Heat the oil in a medium skillet on medium heat. Add the leeks and cook until softened, 7 to 10 minutes. Add the wine and water; continue to cook for 5 minutes, until the liquid has mostly evaporated but the skillet is not completely dry. When the leeks are almost translucent, transfer them to a bowl and let cool.

Preheat the oven to 400°F (200°C). Lightly grease a 9-inch (23 cm) pie plate or spray with cooking oil. Roll out the pastry and line the pie plate (see page 190).

In a small bowl, beat the eggs and egg whites. Add the milk, Parmesan, tarragon, nutmeg, salt (if using) and pepper. Whisk until well combined. Stir in the cooled leeks. Pour into the pie shell.

Bake for 20 minutes or until the center of the quiche is firm. Let cool for 5 minutes. Run a knife around the outside edge of the quiche to loosen the crust. Slice into wedges and serve hot.

PER SERVING: Energy 300 calories; Protein 7 g; Carbohydrates 29 g; Dietary Fiber 2 g; Fat 17 g; Sugar 3 g; Cholesterol 80 mg; Sodium 200 mg

SERVES 8

1 Tbsp (15 mL) grapeseed oil

2 cups (500 mL) thinly sliced leeks (white part only)

½ cup (125 mL) dry white wine

⅓ cup (75 mL) water

1 unbaked single Flaky Pie Crust (page 190)

2 large eggs

4 large egg whites

½ cup (125 mL) whole milk or whipping cream

¼ cup (60 mL) freshly grated Parmesan cheese

1 Tbsp (15 mL) chopped fresh tarragon

¼ tsp (1 mL) nutmeg

¼ tsp (1 mL) salt (optional)

¼ tsp (1 mL) black pepper

MUSHROOM & SPINACH QUICHE

SERVES 8

⅔ cup (150 mL) water

⅓ cup (75 mL) quinoa

1 tsp (5 mL) vegetable oil
or olive oil

2 shallots, finely chopped

2 cloves garlic, minced

4 cups (1 L) packed fresh spinach,
tough stems removed

2 cups (500 mL) chopped
shiitake mushrooms

1½ tsp (7 mL) herbes de Provence

2 large eggs + 4 large egg whites
(or 4 whole, large eggs total)

¼ cup (60 mL) quinoa flour or
all-purpose flour

⅓ cup (75 mL) shredded, reduced-
fat mozzarella cheese

⅓ cup (75 mL) freshly grated
Parmesan cheese

¼ cup (60 mL) milk or 10% cream

¼ tsp (1 mL) nutmeg

¼ tsp (1 mL) salt

Pinch of black pepper

This simple crustless quiche is full of quinoa, shiitake mushrooms and spinach. Herbs and a hint of nutmeg give this quiche an impressive flavor.

Preheat the oven to 350°F (180°C). Lightly grease a 9-inch (23 cm) round baking dish or spray with cooking oil.

Bring the water and quinoa to a boil in a medium saucepan. Reduce to a simmer, cover and cook for 15 minutes. Fluff with a fork and set aside.

Heat ½ tsp (2 mL) of the oil in a medium saucepan on medium-low heat. Add the shallots and cook until transparent and beginning to brown. (Add a spoonful of water if the pan looks dry.) Add the garlic and spinach; cook for 3 to 4 more minutes, until the spinach is wilted. Transfer the mixture to a bowl. Set aside.

Heat the remaining oil in the same saucepan on medium-low heat. Add the mushrooms and herbes de Provence; cook for 7 to 8 minutes, until the mushrooms begin to sweat. Add to the spinach mixture.

In a medium bowl, whisk together eggs and flour. Stir in the cooked quinoa, mozzarella, Parmesan, milk, nutmeg, salt and pepper. Stir in the spinach mixture.

Pour into the baking dish and bake for 45 to 50 minutes, until the center of the quiche is firm. Remove from the oven and let cool for 10 minutes. Run a knife around the outside edge of the quiche. Slice into wedges and serve hot.

PER SERVING: Energy 180 calories; Protein 13 g; Carbohydrates 20 g; Dietary Fiber 4 g; Fat 6 g; Sugar 3 g; Cholesterol 70 mg; Sodium 260 mg

Cooked quinoa already on hand? Add 1 cup (250 mL) cooked quinoa to the eggs.

SOUTHWEST QUICHE

This quiche is satisfying but not heavy. Quinoa flour gives the crust a nutty flavor, and peppers, spices, cheese and fresh cilantro add taste, dramatic color—and even more nutrition.

Preheat the oven to 375°F (190°C). Lightly grease a 9-inch (23 cm) pie plate or spray with cooking oil. Roll out pastry and line the pie plate (see page 190).

In a medium bowl, whisk together the eggs, milk, green onions, cilantro, chili pepper, chili powder, cumin, salt (if using) and black pepper. Stir in the Cheddar cheese, corn and red pepper. Pour the mixture into the pie shell.

Bake for 40 to 45 minutes or until the center of the quiche is set. Let sit for 8 to 10 minutes before cutting into wedges. Serve immediately.

PER SERVING: Energy 250 calories; Protein 11 g; Carbohydrates 16 g; Dietary Fiber 3 g; Fat 16 g; Sugar 3 g; Cholesterol 80 mg; Sodium 160 mg

> Make it crustless! Instead of using a pastry crust, add ⅓ to ½ cup (75 to 125 mL) cooked quinoa to the egg mixture.

SERVES 8

1 unbaked single Flaky Pie Crust (page 190)

2 large eggs + 4 large egg whites (or 4 whole, large eggs total)

1 cup (250 mL) 2% milk or cream

¼ cup (60 mL) chopped green onions

1 Tbsp (15 mL) minced fresh cilantro

1 Tbsp (15 mL) chopped fresh red hot chili pepper

1 tsp (5 mL) chili powder

½ tsp (2 mL) ground cumin

½ tsp (2 mL) salt (optional)

½ tsp (2 mL) black pepper

1 cup (250 mL) shredded reduced-fat aged Cheddar cheese

½ cup (125 mL) thawed frozen corn

½ cup (125 mL) chopped red bell pepper

BARBECUE BEEF LETTUCE WRAPS

SERVES 6

½ cup (125 mL) sodium-reduced
    soy sauce or tamari
    (gluten-free if required)

3 Tbsp (45 mL) brown sugar

2 Tbsp (30 mL) sesame oil

1 Tbsp (15 mL) rice vinegar

1 tsp (5 mL) minced garlic

1 tsp (5 mL) minced fresh ginger

½ tsp (2 mL) hot red pepper
    flakes (optional)

1 lb (450 g) sirloin steak

1 cup (250 mL) water

½ cup (125 mL) quinoa (any color)

2 hearts romaine or 1 head butter
    lettuce, leaves separated

½ cup (125 mL) shredded carrots

¼ cup (60 mL) thinly sliced
    green onions

1 Tbsp (15 mL) sesame seeds

1 can (8 oz/230 g) water chestnuts,
    drained and halved (optional)

Beef bulgogi is a traditional Korean favorite. Include the hot pepper flakes if you prefer a little heat. You can either grill the meat or cook it on your stovetop. Either way, it's easy!

BARBECUE METHOD In a large bowl or resealable plastic bag, combine the soy sauce, brown sugar, sesame oil, vinegar, garlic, ginger and hot pepper flakes (if using). Add the steak. Place in the refrigerator to marinate for at least 1 hour and up to 24 hours.

Bring the water and quinoa to a boil in a medium saucepan. Reduce to a simmer, cover and cook for 15 minutes. Remove from the heat and set aside, covered.

Preheat the barbecue to medium-high. Brush the grill lightly with oil. Remove the steak from the bag and drain off the marinade (discard the marinade). Grill the steak for about 4 minutes per side for medium-rare, or cook to your preferred doneness. Transfer the steak to a cutting board and let rest for 8 minutes. Slice thinly across the grain with a sharp knife.

Fluff quinoa with a fork and spoon onto each romaine leaf. Top with a few beef strips, carrots, green onions, a sprinkle of sesame seeds and water chestnuts (if using). Wrap and serve.

STOVETOP METHOD Freeze the steak for about 30 minutes, until semi-firm. Using a sharp knife, slice into strips ⅛ inch (3 mm) to ¼ inch (5 mm) thick. Place the meat in a large resealable plastic bag or a bowl and add the soy sauce, brown sugar, sesame oil, vinegar, garlic, ginger and hot pepper flakes (if using). Refrigerate for at least 1 hour and up to 24 hours. Cook meat, with the marinade, in a large saucepan on medium-high heat until meat is cooked through.

PER SERVING: Energy 220 calories; Protein 26 g; Carbohydrates 14 g; Dietary Fiber 2 g; Fat 6 g; Sugar 2 g; Cholesterol 60 mg; Sodium 350 mg

If desired, cook marinade on medium heat for 2 minutes and serve cooled with the wraps for dipping.

HEALTHY BAKED QUINOA FALAFELS

MAKES 28 FALAFELS

1 cup (250 mL) water

½ cup (125 mL) quinoa

1½ cups (375 mL) cooked chickpeas (or one 14 oz/ 398 mL can chickpeas, drained and rinsed)

½ cup (125 mL) chopped fresh parsley

2 tsp (10 mL) chopped garlic

1 large egg

3 Tbsp (45 mL) grapeseed oil or vegetable oil

1 tsp (5 mL) ground coriander

1 tsp (5 mL) ground cumin

¼ tsp (1 mL) cayenne pepper

¼ tsp (1 mL) salt (optional)

Enjoy these falafels in a pita or on a plate of greens along with yogurt dip, tomato, cucumbers, green peppers and red onion for a light dinner.

Preheat the oven to 400°F (200°C). Lightly grease or spray with cooking oil a baking sheet or line with parchment.

Bring the water and quinoa to a boil in a medium saucepan. Reduce to a simmer, cover and cook for 15 minutes. Remove from the heat and let sit, covered, for another 10 minutes. The quinoa should be extra-fluffy.

In a food processor, combine the quinoa, chickpeas, parsley and garlic. Pulse until the chickpeas are finely chopped but not a paste. Add the egg, oil, coriander, cumin, cayenne and salt (if using). Pulse a few times to combine. Scoop out tablespoons of the mixture and arrange 1 inch (2.5 cm) apart on the baking sheet. With wet hands, press down on the balls to make patties ½ inch (1 cm) thick.

Bake the falafels for 10 minutes on each side. Let cool for 5 minutes before serving. Enjoy in a pita or on a salad.

PER SERVING: Energy 40 calories; Protein 1 g; Carbohydrates 4 g; Dietary Fiber 1 g; Fat 2 g; Sugar 0 g; Cholesterol 5 mg; Sodium 35 mg

Cooked quinoa already on hand? Make these falafels with 1½ cups (375 mL) extra-fluffy cooked quinoa.

FRESH SPRING ROLLS WITH GINGER LIME PEANUT SAUCE

Full of fresh, lively flavors, this recipe can easily be modified to accommodate your tastes. Be as creative or as colorful as you want. These rolls are terrific in lunches or as appetizers (use smaller wrappers if you prefer).

For the sauce, in a small saucepan whisk together the water, peanut butter, soy sauce and ginger. Bring to a boil on medium heat. Reduce heat and simmer for 2 to 3 minutes, whisking until smooth. If the sauce becomes too thick, add a spoonful of water. Remove from the heat and add lime juice to taste. Set aside.

For the spring rolls, bring the water and quinoa to a boil in a medium saucepan. Reduce to a simmer, cover and cook for 15 minutes. Remove from the heat and let sit, covered, for another 10 minutes. Fluff with a fork and set aside to cool completely.

Fill a large bowl with warm water. Soak 1 rice paper wrapper in the water for 20 seconds, then lay flat on a work surface. In a line at the edge closest to you, sprinkle a small amount of sesame seeds. Top with a few cilantro leaves, a few pieces of cucumber, a strip or two of red pepper, a spoonful or two of shredded carrot and some sliced spinach. Top the vegetables with ¼ cup (60 mL) of cooked quinoa. Fold the sides over the filling and fold the bottom up. Continue to tightly roll the wrapper from the bottom to enclose the filling completely, then press the edges together to seal. (See the instructions on the wrapper packaging for additional clarification.) Repeat with the remaining ingredients. Serve on a platter with the ginger-lime peanut sauce.

PER SERVING: Energy 150 calories; Protein 5 g; Carbohydrates 20 g; Dietary Fiber 2 g; Fat 5 g; Sugar 2 g; Cholesterol 0 mg; Sodium 120 mg

MAKES 8 SPRING ROLLS

SAUCE

⅓ cup (75 mL) water

3 Tbsp (45 mL) smooth or crunchy natural peanut butter

1 Tbsp (30 mL) sodium-reduced soy sauce or tamari (gluten-free if required)

¼ tsp (1 mL) grated fresh ginger

Squeeze of fresh lime juice to taste

SPRING ROLLS

1⅓ cups (325 mL) water

⅔ cup (150 mL) quinoa

8 rice paper wrappers (8 ½ inches/21 cm)

2 Tbsp (30 mL) sesame seeds

¼ cup (60 mL) whole cilantro leaves

1 cup (250 mL) unpeeled English cucumber cut into thin half-moons

¼ cup (60 mL) thinly sliced red bell pepper

1 cup (250 mL) shredded carrot

1 cup (250 mL) thinly sliced baby spinach

Feeling experimental? Try one or more of these ingredients in your spring rolls: green onions, bean sprouts, thin slices of plain omelet, thinly sliced mango, cooked shrimp, thinly sliced pork, avocado slices, chopped peanuts or smoked salmon.

KALE, RED PEPPER & QUINOA TOSS

This recipe can be made in less time than you'd wait for take-out delivery. Satisfy your desire for a super-nutritious hot meal made in 20 minutes.

Combine 1⅓ cups (325 mL) of water and quinoa in a medium saucepan and bring to a boil. Reduce to a simmer, cover and cook for 15 minutes. Remove from the heat and set aside.

Pour ½ cup (125 mL) of water into a large saucepan. Layer the kale, red pepper and cannellini beans in the pan—do not stir. Bring to a boil, reduce to a simmer, cover and cook for 4 to 5 minutes (peek once to ensure the water does not completely cook away) or until the red pepper is tender and the beans are hot. Remove from the heat and drain away any remaining water.

Stir the pesto into the quinoa. Add the quinoa and 2 Tbsp (30 mL) of the Parmesan cheese to the kale mixture; toss well. Spoon the quinoa mixture into a serving bowl and sprinkle with the remaining Parmesan cheese. Sprinkle with lemon juice and serve immediately.

PER SERVING: Energy 230 calories; Protein 11 g; Carbohydrates 32 g; Dietary Fiber 7 g; Fat 7 g; Sugar 2 g; Cholesterol 5 mg; Sodium 170 mg

SERVES 6

1⅓ cups (325 mL) + ½ cup (125 mL) water

⅔ cup (150 mL) quinoa (any color)

4 cups (1 L) chopped kale, center ribs and stems removed

1 cup (250 mL) red bell pepper sliced into 2-inch (5 cm) lengths

1 can (19 oz/540 mL) cannellini or white kidney beans, drained and rinsed

3 Tbsp (45 mL) basil pesto

¼ cup (60 mL) grated Parmesan cheese

2 Tbsp (30 mL) lemon juice

SAVORY MUSHROOM SPINACH CRÊPES

MAKES 12 (6-INCH/15 CM) CRÊPES, SERVING 6

CRÊPES

⅓ cup (75 mL) quinoa flour

¼ cup (60 mL) brown rice flour or whole wheat flour

2 tsp (10 mL) cornstarch

2 large eggs + 2 large egg whites (or 3 whole, large eggs total)

1 cup (250 mL) 1% or 2% milk

FILLING

1 Tbsp (15 mL) salted butter

1 lb (450 g) cremini mushrooms, thinly sliced

¼ tsp (1 mL) salt (optional)

2 tsp (10 mL) minced garlic

1½ tsp (7 mL) minced fresh thyme

¾ tsp (4 mL) minced fresh rosemary

1 bag (10 oz/280 g) fresh baby spinach

¾ cup (175 mL) crumbled soft unripened goat cheese

These delicious and healthful crêpes will not last long! Not only are they great for a light supper with salad, they are wonderful served at brunch. If desired, in place of fresh spinach you can use a 10-oz (284 g) package of frozen spinach, thawed and well drained.

For the crêpes, stir together the quinoa flour, rice flour and cornstarch in a medium bowl. Add the eggs, egg whites and milk. Whisk until smooth.

Heat a lightly oiled 6-inch (15 cm) skillet on medium-high heat. Pour 2 Tbsp (30 mL) of batter into the center of the pan; quickly tilt the pan in a circular motion to spread the batter over the bottom. Flip crêpe when the edges begin to curl, after about 30 to 45 seconds. Cook the other side for another 30 seconds, then remove from the pan. Place the hot crêpe on a plate and cover with foil. Repeat with the remaining batter.

For the filling, melt the butter in a large nonstick skillet on medium heat. Add the mushrooms and salt (if using). Cook, stirring occasionally, for 8 to 10 minutes, until the mushrooms soften. Add the garlic, thyme and rosemary; cook for 30 seconds longer. Stir in the spinach and cook, stirring occasionally, for 4 minutes or until spinach has wilted. Remove from the heat.

Place a crêpe on a plate and spoon 1 Tbsp (15 mL) of crumbled goat cheese and ¼ cup (60 mL) of mushroom mixture in a line down the center. Fold in the edges (like a burrito). Serve immediately.

PER SERVING: Energy 210 calories; Protein 12 g; Carbohydrates 22 g; Dietary Fiber 4 g; Fat 9 g; Sugar 4 g; Cholesterol 80 mg; Sodium 240 mg

INDIVIDUAL MIGHTY MEAT LOAVES

Take the guesswork out of what equals a serving size of meat loaf. This traditional-style meat loaf made with quinoa is baked in individual portions. This recipe makes enough to freeze extra for future meals or to make easy lunch sandwiches the next day.

Preheat the oven to 375°F (190°C). Lightly grease or spray with cooking oil a baking sheet or line with parchment.

Combine the water and quinoa in a medium saucepan and bring to a boil. Reduce to a simmer, cover and cook for 15 minutes. Remove from the heat and leave the lid on for an additional 10 minutes. Fluff with a fork and set aside to cool.

Heat the oil in a small skillet on medium-low heat. Add the onions and cook for about 5 minutes, until the onions are tender. (Add a spoonful of water to the pan if dry.) Add the thyme and garlic; continue to cook for 1 minute. Remove from the heat and let cool slightly.

In a medium bowl, beat the eggs. Add the quinoa, onion mixture, ground beef, parsley, milk, Worcestershire sauce, mustard and salt (if using); mix until combined. Scoop out ½-cup (125 mL) portions of the mixture and shape into 9 oval patties ¾ inch (2 cm) thick. Arrange on the baking sheet about 2 inches (5 cm) apart. Bake for 15 minutes.

Meanwhile, stir together the ketchup, brown sugar and vinegar in a small bowl. Using the back of a spoon, spread an even amount of the topping over each meat loaf. Bake for another 20 minutes or until the loaves have browned and the topping is bubbling. Serve hot.

PER SERVING: Energy 150 calories; Protein 13 g; Carbohydrates 12 g; Dietary Fiber 1 g; Fat 5 g; Sugar 3 g; Cholesterol 70 mg; Sodium 150 mg

MAKES 9 INDIVIDUAL MEAT LOAVES

1 cup (250 mL) water

½ cup (125 mL) quinoa

1 Tbsp (15 mL) grapeseed oil or vegetable oil

1 cup (250 mL) finely chopped onions

2 ¾ tsp (11 mL) chopped fresh thyme (or ¾ tsp/4 mL dried)

1½ tsp (7 mL) minced garlic

2 large eggs

1 lb (450 g) extra-lean ground beef

⅓ cup (75 mL) chopped fresh parsley (or 2 Tbsp/30 mL dried)

¼ cup (60 mL) skim milk

1 Tbsp (15 mL) Worcestershire sauce (gluten-free if required)

2 tsp (10 mL) mild Dijon mustard

½ tsp (2 mL) salt (optional)

½ cup (125 mL) sugar-reduced ketchup

2 Tbsp (30 mL) packed brown sugar

1 tsp (5 mL) apple cider vinegar

MINI MEXICAN MEAT LOAVES

MAKES 6 INDIVIDUAL
MEAT LOAVES

1 cup (250 mL) water

½ cup (125 mL) quinoa

1 large egg

2 large egg whites

1 lb (450 g) ground chicken

¾ cup (175 mL) salsa

1½ tsp (7 mL) chili powder

1¼ tsp (6 mL) dried oregano

1 tsp (5 mL) minced garlic

⅓ cup (75 mL) shredded
    reduced-fat aged
    Cheddar cheese

These individual moist meat loaves are full of Mexican flavor, and making them as individual portions reduces the cooking time. By using quinoa in your favorite dishes such as this one, you can reduce the amount of meat you eat and gain nutrition from another protein source. These meat loaves can easily be frozen.

Preheat the oven to 350°F (180°C). Lightly grease a baking sheet or line with parchment.

Combine the water and quinoa in a medium saucepan and bring to a boil. Reduce to a simmer, cover and cook for 15 minutes. Remove from the heat and leave the lid on for an additional 5 minutes. Fluff with a fork and set aside to cool.

In a medium bowl, beat the egg and egg whites. Add 1½ cups (375 mL) cooked quinoa and the ground chicken, salsa, chili powder, oregano and garlic. Stir until well combined. Scoop out ½-cup (125 mL) portions of the mixture and shape into 6 oval patties ¾ inch (2 cm) thick. Arrange on the baking sheet about 2 inches (5 cm) apart.

Bake for 15 minutes. Sprinkle with the Cheddar. Bake for another 15 minutes or until no longer pink and slightly browned. Serve hot.

PER SERVING: Energy 200 calories; Protein 19 g; Carbohydrates 12 g; Dietary Fiber 2 g; Fat 8 g; Sugar 2 g; Cholesterol 95 mg; Sodium 360 mg

SMOKED SALMON
SANDWICH WITH AVOCADO
& QUINOA SPROUTS

This is a revamped version of the popular lox and cream cheese usually served on a bagel. Add quinoa sprouts and avocado and this open-faced sandwich is nutritious and bursting with flavor. This sandwich is a great way to use up any extra quinoa sprouts.

Toast the bread, if desired. Spread the herbed goat cheese over the bread. Sprinkle with the quinoa sprouts. Top with salmon, avocado and red onion. Serve immediately.

PER SERVING: Energy 240 calories; Protein 13 g; Carbohydrates 24 g; Dietary Fiber 5 g; Fat 11 g; Sugar 1 g; Cholesterol 15 mg; Sodium 420 mg

SERVES 1

1 slice sprouted grain sandwich bread or gluten-free bread

4 tsp (20 mL) herbed goat cheese

2 Tbsp (30 mL) quinoa sprouts (pages 10 and 11)

3 slices smoked wild Alaskan salmon

¼ avocado, peeled and thinly sliced

1 Tbsp (15 mL) thinly sliced red onion

An avocado is ripe when the skin is a dark brown/green color. A ripe avocado will give under gentle pressure.

SMOKY CHIPOTLE BBQ PULLED BEEF WITH RED CABBAGE & SPROUT SLAW

This recipe should be served with the Red Cabbage & Sprout Slaw on page 64. The fresh crunch of the salad along with the smoky chipotle is a spectacular combination. For a pork alternative, use an equivalent weight of pork tenderloin instead.

SERVES 8

PULLED BEEF

2 ½ lb (1.125 kg) inside round beef roast

¼ tsp (1 mL) salt (optional)

¼ tsp (1 mL) black pepper

1 Tbsp (15 mL) grapeseed oil or vegetable oil

2 cups (500 mL) beef stock

8 buns of your choice (optional)

BARBECUE SAUCE

(MAKES ABOUT 2 CUPS/500 ML)

1 cup (250 mL) water or cooking liquid from the slow cooker (fat removed)

1 can (5 ½ oz/156 mL) tomato paste

⅓ cup (75 mL) dark brown sugar

1 Tbsp (15 mL) Worcestershire sauce (gluten-free if required)

1 Tbsp (15 mL) white vinegar

1 Tbsp (15 mL) lemon juice

1 tsp (5 mL) minced garlic

1 tsp (5 mL) fancy molasses

½ tsp (2 mL) salt (optional)

½ tsp (2 mL) minced chipotle pepper in adobo sauce

¼ tsp (1 mL) chili powder

For the pulled beef, pat the roast dry with paper towel and rub with salt (if using) and pepper. Heat the oil in a large skillet on medium-high heat. Add the roast and sear on all sides, using tongs to turn the meat as it browns (each side should take 30 to 60 seconds). Place the roast in a 6-quart (6 L) slow cooker. Add the stock and just enough water to cover the roast. Cook on low for 7 to 8 hours or on high for 5 to 6 hours. Remove the roast when the internal temperature reaches 170°F (75°C). Cool the roast for 10 minutes, then shred the meat using 2 forks. Transfer meat to a medium bowl.

For the barbecue sauce, in a large saucepan, combine the water, tomato paste, brown sugar, Worcestershire sauce, vinegar, lemon juice, garlic, molasses, salt (if using), chipotle pepper and chili powder. Cook on medium-low heat, stirring occasionally, for about 8 minutes, until the sauce is thick enough to coat the back of a spoon. Stir in the shredded meat and cook until heated through. Spoon ⅓ cup (75 mL) pulled beef onto buns (if using). Serve with Red Cabbage & Sprout Slaw.

PER SERVING (without bun): Energy 360 calories; Protein 40 g; Carbohydrates 11 g; Dietary Fiber 1 g; Fat 16 g; Sugar 9 g; Cholesterol 120 mg; Sodium 170 mg

Cook your meat consistently to perfection by using a digital or dial instant-read meat thermometer.

SPICY SALMON BURGERS

These salmon burgers burst with flavor! Sweet mango, creamy avocado, crisp red onion and a bit of heat are a brilliant match for salmon. Toast the buns for the best flavor and texture. Also delicious with grilled pineapple rings, if you like.

For the burgers, bring the water and quinoa to a boil in a medium saucepan. Reduce to a simmer, cover and cook for 15 minutes. Remove from the heat and let sit, covered, for another 5 minutes. Fluff with a fork and set aside to cool.

Preheat the oven to 400°F (200°C). Lightly grease or spray with cooking oil a baking sheet or line with parchment.

Flake the salmon with a fork in a shallow bowl. Add the cooled quinoa, egg, green onions, cilantro, sriracha sauce, honey, ginger and garlic. Mix until well combined. Form into 6 patties and place on the baking sheet. Bake for 7 minutes on each side, flipping gently.

For the yogurt topping, stir together the yogurt, lime juice and lime zest in a small bowl.

Place a cooked salmon burger on half of a toasted bun and top with a few pieces of sliced mango and avocado (or a pineapple ring, if you prefer). Top with a dollop of yogurt topping, a sprinkle of red onion and a sprig of cilantro. Serve immediately.

PER SERVING (with ½ bun): Energy 310 calories; Protein 23 g; Carbohydrates 32 g; Dietary Fiber 5 g; Fat 12 g; Sugar 12 g; Cholesterol 70 mg; Sodium 190 mg

SERVES 6

SALMON BURGERS

⅔ cup (150 mL) water

⅓ cup (75 mL) quinoa

2 cans (7 ½ oz/213 g each) sodium-reduced wild Pacific salmon, drained, larger bones removed

1 large egg, beaten

½ cup (125 mL) thinly sliced green onions

2 Tbsp (30 mL) chopped fresh cilantro

1 Tbsp (15 mL) sriracha or other hot chili sauce

1 tsp (5 mL) liquid honey

½ tsp (2 mL) grated fresh ginger

½ tsp (2 mL) minced garlic

3 whole wheat or gluten-free buns, halved and toasted

YOGURT TOPPING

¾ cup (175 mL) nonfat plain thick Greek yogurt

¾ tsp (4 mL) lime juice

½ tsp (2 mL) grated lime zest

GARNISHES

1 mango, peeled and thinly sliced

1 avocado, peeled and thinly sliced

6 grilled pineapple rings (optional)

¼ cup (60 mL) minced red onion

6 small sprigs fresh cilantro

THE BETTER
BURGER

SERVES 8

1 cup (250 mL) water

½ cup (125 mL) red quinoa

1 Tbsp (15 mL) grapeseed oil
   or vegetable oil

1 cup (250 mL) diced onions

2 cups (500 mL) finely chopped
   cremini or white button
   mushrooms

1 tsp (5 mL) minced garlic

¾ tsp (4 mL) dried marjoram

¼ tsp (1 mL) dried oregano

1 large egg

⅔ cup (150 mL) shredded
   reduced-fat aged
   Cheddar cheese

½ cup (125 mL) toasted pecans,
   finely chopped

⅓ cup (75 mL) quick-cooking rolled
   oats (gluten-free if required)

1 Tbsp (15 mL) sodium-reduced
   soy sauce or tamari
   (gluten-free if required)

This burger *is* better! A meatless meat-lover's burger, this is a full-flavor burger with the perfect combination of toasted pecans, mushrooms, aged Cheddar, herbs and, of course, red quinoa. These patties hold together well for freezing, making for a quick and easy meal.

Preheat the oven to 350°F (180°C). Lightly grease a baking sheet or line with parchment.

Combine the water and quinoa in a medium saucepan. Bring to a boil, reduce to a simmer, cover and cook for 15 minutes. Remove from the heat and let sit, covered, for another 10 minutes. Fluff with a fork and set aside to cool.

Heat the oil in a large saucepan on medium heat. Add the onions and cook for about 5 minutes or until the onions start to become soft and transparent. Add the mushrooms, garlic, marjoram and oregano; cook for another 5 minutes or until the mushrooms are tender. Set aside to cool.

In a medium bowl, beat the egg. Add the quinoa, mushroom mixture, cheese, toasted pecans, oats and soy sauce. Scoop ½-cup (125 mL) portions of the mixture onto the baking sheet and shape into 8 or 9 patties 1 inch (2.5 cm) thick, leaving 1 inch (2.5 cm) between them. Bake for 27 to 30 minutes, until slightly browned and crispy. Serve with your favorite garnishes.

PER SERVING: Energy 150 calories; Protein 7 g; Carbohydrates 13 g; Dietary Fiber 2 g; Fat 9 g; Sugar 2 g; Cholesterol 25 mg; Sodium 130 mg

- These burgers can also be fried in an oiled skillet or grilled on a barbecue baking sheet.

- To toast nuts, preheat the oven to 350°F (180°C). Spread the nuts on a baking sheet and toast in the oven, stirring once if necessary, for 5 to 7 minutes, until fragrant and lightly toasted.

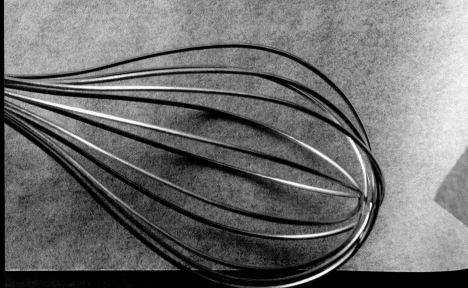

REVOLUTIONIZE
DESSERT

REVOLUTIONIZE DESSERT

NOT just a high-calorie afterthought, a delicious dessert can be healthful and an impressive finale to any meal, whether for guests or even just for yourself. It doesn't have to be full of fat and sugar to taste good, but no one else needs to know that. In this chapter, quinoa seeds, flour and flakes play a star role in desserts. In fact, the flavor of quinoa desserts may pleasantly surprise you.

Many of these satisfying and delectable desserts are a hit for gatherings and entertaining, convenient for weekday family snacks or perfect to take along to the office. For entertaining, try the Lemon Ginger Blueberry Crisp (page 200) or the Country Apple Pecan Pie (page 189). Chocolate Chip Fruit Granola Bars (page 184) make great family snacks that are easy to grab on the run. If you'd like to get the kids involved, try the Banana Mouse Pops (page 170) or Black Forest Goat Cheese Brownies (page 159). Great treats to show off at work include the Almond Butter Blondies (page 154) and the Salted Caramel Pecan Bites (page 160).

For a treat with frosting that has no refined sugar or added fat, try the Chocolate Cream Mini Cupcakes with Avocado Icing (page 179).

ALMOND BUTTER BLONDIES

MAKES 24 SQUARES

¼ cup (60 mL) unsalted
    butter, softened

¾ cup (175 mL) smooth or
    crunchy natural almond butter

2 large eggs

¾ cup (175 mL) brown sugar

1 tsp (5 mL) pure vanilla extract

¾ cup (175 mL) quinoa flour

1 tsp (5 mL) baking powder

¼ tsp (1 mL) salt

1 cup (250 mL) semisweet
    chocolate chips

People likely won't even notice that these delightfully nutty blondies have quinoa in them. Chewy with just a hint of chocolate.

Preheat the oven to 350°F (180°C). Lightly grease or spray with cooking oil an 8-inch (2 L) square cake pan and line pan with parchment.

In a medium bowl, cream the butter and almond butter. Beat in the eggs, sugar and vanilla.

In a small bowl, whisk together the flour, baking powder and salt. Mix into the almond butter mixture. Stir in the chocolate chips. Spread the batter evenly in the prepared pan.

Bake for 18 to 20 minutes or until a toothpick inserted into the center comes out with just a few crumbs on it. Do not overbake. Let cool in the pan for 15 minutes before cutting into 24 squares.

Store in a sealed container in the refrigerator for up to 1 week.

PER SERVING: Energy 140 calories; Protein 3 g; Carbohydrates 13 g; Dietary Fiber 2 g; Fat 9 g; Sugar 9 g; Cholesterol 20 mg; Sodium 70 mg

ALMOND BUTTER
PUFF SQUARES

These squares are so easy to make—and to eat! Rice syrup has a mild sweetness that doesn't overpower in this recipe. Rice syrup, puffed quinoa and almond butter are all widely available at most health-food stores and well-stocked grocery stores.

Lightly grease an 8-inch (2 L) square cake pan.

Measure the puffed quinoa into a large bowl. In a small saucepan, heat the rice syrup and almond butter on medium heat, whisking constantly. When the mixture is hot but not boiling, remove from the heat and stir in the vanilla. Pour the mixture over the puffed quinoa and stir until all puffs are coated. Stir in the almonds until evenly distributed. Firmly press the mixture into the prepared pan and cover with plastic wrap. Refrigerate for 1 hour before cutting into 16 squares.

Store in a sealed container in the refrigerator for up to 1 week.

PER SERVING: Energy 70 calories; Protein 2 g; Carbohydrates 8 g; Dietary Fiber 1 g; Fat 3.5 g; Sugar 4 g; Cholesterol 0 mg; Sodium 10 mg

MAKES 16 SQUARES

3 cups (750 mL) puffed quinoa

⅓ cup (75 mL) rice syrup

¼ cup (60 mL) almond butter

½ tsp (2 mL) pure vanilla extract

⅓ cup (75 mL) sliced almonds

CHOCOLATE PUFF SQUARES

MAKES 16 SQUARES

1 cup (250 mL) seedless raisins

1 cup (250 mL) hot water

1 cup (250 mL) unsalted natural peanut or almond butter

3 Tbsp (45 mL) unsweetened cocoa powder

1 Tbsp (15 mL) flax meal

1 tsp (5 mL) pure vanilla extract

1 tsp (5 mL) sesame oil

3 cups (750 mL) quinoa puffs

Decadent-tasting treats don't have to be made with highly processed ingredients. This simple, naturally sweet snack is scrumptious, but won't make you feel guilty.

Lightly grease or spray with cooking oil an 8-inch (2 L) cake pan. Set aside.

Place the raisins in a small bowl and add the hot water. Soak raisins, covered, for 10 to 15 minutes or until they are plump and soft. Drain. Combine the raisins and peanut butter in a food processor and blend until combined. Add the cocoa, flax meal, vanilla and sesame oil. Process until fairly smooth and no raisin chunks remain.

In a large bowl, combine the quinoa puffs and raisin mixture. Stir to coat the puffs well. Press the mixture into the prepared pan. Refrigerate, covered, until chilled and set. Cut into 16 squares.

Store in a sealed container in the refrigerator for up to 1 month.

PER SERVING: Energy 170 calories; Protein 5 g; Carbohydrates 18 g; Dietary Fiber 4 g; Fat 10 g; Sugar 6 g; Cholesterol 0 mg; Sodium 0 mg

NORI PEANUT BUTTER PUFF BARS

Nori, an edible seaweed, is best known as a sushi wrap. Less well known is that it partners fantastically with peanut butter for a very tasty (as well as nutritious) snack. Did we say tasty? A must-try!

Lightly grease an 8-inch (2 L) cake pan.

Combine the syrup, peanut butter and sesame oil in a large saucepan on medium-low heat. Stir constantly until blended well and hot but not boiling. Use a rubber spatula to stir in the puffed quinoa and nori pieces, stirring until well coated. Press into the prepared pan and allow to set for 1 hour. Cut into 16 pieces.

Store in a sealed container for up to 1 week.

PER SERVING: Energy 130 calories; Protein 3 g; Carbohydrates 18 g; Dietary Fiber 2 g; Fat 5 g; Sugar 6 g; Cholesterol 0 mg; Sodium 45 mg

MAKES 16 BARS

½ cup (125 mL) brown rice syrup

½ cup (125 mL) chunky
    natural peanut butter

1 tsp (5 mL) sesame oil

3 cups (750 mL) puffed quinoa

2 sheets nori, broken into
    ½-inch (1 cm) pieces

BLACK FOREST GOAT CHEESE BROWNIES

A dense and chewy brownie with a sophisticated sweetness. Buttermilk and goat cheese add a fresh flavor along with the familiar cherry goodness of Black Forest cake.

Preheat the oven to 325°F (160°C). Grease or spray with cooking oil a 9-inch (2.5 L) square cake pan and line pan with parchment.

In a small saucepan on medium-low heat, melt the chocolate chips and butter together, stirring until smooth. Set aside to cool.

Place the cherries in a small bowl, cover with boiling water and let sit for 10 minutes to hydrate. Drain the cherries.

Beat the sugar, eggs and vanilla in a medium bowl until combined. Beat in the melted chocolate mixture. Mix in the flour just until blended, then mix in the buttermilk until well blended.

Pour half of the brownie batter into the prepared pan and spread it evenly. Top with the cherries and goat cheese. Pour the other half of the brownie batter on top, spreading evenly.

Bake for 30 minutes or until the middle of the cake springs back when gently pressed. Do not overbake. Cool in the pan. Chill before cutting into 25 squares.

Store in a sealed container in the refrigerator for up to 1 week.

PER SERVING: Energy 160 calories; Protein 3 g; Carbohydrates 17 g; Dietary Fiber 2 g; Fat 10 g; Sugar 11 g; Cholesterol 30 mg; Sodium 30 mg

MAKES 25 BROWNIES

1½ cups (375 mL) semisweet chocolate chips

¾ cup (175 mL) unsalted butter

¾ cup (175 mL) dried whole cherries

½ cup (125 mL) organic cane sugar or white sugar

2 large eggs

1 tsp (5 mL) pure vanilla extract

1 cup (250 mL) quinoa flour

¼ cup (60 mL) buttermilk

1 cup (250 mL) crumbled goat cheese

SALTED CARAMEL PECAN BITES

MAKES 28 PIECES

CARAMEL BITES

1 ¼ cups (300 mL) quinoa flour

¼ tsp (1 mL) baking soda

¼ tsp (1 mL) salt

1 large egg

½ cup (125 mL) unsalted butter, melted and cooled

½ cup (125 mL) brown sugar

1 tsp (5 mL) pure vanilla extract

⅓ cup (75 mL) semisweet chocolate chips

⅓ cup (75 mL) chopped pecans

CARAMEL TOPPING

⅓ cup (75 mL) brown sugar

¼ cup (60 mL) 18% cream

2 ½ Tbsp (37 mL) unsalted butter

½ tsp (2 mL) coarse sea salt

These tasty little morsels are just the right size to satisfy a hankering for sweet and savory, with a bit of chocolate and caramel topped off with the tiniest sprinkle of coarse sea salt.

Preheat the oven to 350°F (180°C). Grease or thoroughly spray with cooking oil two 12-cup muffin pans. (You can use mini muffin pans, if you prefer.)

For the caramel bites, in a medium bowl, whisk together the flour, baking soda and salt. In a small bowl, beat the egg, then stir in the butter, brown sugar and vanilla. Add the butter mixture to the flour mixture and mix well. Stir in the chocolate chips and pecans. Chill the dough for 20 to 30 minutes.

Use a tablespoon to scoop out dough and roll into 1-inch (2.5 cm) balls. Place one ball in each muffin cup. (You will not use all the dough.) Bake for 7 minutes. Do not overbake. Cool in the pan. Repeat with remaining dough.

For the caramel topping, in a medium saucepan, bring the brown sugar, cream and butter to a boil on high heat, stirring. Reduce the heat to medium-low and stir constantly until the mixture is a thick caramel sauce, about 15 minutes. Remove from the heat and let cool for 10 minutes.

Drop a teaspoon of caramel sauce on top of each pecan bite. Top each with a tiny sprinkle of coarse sea salt.

Store in a sealed container in the refrigerator for up to 1 week.

PER SERVING: Energy 100 calories; Protein 1 g; Carbohydrates 10 g; Dietary Fiber 1 g; Fat 7 g; Sugar 5 g; Cholesterol 20 mg; Sodium 75 mg

ALMOND CINNAMON COOKIES

Inspiration for these cookies came from *Fave dei Morti* (or "beans of the dead"), small bean-shaped cakes made by Italians for All Souls' Day. It is the combination of almonds, pine nuts, lemon and cinnamon that makes for such a flavorful combination.

Preheat the oven to 325°F (160°C). Line a baking sheet with parchment.

In a food processor, combine the almonds and pine nuts. Process until the nuts are approximately ¼-inch (5 mm) pieces. Add the flour, honey, egg, egg white, butter, cornstarch, cinnamon and lemon zest. Pulse just until the almonds become the texture of meal but stop before the mixture becomes nut butter. (You will know you have reached this point when there is a small amount of nut butter forming on the edge of the bowl.) Using a teaspoon, drop the dough onto the baking sheet, about 1½ inches (4 cm) apart.

Bake for 12 to 15 minutes, until the edges begin to turn golden. Cool cookies on a rack.

Store in a sealed container for up to 2 weeks.

PER SERVING: Energy 35 calories; Protein 1 g; Carbohydrates 3 g; Dietary Fiber 0 g; Fat 2 g; Sugar 2 g; Cholesterol 5 mg; Sodium 0 mg

¾ cup (175 mL) whole raw almonds

¼ cup (60 mL) pine nuts

⅓ cup (75 mL) quinoa flour

⅓ cup (75 mL) liquid honey

1 large egg

1 large egg white

2 Tbsp (30 mL) unsalted butter, softened

2 Tbsp (30 mL) cornstarch

1 tsp (5 mL) cinnamon

1½ tsp (7 mL) grated lemon zest

Don't like having to grease baking sheets or use parchment? Try a silicone baking sheet liner, available at most kitchen supply stores. Liners make for easy cleanup and aid even heat distribution.

PEANUT BUTTER CHIA COOKIES

MAKES 30 COOKIES

½ cup (125 mL) natural
   peanut butter

½ cup (125 mL) unsalted
   butter, softened

¾ cup (175 mL) brown sugar

1 large egg

1 tsp (5 mL) pure vanilla extract

1 cup (250 mL) quinoa flour

¾ tsp (4 mL) baking soda

½ tsp (2 mL) baking powder

2 Tbsp (30 mL) chia seeds

½ cup (125 mL) chopped
   unsalted peanuts

These cookies are soft, sweet and simple, with a delicious crisp texture and the added crunch of peanuts. Chia seeds do not need to be ground before eating. They provide additional calcium, fiber and omega-3s.

Preheat the oven to 375°F (190°C). Grease a baking sheet or line with parchment.

In a large bowl, beat the peanut butter, butter, sugar, egg and vanilla until combined well. In a medium bowl, whisk together the flour, baking soda and baking powder. Stir in the chia seeds and peanuts. Add the flour mixture to the peanut butter mixture and mix well. Scoop the dough into 1-inch (2.5 cm) balls and place them 2 inches (5 cm) apart on the baking sheet.

Bake for 10 minutes or until bottoms are lightly golden. Allow the cookies to sit for 4 minutes before transferring to a rack to cool.

Store in a sealed container for up to 1 week or freeze for up to 1 month.

PER SERVING: Energy 100 calories; Protein 2 g; Carbohydrates 8 g; Dietary Fiber 1 g; Fat 7 g; Sugar 4 g; Cholesterol 15 mg; Sodium 60 mg

DOUBLE CHOCOLATE MINT COOKIES

Everyone loves these soft and chewy chocolate cookies with the fresh flavor of mint.

Preheat the oven to 375°F (190°C).

Cream the butter with the sugar in a large bowl until light and fluffy. Beat in the eggs until well combined. Beat in the mint extract until the mixture is smooth. In another large bowl, whisk together the flour, cocoa, baking soda and salt. Add the butter mixture to the flour mixture and blend well. Stir in the chocolate chips. Roll dough into 1¼-inch (3 cm) balls. Place the balls 2 inches (5 cm) apart on a baking sheet and flatten slightly with the palm of your hand.

Bake for 8 to 10 minutes or until the edges are slightly crispy but cookies are still soft and chewy. Allow the cookies to sit on the baking sheet for 5 minutes before transferring them to a rack to cool.

Store in a sealed container for up to 1 week or freeze for up to 1 month.

PER SERVING: Energy 120 calories; Protein 2 g; Carbohydrates 14 g; Dietary Fiber 2 g; Fat 7 g; Sugar 8 g; Cholesterol 25 mg; Sodium 85 mg

MAKES 24 COOKIES

½ cup (125 mL) unsalted butter, softened

¾ cup (175 mL) brown sugar

2 large eggs, beaten

½ tsp (2 mL) pure mint or peppermint extract

1¼ cups (300 mL) quinoa flour

⅓ cup (75 mL) sifted unsweetened cocoa powder

1 tsp (5 mL) baking soda

¼ tsp (1 mL) salt

1 cup (250 mL) semisweet chocolate chips

OATMEAL DATE SANDWICH COOKIES

MAKES 24 COOKIES

2 cups (500 mL) large-flake rolled oats (gluten-free if required)

2 cups (500 mL) quinoa flour

½ tsp (2 mL) baking powder

¼ tsp (1 mL) baking soda

½ cup (125 mL) unsalted butter, softened

⅔ cup (150 mL) brown sugar

½ cup (125 mL) unsweetened applesauce

½ cup (125 mL) buttermilk

1 tsp (5 mL) pure vanilla extract

1¼ cups (300 mL) chopped pitted dates

⅔ cup (150 mL) water

⅓ cup (75 mL) organic cane sugar or white sugar

1 tsp (5 mL) lemon juice

An old-fashioned favorite transformed. Oats, vanilla and lemony dates complement the nutty fragrance of quinoa flour.

Preheat the oven to 350°F (180°C). Lightly grease a baking sheet or line with parchment.

In a large bowl, whisk together the oats, flour, baking powder and baking soda. In a separate bowl, cream the butter with the sugar until light and fluffy. Stir in the applesauce, buttermilk and vanilla. Pour the butter mixture into the flour mixture and blend until well combined. Place tablespoons of dough 2 inches (5 cm) apart on the baking sheet and gently flatten with the palm of your hand. (If dough is too sticky, place in the refrigerator for 15 to 20 minutes first.)

Bake for 13 to 15 minutes, until the edges are just starting to brown. Allow the cookies to cool for 10 minutes before transferring them to a rack to cool.

In a medium saucepan, combine the dates, water and sugar. Bring to a boil, reduce the heat to medium, and continue to cook, stirring frequently, until the mixture is thick and fairly smooth. Stir in the lemon juice. Set aside to cool for 10 minutes.

Spread ½ tsp (2 mL) of the date mixture on the bottom of one cookie and sandwich it with another cookie. Repeat with remaining cookies.

Store in a sealed container in the refrigerator for up to 1 week.

PER SERVING: Energy 160 calories; Protein 3 g; Carbohydrates 26 g; Dietary Fiber 3 g; Fat 5 g; Sugar 13 g; Cholesterol 10 mg; Sodium 30 mg

PEANUT BUTTER & JELLY SANDWICH COOKIES

These easy-to-make bite-size treats will satisfy your childhood urge for a PB&J sandwich.

Preheat the oven to 350°F (180°C). Lightly grease or spray with cooking oil a baking sheet or line with parchment.

In a large bowl, beat the peanut butter, sugar, quinoa flakes and egg until combined. If texture appears crumbly, add 1 to 2 Tbsp (15 to 30 mL) water and massage into dough until no longer crumbly. Measure out teaspoons of dough and place them ½ inch (1 cm) apart on the baking sheet. Flatten to about 1 inch (2.5 cm) across with the palm of your hand.

Bake for 5 minutes, until the bottoms are slightly golden. Transfer to a rack to cool.

Spread ¼ tsp (1 mL) of jam on the bottom of one cookie and sandwich it with another cookie. Repeat with remaining cookies.

Store in a sealed container in the refrigerator for up to 1 week.

PER SERVING: Energy 90 calories; Protein 3 g; Carbohydrates 8 g; Dietary Fiber 1 g; Fat 6 g; Sugar 4 g; Cholesterol 5 mg; Sodium 60 mg

MAKES 30 COOKIES

1 ¼ cups (300 mL) natural peanut butter

½ cup (125 mL) organic cane sugar or white sugar

¼ cup (125 mL) quinoa flakes

1 large egg

3 Tbsp (45 mL) low-sugar raspberry or strawberry jam

PUMPKIN CHOCOLATE PECAN COOKIES

MAKES 40 COOKIES

½ cup (125 mL) unsalted
  butter, softened

¾ cup (175 mL) brown sugar

1 large egg

1½ cups (375 mL) pumpkin purée

1¾ cups (425 mL) quinoa flour

1 tsp (5 mL) baking soda

¼ tsp (1 mL) salt

1½ tsp (7 mL) cinnamon

1 tsp (5 mL) nutmeg

1 tsp (5 mL) ground ginger

½ tsp (2 mL) ground cloves

½ cup (125 mL) semisweet
  chocolate chips

⅓ cup (75 mL) chopped pecans

Full of pumpkin spice, these small cookies are soft, moist and nutty. If you prefer a larger cookie, increase size to 2-inch (5 cm) balls and bake for 15 minutes instead.

Preheat the oven to 350°F (180°C). Grease 2 baking sheets or line with parchment.

In a large bowl, cream the butter with the sugar until light and fluffy. Add the egg and pumpkin; stir well. In a medium bowl, whisk together the flour, baking soda, salt, cinnamon, nutmeg, ginger and cloves; stir into the pumpkin mixture until combined. Stir in the chocolate chips and pecans. Roll dough into 1¼-inch (3 cm) balls and place 2 inches (5 cm) apart on the baking sheets.

Bake cookies, 1 sheet at a time, for 12 to 13 minutes, until cookies are golden on the edges. Do not overbake. Allow to cool for 10 minutes before transferring to a rack to cool completely.

Store in a sealed container for up to 1 week.

PER SERVING: Energy 70 calories; Protein 1 g; Carbohydrates 8 g; Dietary Fiber 1 g; Fat 4 g; Sugar 4 g; Cholesterol 10 mg; Sodium 35 mg

RAISIN SPICE COOKIES

This soft cookie is full of chewy raisins and the warm aroma of spices and nuts. If you prefer a smaller cookie, simply make 1-inch (2.5 cm) balls and decrease the cooking time to 10 minutes.

Preheat the oven to 350°F (180°C). Grease or spray with cooking oil 2 baking sheets or line with parchment.

Place the raisins in a small bowl, cover with boiling water and let sit for 10 minutes to hydrate.

Meanwhile, in a medium bowl, beat the butter with the sugar until smooth and fluffy. Beat in the eggs, then beat in the vanilla until well blended. In a large bowl, whisk together the quinoa flour, almond flour, baking soda, salt, cinnamon, nutmeg and cloves. Add the butter mixture to the flour mixture and stir until mixed well. Drain the raisins and fold them and the walnuts into the dough until well mixed.

Scoop the dough into 2-inch (5 cm) balls and place 2 inches (5 cm) apart on the baking sheets.

Bake cookies, 1 sheet at a time, for 12 minutes or until edges are light golden. Allow cookies to cool 10 minutes before transferring to a rack to cool completely.

Store in a sealed container in the refrigerator for up to 1 week or freeze for up to 2 weeks.

PER SERVING: Energy 190 calories; Protein 3 g; Carbohydrates 17 g; Dietary Fiber 2 g; Fat 13 g; Sugar 10 g; Cholesterol 35 mg; Sodium 85 mg

1 cup (250 mL) seedless raisins

½ cup (125 mL) unsalted butter, softened

¾ cup (175 mL) organic cane sugar or white sugar

2 large eggs, beaten

1 tsp (5 mL) pure vanilla extract

1½ cups (375 mL) quinoa flour

½ cup (125 mL) almond flour

1 tsp (5 mL) baking soda

¼ tsp (1 mL) salt

1½ tsp (7 mL) cinnamon

½ tsp (2 mL) nutmeg

½ tsp (2 mL) ground cloves

1 cup (250 mL) chopped walnuts

APRICOT COCONUT SNOWBALLS

MAKES 70 BALLS

½ cup (125 mL) unsweetened
    shredded coconut

2 cups (500 mL) dried apricots

1½ cups (375 mL) quinoa flakes

1 cup (250 mL) seedless raisins

1 tsp (5 mL) grated orange zest

⅓ cup (75 mL) freshly
    squeezed orange juice

Feeling peckish? These treats are ideal for popping in your mouth when you need that after-dinner sweet fix. Also perfect for giving, these snowballs make great fare for a Christmas or New Year's snack tray.

Preheat the oven to 350°F (180°C). Spread the coconut on a baking sheet and toast until light golden, about 3 minutes. (Watch the coconut closely, as it burns quickly.) Set aside in a shallow bowl to cool.

Place the apricots, quinoa flakes, raisins, orange zest and orange juice in a food processor; process until relatively smooth and no apricot or raisin chunks remain.

Spoon out apricot mixture with a teaspoon and roll into a ball. Roll in toasted coconut.

Store in a sealed container with each layer separated by parchment or waxed paper. Store in the refrigerator for up to 1 month.

PER SERVING: Energy 45 calories; Protein 1 g; Carbohydrates 9 g; Dietary Fiber 1 g; Fat 1 g; Sugar 3 g; Cholesterol 0 mg; Sodium 60 mg

NO-BAKE CHOCOLATE MACAROONS

We've reinvented the chocolate macaroon in this naturally sweetened, deliciously chewy, no-bake recipe.

Line a baking sheet with parchment or waxed paper.

Melt the honey and butter together in a large saucepan on medium heat. Stir until combined. Stir in the cocoa and vanilla until smooth. When mixture is heated through, remove from the heat. Add the quinoa flakes, oats, coconut and flax meal; stir until the dry ingredients are completely coated. Using a tablespoon, scoop the mixture into mounds on the baking sheet. Reshape any mounds that fall apart. Leave macaroons to sit at room temperature or colder for 1 hour or more to set.

Store macaroons in a sealed container, with each layer separated by parchment or waxed paper. Store at room temperature for up to 1 week or refrigerated for up to 1 month.

PER SERVING: Energy 100 calories; Protein 2 g; Carbohydrates 15 g; Dietary Fiber 2 g; Fat 4.5 g; Sugar 7 g; Cholesterol 5 mg; Sodium 60 mg

MAKES 36 MACAROONS

1 cup (250 mL) honey

⅓ cup (75 mL) salted butter

½ cup (125 mL) unsweetened cocoa powder

1½ tsp (7 mL) pure vanilla extract

1½ cups (375 mL) quinoa flakes

1¼ cups (300 mL) quick-cooking rolled oats (gluten-free if required)

1¼ cups (300 mL) unsweetened shredded coconut

⅓ cup (75 mL) flax meal

BANANA MOUSE POPS

SERVES 1

1 small unpeeled banana

1 Tbsp (15 mL) quinoa flakes

1 Tbsp (15 mL) unsweetened
    shredded or flaked coconut

1 Tbsp (15 mL) + 1 tsp (5 mL)
    smooth natural peanut butter

1 large dried apricot, halved
    crosswise

3 dried currants

Scrumptious and fun, these quinoa pops can be made with marshmallow ears and chocolate chip eyes, or apricot ears and currant eyes for a healthier version. Easily multiply the ingredients to make as many pops as you please.

Cut 1 inch (2.5 cm) from the stem end of the banana. Insert a wooden food stick into cut end, pushing it in 2 to 3 inches (5 to 8 cm). (If desired, insert the stick into the underside of the banana, as shown.) Remove banana peel, cover banana with plastic wrap and freeze until firm, 3 to 4 hours.

Meanwhile, preheat the oven to 350°F (180°C). Spread the quinoa flakes and coconut on a baking sheet and bake until fragrant and toasted, about 5 minutes. Set aside to cool.

Remove plastic wrap from the frozen banana and spread 1 Tbsp (15 mL) of the peanut butter over the banana. Place the quinoa-coconut mixture on a plate. Roll the banana in the flakes, making sure to cover the entire banana. Using the remaining 1 tsp (5 mL) peanut butter as glue, attach the apricot halves for ears and currants for eyes and nose. Serve immediately.

PER SERVING: Energy 250 calories; Protein 7 g; Carbohydrates 34 g; Dietary Fiber 5 g; Fat 12 g; Sugar 14 g; Cholesterol 0 mg; Sodium 180 mg

ROSEMARY WALNUT CRISPS WITH CRANBERRIES

MAKES 72 COOKIES

¾ cup (175 mL) quinoa flour

¼ cup (60 mL) brown rice flour

2 Tbsp (30 mL) cornstarch

½ tsp (2 mL) baking powder

½ tsp (2 mL) salt

½ cup (125 mL) sweetened
    dried cranberries

⅓ cup (75 mL) chopped walnuts

2 tsp (10 mL) chopped fresh
    rosemary

1 cup (250 mL) reduced-fat
    or regular sour cream
    (gluten-free if required)

⅓ cup (75 mL) light brown sugar

1 large egg

2 tsp (10 mL) fancy molasses

Similar to a biscotti, these twice-baked thin, crunchy crisps are delicious eaten as-is or dipped in coffee.

Preheat the oven to 350°F (180°C). Lightly grease a 9- × 5-inch (2 L) loaf pan. Line the bottom with parchment.

In a medium bowl, whisk together the quinoa flour, rice flour, cornstarch, baking powder and salt. Stir in the cranberries, walnuts and rosemary. In a small bowl, whisk together the sour cream, brown sugar, egg and molasses. Pour the wet mixture into the flour mixture and stir just until combined. Pour the batter into the loaf pan, using a spatula to level the top evenly.

Bake for 30 minutes or until the loaf has risen slightly and a toothpick inserted in the center comes out clean. Cool completely in the pan.

Turn the loaf out onto a cutting board. Slice in half lengthwise. Holding the loaf together carefully with one hand and using a sharp knife, cut into thin slices (¼ inch/5 mm). If the loaf crumbles and is difficult to slice, wrap it in plastic wrap and place in the refrigerator for at least 1 hour or overnight.

Place the oven racks one above and one below the center of the oven. Preheat the oven to 300°F (150°C). Line 2 baking sheets with parchment.

Arrange the slices on the baking sheets. Bake for 15 minutes. Turn the crisps over. Place baking sheets in opposite positions and bake for another 15 minutes, keeping an eye on them in the last 5 minutes to make sure they do not get too dark. Let cool and dry out on the baking sheets.

Store in a sealed container for up to 1 month.

PER SERVING: Energy 25 calories; Protein 0 g; Carbohydrates 3 g; Dietary Fiber 0 g; Fat 1 g; Sugar 1 g; Cholesterol 5 mg; Sodium 25 mg

BLUEBERRY ALMOND MUFFINS

Healthy blueberry muffins are here! No white flour necessary. Filled with wholesome almonds, blueberries and quinoa, these aren't just a super dessert but make a terrific snack any time of the day.

Preheat the oven to 400°F (200°C). Lightly grease or spray with cooking oil a 12-cup muffin pan or line with paper liners.

In a small saucepan, bring the water and quinoa to a boil. Reduce to a simmer, cover and cook for 15 minutes. Remove from the heat and leave covered for another 10 minutes. The quinoa must be fluffy.

In a blender, combine the eggs, applesauce, brown sugar, oil, vanilla and ¼ cup (60 mL) of the quinoa. Blend until smooth. Repeat adding ¼ cup (60 mL) quinoa, puréeing after each addition, until you have added 1½ cups (375 mL).

In a large bowl, whisk together the almond flour, oats, cornstarch, baking powder, baking soda and salt. Add the blueberries and stir to coat with flour mixture. Add the quinoa purée, using a spatula to get all the purée out. Stir just until blended. Divide batter among muffin cups.

Bake for 30 minutes or until a toothpick inserted in the center comes out clean. Transfer to a rack to cool.

Store in a sealed container for up to 1 week.

PER SERVING: Energy 160 calories; Protein 4 g; Carbohydrates 17 g; Dietary Fiber 2 g; Fat 9 g; Sugar 6 g; Cholesterol 30 mg; Sodium 160 mg

MAKES 12 MUFFINS

1 cup (250 mL) water

½ cup (125 mL) white quinoa

2 large eggs, beaten

1 cup (250 mL) unsweetened applesauce

¼ cup (60 mL) lightly packed brown sugar

¼ cup (60 mL) grapeseed oil or vegetable oil

1 tsp (5 mL) pure vanilla extract

⅔ cup (150 mL) almond flour

⅓ cup (75 mL) quick-cooking rolled oats (gluten-free if required)

3 Tbsp (45 mL) cornstarch

1 tsp (5 mL) baking powder

½ tsp (2 mL) baking soda

¼ tsp (1 mL) salt

1 cup (250 mL) fresh or frozen blueberries

CHAI CHOCOLATE CHIP MUFFINS

MAKES 12 MUFFINS

1½ cups (375 mL) quinoa flour

1½ tsp (7 mL) baking powder

½ tsp (2 mL) baking soda

¼ tsp (1 mL) salt

½ tsp (2 mL) ground cardamom

¼ tsp (1 mL) cinnamon

¼ tsp (1 mL) ground ginger

¼ tsp (1 mL) ground cloves

¼ tsp (1 mL) black pepper

¼ cup (60 mL) unsalted butter, softened

¼ cup (60 mL) organic cane sugar or white sugar

2 large eggs

¼ cup (60 mL) buttermilk

1 cup (250 mL) unsweetened applesauce

½ cup (125 mL) semisweet chocolate chips

2 Tbsp (30 mL) sliced almonds

The warm, spicy blend of chai seasoning makes these quinoa muffins great with hot tea or coffee—or whenever you need a treat to awaken your senses.

Preheat the oven to 400°F (200°C). Lightly grease a 12-cup muffin pan.

In a large bowl, whisk together the quinoa flour, baking powder, baking soda, salt, cardamom, cinnamon, ginger, cloves and pepper. In a medium bowl, cream the butter and sugar together just until blended. Beat in the eggs, 1 at a time. Beat in the buttermilk and applesauce. Add this mixture to the flour mixture and stir just until blended. Stir in the chocolate chips. Use a large spoon or ice-cream scoop to divide the batter evenly among the muffin cups. Top each muffin with 2 or 3 almond slices.

Bake for 16 to 18 minutes or until a toothpick inserted into the center of a muffin comes out clean. Cool in the pan.

Store in a sealed container for up to 1 week.

PER SERVING: Energy 170 calories; Protein 4 g; Carbohydrates 22 g; Dietary Fiber 3 g; Fat 8 g; Sugar 10 g; Cholesterol 40 mg; Sodium 180 mg

CHOCOLATE BROWNIE SOUR CREAM MUFFINS

Mmm . . . are they muffins or cupcakes? Without frosting it is a muffin, and with frosting it's a cupcake. Either way, it's a moist and delicious dessert or snack.

Preheat the oven to 400°F (200°C). Lightly grease or spray with cooking oil a 12-cup muffin pan or line with paper liners.

In a medium bowl, whisk together the flour, cocoa, sugar, baking powder, baking soda and salt. In a small bowl, beat the egg; whisk in the sour cream, milk, oil and vanilla. Add this mixture to the flour mixture and stir just until combined. Stir in the chocolate chips and nuts. Evenly divide the batter among the muffin cups.

Bake for 15 minutes or until a toothpick inserted in the center of a muffin comes out clean. Cool in the pan.

Store in a sealed container in the refrigerator for up to 1 week.

PER SERVING: Energy 220 calories; Protein 5 g; Carbohydrates 24 g; Dietary Fiber 3 g; Fat 13 g; Sugar 11 g; Cholesterol 25 mg; Sodium 280 mg

MAKES 12 MUFFINS

1¼ cups (300 mL) quinoa flour

½ cup (125 mL) sifted unsweetened cocoa powder

½ cup (125 mL) organic cane sugar or white sugar

2½ tsp (12 mL) baking powder

½ tsp (2 mL) baking soda

½ tsp (2 mL) salt

1 large egg

1 cup (250 mL) reduced-fat sour cream (gluten-free if required)

¾ cup (175 mL) 1% milk

⅓ cup (75 mL) grapeseed oil or vegetable oil

1 tsp (5 mL) pure vanilla extract

¼ cup (60 mL) semisweet mini chocolate chips

¼ cup (60 mL) chopped toasted walnuts or pecans

- To toast nuts, preheat the oven to 350°F (180°C). Spread the nuts on a baking sheet and toast in the oven, stirring once if necessary, for 5 to 7 minutes, until fragrant and lightly toasted.

- If you plan to frost the muffins, we suggest that you omit the nuts.

SWEET POTATO DATE MUFFINS

1 ¾ cups (425 mL) quinoa flour

1 tsp (5 mL) baking powder

1 tsp (5 mL) baking soda

¼ tsp (1 mL) salt

¼ tsp (1 mL) ground cloves

¼ tsp (1 mL) nutmeg

⅓ cup (75 mL) unsalted butter, softened

⅓ cup (75 mL) organic cane sugar or white sugar

2 Tbsp (30 mL) pure maple syrup

2 large eggs

2 cups (500 mL) mashed cooked sweet potato

¾ cup (175 mL) chopped pitted dates

Light quinoa flour, moist sweet potatoes and soft dates make a tasty combination in these fluffy, satisfying muffins.

Preheat the oven to 375°F (190°C). Lightly grease a 12-cup muffin pan or line with paper liners.

In a large bowl, whisk together the quinoa flour, baking powder, baking soda, salt, cloves and nutmeg. In a medium bowl, cream the butter, sugar and maple syrup. Beat in the eggs, 1 at a time. Whisk in the sweet potato. Add this mixture to the flour mixture and stir just until blended. Add the dates, mixing until well distributed. Use a large spoon or ice-cream scoop to divide the batter evenly among the muffin cups.

Bake for 18 to 20 minutes or until a toothpick inserted into the center of a muffin comes out clean. Cool in the pan.

Store in a sealed container in the refrigerator for up to 1 week.

PER SERVING: Energy 230 calories; Protein 4 g; Carbohydrates 37 g; Dietary Fiber 4 g; Fat 7 g; Sugar 16 g; Cholesterol 45 mg; Sodium 230 mg

PUMPKIN CUPCAKES

These cupcakes are soft, moist and bursting with pumpkin flavor. Plain or topped with cream cheese frosting, pumpkin is always in season! Decorate to match all of your year-round celebrations, including birthdays, Halloween and even Valentine's Day.

Preheat the oven to 375°F (190°C). Lightly grease a 12-cup muffin pan or line with paper liners.

In a medium bowl, whisk together the quinoa flour, baking powder, baking soda, salt, cinnamon, ginger, cloves and nutmeg. In a large bowl, beat the eggs; add the pumpkin, sugar, buttermilk, apple-sauce and oil. Whisk until smooth. Add the pumpkin mixture to the flour mixture; gently stir just until blended. Use a large spoon or ice-cream scoop to divide the batter evenly among the muffin cups.

Bake for 15 minutes or until a toothpick inserted into the center of a muffin comes out clean. Cool in the pan. If frosting, refrigerate for 2 hours beforehand.

Store in a sealed container in the refrigerator for up to 1 week.

PER SERVING: Energy 170 calories; Protein 4 g; Carbohydrates 29 g; Dietary Fiber 3 g; Fat 4.5 g; Sugar 13 g; Cholesterol 30 mg; Sodium 280 mg

MAKES 12 CUPCAKES

2 cups (500 mL) quinoa flour

2½ tsp (12 mL) baking powder

½ tsp (2 mL) baking soda

½ tsp (2 mL) salt

1 tsp (5 mL) cinnamon

1 tsp (5 mL) ground ginger

½ tsp (2 mL) ground cloves

½ tsp (2 mL) nutmeg

2 large eggs

1 cup (250 mL) pumpkin purée

¾ cup (175 mL) organic
    cane sugar or white sugar

½ cup (125 mL) buttermilk

⅓ cup (75 mL) unsweetened
    applesauce

2 Tbsp (30 mL) vegetable oil

Really want to celebrate? Turn this into a double layer cake by evenly dividing the batter between 2 greased 8-inch (1.2 L) cake pans and bake for 20 to 22 minutes.

CHOCOLATE CREAM MINI CUPCAKES WITH AVOCADO ICING

These quinoa cupcakes will definitely satisfy your sweet tooth. The cupcakes can be made the day before, but the avocado icing is best made fresh on the day you are going to serve them.

Preheat the oven to 350°F (180°C). Line a 24-cup mini muffin pan with paper liners.

For the cupcakes, in a medium saucepan, bring the water and quinoa to a boil. Reduce to a simmer, cover and cook for 15 minutes. Remove from the heat and let sit with the cover on for another 15 minutes. The quinoa must be extra-fluffy.

In a blender, combine the sour cream, honey, egg, egg white, oil and vanilla. Blend until combined. Add ¼ cup (60 mL) of the quinoa and blend until completely smooth. Repeat adding ¼ cup (60 mL) quinoa, puréeing after each addition, until all the quinoa has been added.

In a medium bowl, whisk together the cocoa, baking powder, baking soda and salt until no lumps of cocoa powder remain. Add the puréed mixture. Stir just until blended. Divide the batter evenly among the cupcake liners.

Bake for 12 to 15 minutes, until a toothpick inserted in the center of a cupcake comes out clean. Cool in the pan.

For the icing, peel the avocado and in a small bowl, mash it with a fork until no big lumps remain. Place in a blender with the honey and vanilla. Purée until smooth. Add the cocoa powder and blend until completely incorporated. Transfer the icing to a piping bag (or a resealable plastic bag, then cut off one corner). Pipe the icing onto the cooled cupcakes.

Store in a sealed container in the refrigerator for up to 4 days (with the avocado icing).

PER SERVING (with icing): Energy 60 calories; Protein 1 g; Carbohydrates 7 g; Dietary Fiber 1 g; Fat 4 g; Sugar 3 g; Cholesterol 10 mg; Sodium 60 mg

MAKES 24 MINI CUPCAKES

CUPCAKES

⅔ cup (150 mL) water

⅓ cup (75 mL) white quinoa

¼ cup (60 mL) reduced-fat sour cream (gluten-free if required)

¼ cup (60 mL) liquid honey

1 large egg

1 large egg white

3 Tbsp (45 mL) grapeseed oil or light-tasting vegetable oil

½ tsp (125 mL) pure vanilla extract

⅓ cup (75 mL) sifted unsweetened cocoa powder

¾ tsp (4 mL) baking powder

¼ tsp (1 mL) baking soda

¼ tsp (1 mL) salt

ICING

1 ripe avocado

1 Tbsp (15 mL) liquid honey

1 tsp (5 mL) pure vanilla extract

¼ cup (60 mL) unsweetened cocoa powder

APPLE CINNAMON ENERGY BARS

MAKES 16 BARS

½ cup (125 mL) quinoa

2 ½ cups (625 mL) unsalted raw almonds chopped into ¼-inch (5 mm) pieces

¼ cup (60 mL) peanuts chopped into ¼-inch (5 mm) pieces

¼ cup (60 mL) raw sesame seeds

1 cup (250 mL) dried apple chopped into ¼-inch (5 mm) to ½-inch (1 cm) pieces

¼ cup (60 mL) chopped raisins or whole dried currants

¼ cup (60 mL) honey

¼ cup (60 mL) pure maple syrup

1 Tbsp (15 mL) unsalted butter

1 tsp (5 mL) cinnamon

1 tsp (5 mL) pure vanilla extract

Look no further for that healthful and tasty granola bar for your family. This perfect blend of cinnamon, apple and nuts will be the first thing you grab when you need something healthy for lunches, hiking, camping or keeping in the glove compartment for those times you're stuck in traffic.

Preheat the oven to 350°F (180°C). Line bottom and sides of a 13- × 9-inch (3 L) cake pan with parchment or waxed paper. Cut another piece to cover the top.

Place the quinoa in a resealable plastic bag and gently roll over it with a rolling pin to crack the seeds slightly. Spread the quinoa, almonds, peanuts and sesame seeds evenly on a baking sheet. Bake for 5 minutes, then stir. Bake for another 5 minutes or until lightly toasted and fragrant. Pour the mixture into a large bowl, then add the apple and raisins. Mix with your hands to separate the fruit pieces.

Combine the honey, maple syrup, butter, cinnamon and vanilla in a small saucepan. Heat on medium heat, stirring, until bubbling. Pour over the quinoa mixture and stir to coat thoroughly.

Pour into the prepared pan and spread evenly with a spatula. Place the piece of parchment or waxed paper on top and press firmly all over. Let cool for 2 to 3 hours, then cut into 16 bars.

Wrap individual bars in plastic wrap or store in a sealed container for up to 1 month.

PER SERVING: Energy 190 calories; Protein 5 g; Carbohydrates 21 g; Dietary Fiber 3 g; Fat 10 g; Sugar 12 g; Cholesterol 0 mg; Sodium 20 mg

CASHEW APRICOT ENERGY BARS

Hearty and loaded with flavor, these granola bars will definitely satisfy your hunger. They're especially great for that mid-afternoon snack.

Preheat the oven to 350°F (180°C). Line bottom and sides of a 13- × 9-inch (3 L) cake pan with parchment or waxed paper. Cut another piece to cover the top.

Place the quinoa in a resealable plastic bag and gently roll over it with a rolling pin to crack the seeds slightly. Spread the quinoa, cashews, almonds, coconut and sunflower seeds evenly on a baking sheet. Bake for 5 minutes, then stir. Bake for another 5 minutes or until lightly toasted and fragrant. Stir again and set aside to cool slightly.

Pour the quinoa mixture into a large bowl, then add the apricots. Mix with your hands to separate the apricot pieces.

Heat the honey and vanilla in a small saucepan on medium heat, stirring often. Remove from the heat when honey is bubbling. Pour over the quinoa mixture and stir until evenly distributed.

Pour into the prepared pan and spread evenly with a spatula. Place the piece of parchment or waxed paper on top and press firmly all over. Let cool for 2 to 3 hours, then cut into 18 bars.

Wrap individual bars in plastic wrap or store in a sealed container for up to 1 month.

PER SERVING: Energy 160 calories; Protein 4 g; Carbohydrates 20 g; Dietary Fiber 2 g; Fat 9 g; Sugar 12 g; Cholesterol 0 mg; Sodium 0 mg

MAKES 18 BARS

½ cup (125 mL) quinoa

1 cup (250 mL) unsalted raw cashews, finely chopped (same size as a sunflower seed)

1 cup (250 mL) unsalted raw almonds, finely chopped (same size as a sunflower seed)

½ cup (125 mL) unsweetened shredded coconut

¼ cup (60 mL) unsalted raw sunflower seeds

1 cup (250 mL) finely chopped dried apricots

½ cup (125 mL) honey

¼ tsp (1 mL) pure vanilla extract

MIXED BERRIES WITH BLACK QUINOA & BLACK CURRANT YOGURT

SERVES 4

⅔ cup (150 mL) water

⅓ cup (75 mL) black quinoa

2 cups (500 mL) fresh raspberries

1 cup (250 mL) fresh blackberries

1 Tbsp (15 mL) organic
cane sugar or white sugar

1⅓ cups (325 mL) low-fat
plain yogurt

1 Tbsp (15 mL) pure maple syrup

5 Tbsp (75 mL) Ribena black
currant concentrate or 3 Tbsp
(45 mL) crème de cassis +
1 Tbsp (15 mL) sugar

A light dessert with a sophisticated flavor and a dramatic appearance.

Bring the water and quinoa to a boil in a medium saucepan. Reduce to a simmer, cover and cook for 15 minutes. Fluff with a fork and set aside to cool completely.

Combine the quinoa, 1½ cups (375 mL) of the raspberries and ¾ cup (175 mL) of the blackberries in a medium bowl. Sprinkle on the cane sugar and toss gently. Set aside for about 5 minutes to draw out the juices.

In another bowl, stir together the yogurt, maple syrup and black currant concentrate until combined. Spoon the fruit mixture into 4 dessert bowls. Divide the yogurt on top of each serving and garnish with the remaining raspberries and blackberries. Serve chilled.

PER SERVING: Energy 200 calories; Protein 8 g; Carbohydrates 37 g; Dietary Fiber 6 g; Fat 2.5 g; Sugar 22 g; Cholesterol 5 mg; Sodium 60 mg

For a yummy alternative, try this recipe with 2 ripe peaches, pitted and sliced.

CHOCOLATE CHIP FRUIT GRANOLA BARS

MAKES 12 BARS

½ cup (125 mL) rice syrup or
    liquid honey

¼ cup (60 mL) grapeseed oil
    or vegetable oil

1 tsp (5 mL) pure vanilla extract

3 cups (750 mL) quinoa flakes

½ cup (125 mL) sweetened
    dried cranberries

¼ cup (60 mL) semisweet
    mini chocolate chips or
    mini carob chips

Easy to make, no-fuss bars. Switch up the fruit for variety—try coarsely chopped dried cherries or dried blueberries, or even peanuts. Rice syrup is a nice alternative to the usual sweeteners because it has a milder sweetness. Mini chocolate chips are essential, as larger chips will make the bar crumbly.

Preheat the oven to 350°F (180°C). Line an 8-inch (2 L) square cake pan with a piece of parchment large enough to come up sides of pan.

In a large bowl, stir together the syrup, oil and vanilla until well blended. Add the quinoa flakes, dried cranberries and chocolate chips. Stir until the flakes are completely covered with syrup and the chocolate chips and cranberries are evenly dispersed. Press evenly and firmly into the baking dish, using another piece of parchment over the top. (The mixture is very sticky.) Once firmly packed, remove and discard the top piece of parchment.

Bake for 20 minutes. Let cool for 30 minutes, then remove from the pan by lifting the parchment. Transfer to a cutting board and remove the parchment. Cut into 12 bars.

Store in a sealed container for up to 2 weeks.

PER SERVING: Energy 230 calories; Protein 4 g; Carbohydrates 40 g; Dietary Fiber 2 g; Fat 7 g; Sugar 13 g; Cholesterol 0 mg; Sodium 280 mg

APPLE SPICE CAKE

Full of apple-spiced goodness, this tasty cake is moist and gluten-free!

Combine the water and quinoa in a medium saucepan and bring to a boil. Reduce to a simmer, cover and cook for 15 minutes. Remove from the heat and let sit, covered, for another 10 minutes. The quinoa should be fluffy. Fluff with a fork and set aside to cool.

Preheat the oven to 350°F (180°C). Lightly grease or spray with cooking oil a 9- or 10-inch (2 or 3 L) Bundt pan.

Combine the eggs, egg whites, butter, applesauce and vanilla in a blender. Blend until smooth. Add ½ cup (125 mL) of the cooked quinoa and blend until smooth. Add 3 more ½-cup (125 mL) portions of quinoa, for a total of 2 cups (500 mL), blending until smooth after each addition.

In a medium bowl, whisk together the sugar, cornstarch, baking powder, baking soda, salt, cinnamon, allspice and nutmeg. Stir in the grated apple, raisins and walnuts (if using). Pour the quinoa purée into the bowl and stir just until combined. Pour the batter into the prepared pan and spread evenly.

Bake for 45 minutes or until a toothpick inserted in the cake comes out clean. Let the cake rest in the pan for about 15 minutes. (The cake may fall slightly after it's removed from the oven.) Turn upside down onto a large plate and lift off the pan. While still warm, drizzle the cake with maple syrup and lightly sprinkle with icing sugar. Serve warm.

Store in a sealed container in the refrigerator for up to 1 week.

PER SERVING: Energy 220 calories; Protein 4 g; Carbohydrates 33 g; Dietary Fiber 2 g; Fat 9 g; Sugar 19 g; Cholesterol 50 mg; Sodium 320 mg

SERVES 10

1⅓ cups (325 mL) water

⅔ cup (150 mL) white quinoa

2 large eggs

2 large egg whites

¼ cup (60 mL) unsalted butter, melted and cooled to room temperature

¼ cup (60 mL) unsweetened applesauce

1 tsp (5 mL) pure vanilla extract

½ cup (125 mL) organic cane sugar or white sugar

⅓ cup (75 mL) cornstarch

2½ tsp (12 mL) baking powder

½ tsp (2 mL) baking soda

½ tsp (2 mL) salt

1½ tsp (7 mL) cinnamon

1 tsp (5 mL) ground allspice

½ tsp (2 mL) nutmeg

1½ cups (375 mL) peeled and grated Granny Smith apples (about 2)

⅓ cup (75 mL) raisins

⅓ cup (75 mL) chopped walnuts (optional)

3 Tbsp (45 mL) pure maple syrup

Icing sugar for garnish

Cooked quinoa already on hand? Purée 2 cups (500 mL) extra-fluffy cooked quinoa in this recipe.

CHERRY LAVENDER CAKE

SERVES 9

¼ cup (60 mL) organic
    cane sugar or white sugar

¼ cup (60 mL) water

1 Tbsp (15 mL) lemon juice

1 tsp (5 mL) cornstarch

2 cups (500 mL) pitted
    fresh cherries

1 cup (250 mL) quinoa flour

⅓ cup (75 mL) organic
    cane sugar or white sugar

1 Tbsp (15 mL) chopped dried
    lavender leaves (edible grade)

1¾ tsp (8 mL) baking powder

1 tsp (5 mL) salt

1 large egg

½ cup (125 mL) whole milk

¼ cup (60 mL) unsalted butter,
    melted and cooled

¼ cup (60 mL) unsweetened
    applesauce

Lavender—both the leaves and the flowers—is the latest trend in new and unusual baking ingredients. An edible herb, it contains vitamin A, calcium and iron. A touch of lavender adds a new dimension to this fluffy quinoa cake. Similar to a pudding cake, it is saucy and loaded with baked fresh cherries. It makes a completely different, sweet surprise for your afternoon tea. If you're new to lavender in baking and unsure if you'll like the taste, you may want to use half the amount given in the recipe the first time you make it.

Preheat the oven to 375°F (190°C). Grease or lightly spray with cooking oil a 9-inch (2 L) square cake pan.

In a medium saucepan, whisk together the sugar, water, lemon juice and cornstarch. Add the cherries and bring to a boil. Reduce to a simmer and stir until the mixture thickens slightly, 4 to 5 minutes. Remove from the heat and set aside.

In a medium bowl, whisk together the flour, sugar, lavender, baking powder and salt. In a small bowl, beat the egg, then whisk in the milk, butter and applesauce. Add the egg mixture to the flour mixture, mixing just until combined. Spread the batter in the prepared pan. Pour the cherry mixture evenly over the top.

Bake for 25 minutes, or until a toothpick inserted in the center comes out clean. Serve warm.

Store in a sealed container in the refrigerator for up to 3 days.

PER SERVING: Energy 190 calories; Protein 3 g; Carbohydrates 29 g; Dietary Fiber 3 g; Fat 7 g; Sugar 18 g; Cholesterol 35 mg; Sodium 280 mg

HUMMINGBIRD COFFEE CAKE

Here is a new version of hummingbird cake, made with bananas, pineapple and pecans. It is perfect during coffee with friends. Decorate with cream cheese icing, if you like.

Preheat the oven to 350°F (180°C). Lightly grease or spray with cooking oil a 9-inch (2.5 L) square cake pan.

In a medium bowl, whisk together the flour, potato starch, baking powder, baking soda and cinnamon. Stir in the pecans. In a small bowl, beat the eggs, then whisk in the pineapple, bananas, sugar, oil and vanilla. Pour banana mixture into the flour mixture and stir just until combined. Pour batter into the prepared pan.

Bake for 40 to 45 minutes or until a toothpick inserted in the center comes out clean. Cool in the pan. Frost with your favorite light cream cheese icing recipe, if desired.

Store in a sealed container in the refrigerator for up to 1 week.

PER SERVING (unfrosted): Energy 140 calories; Protein 2 g; Carbohydrates 19 g; Dietary Fiber 2 g; Fat 7 g; Sugar 7 g; Cholesterol 25 mg; Sodium 105 mg

SERVES 16

¾ cup (175 mL) quinoa flour

½ cup (125 mL) potato starch
  or fine rice flour

2 ½ tsp (12 mL) baking powder

¼ tsp (1 mL) baking soda

1 ¼ tsp (6 mL) cinnamon

½ cup (125 mL) chopped pecans

2 large eggs

1 can (8 oz/227 g) crushed
  pineapple, drained well

1 ½ cups (375 mL) mashed bananas

¼ cup (60 mL) organic
  cane sugar or white sugar

¼ cup (60 mL) grapeseed oil
  or vegetable oil

1 ½ tsp (7 mL) pure vanilla extract

ORANGE GINGERBREAD

SERVES 10

GINGERBREAD

1½ cups (375 mL) quinoa flour

1½ cups (375 mL) almond flour

⅓ cup (75 mL) organic
    cane sugar or white sugar

1½ tsp (7 mL) baking soda

½ tsp (2 mL) salt

1 tsp (5 mL) ground ginger

2 large eggs, lightly beaten

¾ cup (175 mL) buttermilk

½ cup (125 mL) unsweetened
    applesauce

¼ cup (60 mL) vegetable oil

¼ cup (60 mL) fancy molasses

1 Tbsp (15 mL) grated orange zest

1 Tbsp (15 mL) freshly
    squeezed orange juice

GLAZE

(OPTIONAL)

1¼ cups (300 mL) icing sugar

3 Tbsp (45 mL) freshly
    squeezed orange juice

This classic gingerbread has the goodness of quinoa and a rustic texture from almond flour. It is moist and fluffy, with the slight scent of orange. For an extra bit of sweetness, drizzle with the optional orange glaze.

Preheat the oven to 350°F (180°C). Lightly grease or spray with cooking oil a 9- × 5-inch (2 L) loaf pan.

For the gingerbread, in a large bowl, whisk together the quinoa flour, almond flour, sugar, baking soda, salt and ginger. Add the eggs, buttermilk, applesauce, oil, molasses, orange zest and orange juice. Mix well. Pour into the prepared pan.

Bake for 45 to 50 minutes or until a toothpick inserted in the center comes out clean. Cool completely in the pan.

For the glaze (if using), whisk together the icing sugar and orange juice. Turn the gingerbread out of the pan and poke holes in the top of the loaf. Cover with glaze.

Store in a sealed container in the refrigerator for up to 1 week.

PER SERVING (without glaze): Energy 300 calories; Protein 8 g; Carbohydrates 31 g; Dietary Fiber 4 g; Fat 16 g; Sugar 14 g; Cholesterol 40 mg; Sodium 350 mg

COUNTRY APPLE PECAN PIE

A homemade treat! The wonderful aroma of tender apples, cinnamon and toasted pecans will fill your whole home. Serve à la mode if desired. Cripps Pink apples are also sold as Pink Lady.

Place a baking sheet on the lowest rack of the oven and preheat the oven to 350°F (180°C). Lightly grease or spray with cooking oil a 9-inch (23 cm) pie plate. Roll out the pastry and line the pie plate (see page 190).

In a medium bowl, toss the apples with the lemon juice. Pour in the maple syrup and add the cornstarch, cinnamon and salt (if using). Toss well. Pour the apples into the pie shell, evenly distributing and flattening them.

In a small bowl, whisk together the oats, pecans, brown sugar, cornstarch and cinnamon. With your fingers, rub in the butter until evenly distributed. Sprinkle the topping evenly over the apples, then use the palm of your hand to gently press it onto the pie.

Bake for 60 to 70 minutes or until the apples are tender. Place foil over the pie if the crust becomes too dark. Let sit for 30 minutes before serving.

Store in a sealed container in the refrigerator for up to 1 week.

PER SERVING: Energy 380 calories; Protein 3 g; Carbohydrates 55 g; Dietary Fiber 5 g; Fat 18 g; Sugar 21 g; Cholesterol 35 mg; Sodium 190 mg

SERVES 8

1 unbaked single Flaky Pie Crust (page 190)

6 cups (1.5 L) peeled, cored and thinly sliced Golden Delicious or Cripps Pink apples

1 Tbsp (15 mL) lemon juice

¼ cup (60 mL) pure maple syrup

2 Tbsp (30 mL) cornstarch

½ tsp (2 mL) cinnamon

Pinch of salt (optional)

½ cup (125 mL) quick-cooking rolled oats (gluten-free if required)

⅓ cup (75 mL) chopped toasted pecans

3 Tbsp (45 mL) brown sugar

1 Tbsp (15 mL) cornstarch

¼ tsp (1 mL) cinnamon

1 Tbsp (15 mL) salted butter, softened

To toast nuts, preheat the oven to 350°F (180°C). Spread the nuts on a baking sheet and toast in the oven, stirring once if necessary, for 5 to 7 minutes, until fragrant and lightly toasted.

FLAKY PIE CRUST

MAKES ONE 10-INCH (25 CM) CRUST

½ cup (125 mL) quinoa flour

½ cup (125 mL) brown rice flour

½ cup (125 mL) potato starch

1 Tbsp (15 mL) organic
    cane sugar or white sugar

¼ tsp (1 mL) salt

½ cup (125 mL) cold unsalted
    butter, cut into pieces

⅓ cup (75 mL) + 2 Tbsp (30 mL)
    cold water

This flaky pie crust has a blend of flours for a mild, pleasing flavor. It can be used for a variety of sweet or savory fillings. If you need a top crust, simply double the recipe.

Combine the quinoa flour, rice flour, potato starch, sugar and salt in a medium bowl. Whisk together well. Add the cold butter. Cut in the butter with a pastry blender or two knives until the butter is in pea-sized pieces. While gently stirring, add the cold water slowly just until combined. Form dough into a ball and flatten into a disk. Wrap with plastic wrap and place in the refrigerator for 1 hour.

Let the dough sit at room temperature until soft enough to be rolled. Dust your work surface with potato starch or flour and place the pastry dough on top. Lightly dust the top of the pastry with potato starch or flour. Roll from the center out, turning every two or three rolls to ensure the bottom does not stick to your rolling surface. Roll into a round ³⁄₁₆ inch (5 mm) thick and at least 12 inches (30 cm) wide.

Drape the pastry over the rolling pin and gently unroll it over the pie plate. Press the pastry into the bottom of the plate. Press any tears or cracks together, then trim the edge with a knife, allowing ½ inch (1 cm) overhang. For a single pie crust, flute the edges by pressing the dough from the inside with one finger and pinching it gently between two fingers on the outside.

MAKING A DOUBLE-CRUST PIE Roll out the second disk of dough on a piece of parchment until it is ³⁄₁₆ inch (5 mm) thick (so it will brown and bake properly). Turn the crust over onto the filled pie shell and peel off the parchment. Press the edges together and flute them (see above). Brush all over with egg wash (1 egg beaten with 1 tsp/5 mL water). Cut several steam vents in the top.

BAKING AN UNFILLED SINGLE PIE CRUST Pierce crust on sides and bottom. Bake an unfilled single pie shell at 450°F (230°C) for 15 minutes or until crust is a very light brown.

BAKING WITH FILLING OR A DOUBLE CRUST Bake a single pie crust with filling or a double-crust fruit pie on the bottom oven rack at 450°F (230°C) for 10 minutes, then reduce the temperature to 350°F (180°C) and bake for another 30 to 60 minutes, depending on the filling. Cooked fillings generally take 30 minutes, while fillings that need to cook can take up to 60 minutes.

PER SERVING (⅛ pie, single crust, without filling): Energy 210 calories; Protein 2 g; Carbohydrates 24 g; Dietary Fiber 1 g; Fat 12 g; Sugar 2 g; Cholesterol 30 mg; Sodium 180 mg

OLD-FASHIONED SWEET POTATO PIE

SERVES 8

1 unbaked single Flaky
    Pie Crust (page 190)

1½ cups (375 mL) mashed
    cooked sweet potato

¾ cup (175 mL) 2% evaporated milk

⅓ cup (75 mL) light brown sugar

2 Tbsp (30 mL) pure maple syrup

1½ tsp (7 mL) cinnamon

1 tsp (5 mL) pure vanilla extract

1 large egg

1 large egg white

Traditionally served for Thanksgiving dinner, this pie is now being enjoyed throughout the year because of the nutrition of sweet potatoes. They are rich in vitamin A, beta-carotene and vitamin C. Serve this pie with whipped cream sweetened with maple syrup, if desired.

Position oven rack on the bottom level and preheat the oven to 450°F (230°C). Lightly grease or spray with cooking oil a 9-inch (23 cm) pie plate. Roll out the pastry and line the pie plate (see page 190).

In a medium bowl, combine the sweet potato, evaporated milk, brown sugar, maple syrup, cinnamon, vanilla, egg and egg white. Beat with an electric mixer on medium speed until filling is smooth and uniform. Pour into the prepared crust.

Bake for 20 minutes, then reduce temperature to 325°F (160°C) and bake for another 30 minutes or until a knife inserted in the center comes out clean. If the crust begins to get too dark, cover the edges with a piece of foil.

Serve cool or at room temperature with whipped cream, if desired.

Store in a sealed container in the refrigerator for up to 1 week.

PER SERVING: Energy 330 calories; Protein 5 g; Carbohydrates 47 g; Dietary Fiber 3 g; Fat 13 g; Sugar 16 g; Cholesterol 60 mg; Sodium 240 mg

BLACKBERRY BRÛLÉE

Fluffy quinoa is puréed silky smooth with whole milk or cream, loaded with blackberries and topped with a sweet, crunchy caramelized topping. A decadent dessert that's packed with nutrition.

Lightly grease four 1-cup (250 mL) ramekins or an 8-inch (2 L) square baking dish.

Combine the water and quinoa in a medium saucepan. Bring to a boil, reduce to a simmer, cover and cook for 15 minutes. The quinoa must be extra-fluffy. Fluff with a fork and set aside to cool.

Position oven rack at the center of the oven. Preheat the broiler to 500°F (260°C).

In a blender or food processor, combine the cooked quinoa, milk, ¼ cup (60 mL) brown sugar, cinnamon and vanilla. Purée well, for at least 2 to 3 minutes. The mixture should be thick and very smooth. Pour into a small bowl and toss with the blackberries. Scoop into ramekins or the baking dish. Top evenly with 3 Tbsp (45 mL) brown sugar.

Broil for 6 to 8 minutes, until the brown sugar topping is caramelized. Serve warm.

Store in a sealed container in the refrigerator for up to 4 days.

PER SERVING: Energy 180 calories; Protein 5 g; Carbohydrates 35 g; Dietary Fiber 3 g; Fat 3 g; Sugar 19 g; Cholesterol 5 mg; Sodium 25 mg

SERVES 4

1 cup (250 mL) water

½ cup (125 mL) quinoa

¾ cup (175 mL) whole milk or cream

¼ cup (60 mL) + 3 Tbsp (45 mL) brown sugar

1 tsp (5 mL) cinnamon

½ tsp (2 mL) pure vanilla extract

¾ cup (175 mL) whole fresh blackberries

Cooked quinoa already on hand? Add 1½ cups (375 mL) extra-fluffy cooked quinoa to the milk mixture and proceed from there.

CAFÉ MOCHA PUDDING

Here, quinoa is simmered in bold coffee, then blended into a rich and creamy chocolate pudding. If children won't be eating it and you prefer the kick of caffeine, you can swap out the decaf for the real thing.

Combine the coffee and quinoa in a medium saucepan. Bring to a boil, reduce to a simmer, cover and cook for 25 minutes. The quinoa should be extra-fluffy. Fluff with a fork and set aside to cool.

In a blender or food processor, combine the quinoa, milk, sugar, cocoa and vanilla. Purée well, for at least 2 to 3 minutes. The mixture should be very thick and smooth. Scoop into individual serving dishes. Chill for at least 1 hour (or overnight) before serving. Serve garnished with vanilla whipped cream (if using).

Store in a sealed container in the refrigerator for up to 4 days.

PER SERVING: Energy 180 calories; Protein 6 g; Carbohydrates 36 g; Dietary Fiber 4 g; Fat 3 g; Sugar 17 g; Cholesterol 5 mg; Sodium 20 mg

SERVES 4

1 ½ cups (375 mL) strong decaffeinated coffee or espresso

½ cup (125 mL) quinoa

½ cup (125 mL) whole milk

⅓ cup (75 mL) organic cane sugar or white sugar

⅓ cup (75 mL) unsweetened cocoa powder

½ tsp (2 mL) pure vanilla extract

Whipping cream whipped with ¼ tsp (1 mL) pure vanilla extract for garnish (optional)

CHOCOLATE HAZELNUT CREAM

SERVES 6

1 cup (250 mL) water

½ cup (125 mL) quinoa

½ cup (125 mL) toasted
    flaked hazelnuts

½ cup (125 mL) unsweetened
    cocoa powder

⅓ cup (75 mL) organic
    cane sugar or white sugar

½ tsp (2 mL) pure vanilla extract

1¼ cups (300 mL) whole milk

Whipped cream for garnish
    (optional)

Fluffy quinoa is puréed into a thick, decadent pudding with whole milk, cocoa and toasted hazelnuts. A superb dessert with a wow factor that makes you completely forget it's good for you!

Combine the water and quinoa in a medium saucepan. Bring to a boil, reduce to a simmer, cover and cook for 15 minutes. The quinoa should be extra-fluffy. Fluff with a fork and set aside to cool.

Set aside 1 Tbsp (15 mL) of the hazelnuts for garnish. In a blender or food processor, combine the remaining hazelnuts, quinoa, cocoa, sugar and vanilla. Add milk ¼ cup (60 mL) at a time, blending well and scraping down the sides (when necessary) after each addition. Purée well, for at least 2 to 3 minutes. The mixture should be very thick and smooth. Scoop into individual serving dishes. Chill for 1 hour before serving. Serve garnished with the remaining hazelnuts and whipped cream (if using).

Store in a sealed container in the refrigerator for up to 4 days.

PER SERVING: Energy 200 calories; Protein 6 g; Carbohydrates 28 g; Dietary Fiber 4 g; Fat 9 g; Sugar 14 g; Cholesterol 5 mg; Sodium 25 mg

- Cooked quinoa already on hand? Use 1½ cups (375 mL) of extra-fluffy cooked quinoa in this recipe.

- To toast nuts, preheat the oven to 350°F (180°C). Spread the nuts on a baking sheet and toast in the oven, stirring once if necessary, for 5 to 7 minutes, until fragrant and lightly toasted.

PERFECT PUMPKIN PUDDING

Enjoy the taste of pumpkin pie without the crust (and extra calories). This perfect blend of spices in a creamy quinoa pudding makes for a thick, delicious and healthy option. Top each slice with maple whipped cream and toasted pecans. This dessert can be made the day before serving.

For the pudding, combine the water and quinoa in a medium saucepan and bring to a boil. Reduce to a simmer, cover and cook for 17 minutes. The quinoa should be extra-fluffy. Fluff with a fork and set aside to cool.

Preheat the oven to 400°F (200°C). Lightly grease an 8-inch (2 L) square baking dish.

In a medium bowl, beat the egg. Add the pumpkin and whisk until thoroughly combined.

In a medium saucepan, combine the milk, sugar, cinnamon, ginger, cloves, cardamom and salt. Bring to a boil on medium heat, stirring constantly. Whisk in the pumpkin mixture and continue to heat, stirring, until bubbling and thickened slightly, about 2 minutes. Stir in the quinoa and vanilla. Pour into the baking dish.

Bake for 30 minutes or until set. Let cool. Cut into 8 pieces.

For the topping (if using), in a medium bowl, whip the cream with the maple syrup until stiff peaks form.

Serve pudding topped with maple cream and garnished with a candied or toasted pecan.

Store in a sealed container in the refrigerator for up to 4 days.

PER SERVING: Energy 230 calories; Protein 9 g; Carbohydrates 39 g; Dietary Fiber 2 g; Fat 3.5 g; Sugar 23 g; Cholesterol 55 mg; Sodium 150 mg

SERVES 4

PUDDING

1 cup (250 mL) water

½ cup (125 mL) white quinoa

1 large egg

1 cup (250 mL) pumpkin purée

2 cups (500 mL) 1% milk

⅓ cup (75 mL) organic cane sugar or white sugar

½ tsp (2 mL) cinnamon

¼ tsp (1 mL) ground ginger

Pinch each of ground cloves, ground cardamom and salt

1 tsp (5 mL) pure vanilla extract

TOPPING
(OPTIONAL)

¾ cup (175 mL) whipping cream

2 Tbsp (30 mL) pure maple syrup

8 toasted pecans

- Cooked quinoa already on hand? Add 1½ cups (375 mL) extra-fluffy cooked quinoa to the pudding mixture.
- To toast nuts, preheat the oven to 350°F (180°C). Spread the nuts on a baking sheet and toast in the oven, stirring once, for 5 to 7 minutes, until fragrant and lightly toasted.

RASPBERRY ALMOND CUSTARD

SERVES 4

1 cup (250 mL) water

½ cup (125 mL) white quinoa

1 can (12 ounces/370 mL)
    evaporated partly
    skimmed milk

¼ cup (60 mL) brown sugar

1 large egg

1 large egg white

1 tsp (5 mL) pure almond extract

½ cup (125 mL) fresh raspberries

¼ cup (60 mL) toasted
    sliced almonds

A new twist on custard. This creamy custard is made with quinoa and topped with fresh raspberries and toasted almonds.

Combine the water and quinoa in a small saucepan. Bring to a boil, reduce to a simmer, cover and simmer for 15 minutes. The quinoa should be extra-fluffy. Fluff with a fork and set aside to cool.

Heat the evaporated milk and brown sugar in a medium saucepan on medium-high heat. In a small bowl, beat the egg and egg white. Whisk a spoonful of the warm milk into the egg to temper it. Continue with 6 more spoonfuls of milk, whisking after each addition. Whisk the egg mixture gently into the milk mixture. Continue to heat for 3 minutes, stirring constantly. Stir in 1½ cups (375 mL) of the cooked quinoa and the almond extract. Remove from the heat and divide among 4 individual ramekins. Place plastic wrap directly on surface of custard and refrigerate until cool. Serve topped with fresh raspberries and toasted almonds.

Store in a sealed container in the refrigerator for up to 4 days.

PER SERVING: Energy 310 calories; Protein 14 g; Carbohydrates 36 g; Dietary Fiber 3 g; Fat 13 g; Sugar 20 g; Cholesterol 75 mg; Sodium 140 mg

To toast nuts, preheat the oven to 350°F (180°C). Spread the nuts on a baking sheet and toast in the oven, stirring once if necessary, for 5 to 7 minutes, until fragrant and lightly toasted.

STEWED SUMMER FRUIT WITH CINNAMON & LEMON

Each European country has its own version of a fruit "soup" made of delicious combinations of fresh and dried fruit and served with cream. While very tasty, traditionally these recipes can have a large amount of unnecessary sugar. Not this one! We've revamped it so you can enjoy this refreshing dessert worry-free. Enjoy it hot or cold.

In a large saucepan, combine the water, quinoa, rhubarb, strawberries, prunes, raisins, lemon, honey and cinnamon stick. Bring to a boil, reduce to a simmer, cover and cook, stirring occasionally, for 45 minutes or until the strawberries and rhubarb have cooked down and become part of the sauce. Remove from the heat, stir and remove the cinnamon stick and lemon pieces. Let cool slightly before serving, or chill, if desired.

Stir the yogurt and maple syrup together in a small bowl. Spoon stewed fruit into individual serving dishes. Serve hot or cold, topped with the maple yogurt.

Store in a sealed container in the refrigerator for up to 4 days.

PER SERVING: Energy 160 calories; Protein 5 g; Carbohydrates 33 g; Dietary Fiber 3 g; Fat 1 g; Sugar 17 g; Cholesterol 0 mg; Sodium 15 mg

SERVES 8

3 ⅓ cups (825 mL) water

⅔ cup (150 mL) quinoa

1 ½ cups (375 mL) sliced fresh or frozen unsweetened rhubarb

1 ½ cups (375 mL) halved fresh or frozen strawberries

½ cup (125 mL) quartered pitted prunes

⅓ cup (75 mL) seedless raisins or dried currants

½ lemon (see Tip)

3 Tbsp (45 mL) honey

1 cinnamon stick

1 cup (250 mL) nonfat plain thick Greek yogurt

1 Tbsp (15 mL) pure maple syrup

If you would like to keep the lemon in the stewed fruit mixture, slice it thinly. However, if you want the option of removing it before serving, slice it very thick so it is easy to pull out.

LEMON GINGER BLUEBERRY CRISP

SERVES 6

6 cups (1.5 L) fresh or thawed
    frozen blueberries

¼ cup (60 mL) lightly packed
    brown sugar

1 tsp (5 mL) cinnamon

1 tsp (5 mL) grated lemon zest

1 Tbsp (15 mL) lemon juice

1¼ cups (300 mL) quinoa flakes

½ cup (125 mL) sliced almonds

2 Tbsp (30 mL) unsalted
    butter, melted

1 Tbsp (15 mL) brown sugar

½ tsp (2 mL) ground ginger

A lively dessert, with a delightful combination of lemon and blueberries and a hint of ginger. Top with ice cream, if desired.

Preheat the oven to 350°F (180°C). Lightly grease or spray with cooking oil an 11- × 7-inch (2 L) baking dish.

Combine the blueberries, brown sugar, cinnamon, lemon zest and lemon juice in a medium bowl. Toss until blueberries are evenly coated. Pour into the baking dish and spread evenly.

In the same bowl, combine the quinoa flakes, almonds, butter, brown sugar and ginger. Stir until the flakes are coated with the butter mixture. Sprinkle evenly over the blueberries.

Bake for 30 minutes or until the blueberry filling is hot. Serve warm with ice cream, if desired.

Store in a sealed container in the refrigerator for up to 4 days.

PER SERVING: Energy 280 calories; Protein 6 g; Carbohydrates 49 g; Dietary Fiber 6 g; Fat 10 g; Sugar 22 g; Cholesterol 10 mg; Sodium 210 mg

ACKNOWLEDGMENTS

Most importantly, our deepest gratitude to our family, Paul and Ian, and always our amazing Sydney, Alyssa and Aston. We are also grateful for the support of Vera Friesen, Swen Runkvist and the Green family.

Thank you to numerous industry advisors, supporters and friends: Sergio Nuñez de Arco, Tania Petricevic, Marcos Guevara, Laurie Scanlin & Claire Burnett, Jeffrey & Amy Barnes, Marjorie & Bob Leventry, Francisco & Magdalena Diez-Canseco, Olivier & Didier Perreol, Gordon Kirke, Jocelyn Campanaro & Craig Billington, Stefani Farkas, Terry Paluszkiewicz, Annica Sjoberg, Rose Gage, the Addersons, Brenda & Ingrid Wicklund, Linda Beaudoin, Theresa Kyi, Frank Dyson, Shela Shapiro, Shaundra Carvey-Parker, Heather Dyer, Bert Leat & Julie Roberts, Sara & Jim Busby, Kerri Rosenbaum Barr, Billijon Morgan, Jeanette Young-Laroque, Liz Boily, Megan Portello & family, the Vanderwater family, the Atom Girls Hockey Family (you know who you are), Terri Peters, Tammy Martel, Vitaliy Prokopets, Grant & Patricia Wood, Nancy Midwicki, Shannon Goodspeed, Ryan Szulc, Madeleine Johari and Uncle John & Aunt Beryl and all of those brilliant Barbers in England!

We must acknowledge Verna Deason and the entire Deason family. We were always watching, listening and inspired by you. You have all been a tremendous influence on us, and we thank you.

INDEX

SHLOMO BARAK

SPACE

IS ALL THERE IS

A THEORY OF EVERYTHING - TOE
THE PHYSICAL REALITY AS
SPACE DEFORMATIONS AND WAVES

Producer & International Distributor
eBookPro Publishing
www.ebook-pro.com

Space Is All There Is
Shlomo Barak

Editor: Roger M. Kaye

Copyright © 2020 Shlomo Barak

All rights reserved; No parts of this book may be reproduced or transmitted
in any form or by any means, electronic or mechanical, including photo-
copying, recording, taping, or by any information retrieval system, without
the permission, in writing, of the author.

Contact: shlomobarak@yahoo.com
ISBN 978-965-90727-5-0

SPACE

IS ALL THERE IS

A THEORY OF EVERYTHING - TOE
THE PHYSICAL REALITY AS
SPACE DEFORMATIONS AND WAVES

DR. SHLOMO BARAK

EDITED BY ROGER M. KAYE

CONTENTS

Dear readers,

This book is for you scientists, engineers, mathematicians, teachers and for you who are seeking knowledge. Here I present, in a simple way, my theory that explains light particles, the particles that make up atoms, and subjects relating to the entire universe. Physicists name this kind of a total theory of the physical reality A Theory of Everything – TOE. My TOE is based on 22 of my scientific papers, published recently, and a book, listed in Chapter W.

In my theory, Space is all there is and nothing is alien to it. "All there is" are space deformations and waves: some are straight-moving wavepackets, like the particles of light, and others are circulating wavepackets like electrons. This theory yields both theoretical results and calculations that so far, no other theory has been able to provide. More than that, it is a realization of Einstein's vision, expressed by him in many of his articles and books.

This book is important for physicists, since it presents a paradigm shift, and resolves many of the cardinal issues that have been left open. Mathematicians will find in my book my new geometry of deformed spaces that complements the Riemannian geometry of bent manifolds. The beginning of this book is simple but becomes more complicated from each chapter to the next.

ENJOY

PROLOGUE (Recommended for physicists)

The Current Paradigm

The current paradigm in physics, despite the successes of the excellent theories that construct it, is facing many obstacles. Many principles remain unproven, attributes of elementary particles cannot be derived and calculated, and mysteries are un-resolved. This situation results from the lack of a deeper theoretical layer.

The GDM – My Theory of Everything (TOE)

The missing theoretical layer is my **GeometroDynamic Model (GDM)** of reality, in which **Space Is All There Is**. The GDM provides answers as to what are: **charge, elementary particles, inertia (mass), gravitation**, and relates to additional fundamental subjects. The GDM does not, at large, contradict the paradigm; it simply serves as a realistic and tangible deeper theoretical layer – **simplicity and beauty at its peak.**

GDM RESULTS (The first of their kind in physics)

Some results, the **masses and radii of the elementary particles**, out of the many published in the Barak papers, are presented below. The Standard Model of elementary particles and String Theory, **wrongly** consider elementary particles to be alien to space, point-like or string-like, and structureless. This is why both theories **fail** to derive and calculate these masses and radii.

Electron/Positron Mass

$$M_e = \frac{s^2\sqrt{2}}{\pi(1+\pi\,\alpha)} \cdot \sqrt{G^{-1}\alpha\hbar c^{-3}}$$

$s = 1 \quad [s] = LT^{-1}$

For the electron/positron charge, which is a white/black hole, s is light velocity at the event horizon, as the far-away observer measures.

M_e (calculated) = $0.91036 \cdot 10^{-27}$gr

M_e (measured) = $0.910938356(11) \cdot 10^{-27}$gr

M_e (measured) / M_e (calculated) = 1.0006   **!!!**

Muon/Anti-Muon Mass

M_μ (calculated) = 112.5 ·Mev/c^2

M_μ (measured) = 105.8·Mev/c^2

Quarks/Anti-Quarks Masses

M_d (calculated) = $9M_e$ = 4.5 MeV/c^2

M_d (measured) = 4.8 $\pm$ 0.5 MeV/c^2

$M_{\tilde{u}}$ (calculated) = $4.5M_e$ = 2.25 MeV/c^2

$M_{\tilde{u}}$ (measured) = 2.3 $\pm$ 0.8 MeV/c^2

The Elementary Charge Radius

$r_p = \sqrt{2}/(2s^2) \cdot \sqrt{G\alpha\hbar c}$

r_p(calculated) = 0.8774 ·10^{-13}cm

r_p(measured) = 0.8768(69) ·10^{-13}cm

r_p(calculated)/r_p(measured) = 1.0007   !!!

11

The Extended (unified) General Relativity (GR) Equation

By defining charge as nothing but curved space and using the Lorentz Transformation we derive the entire Maxwellian Electromagnetic theory, without any phenomenology. This result enables us to extend Einstein's equation of General Relativity (GR) to become an equation that incorporates not only the energy/momentum tensor ($T_m^{\mu\nu}$), but also the charge/current tensor ($T_q^{\mu\nu}$).

This equation becomes a macroscopic/microscopic equation of the entire physical reality. Charge and angular momentum are quantized and thus we predict that the curvature of spacetime is also quantized.

$$R^{\mu\nu} - 1/2 R g^{\mu\nu} = 8\pi G/c^4 \cdot T_m^{\mu\nu} + 4\pi G^{1/2}/s^2 \cdot T_q^{\mu\nu}$$

where $S = 1$ and $[S] = LT^{-1}$. In the GDM $[L] = $ cm and $[T] = $ sec.

In the past, efforts were made to incorporate the energy/momentum tensor of the electromagnetic field in the GR equation. The common denominator of all these efforts to unify gravitation and electromagnetism was the idea that only energy/momentum curves spacetime. In contrast, we show that the right-hand-side of the GR

12

equation expresses curving by angular momentum and charge. Curving by angular momentum is related to frame dragging, by the elementary spins, whereas charge is simply curved space. Charge and angular momentum are quantized and thus we predict that curvature of spacetime is also quantized. Thus, the creation or annihilation of pairs is supposed to result in a double quantum change in curvature

The GDM Idea

The elastic and vibrating three-dimensional Space Lattice **is all there is**.

Elementary particles are Transversal or Longitudinal wavepackets of this vibrating space.

The GDM Method of Unification

The GDM approach to the issue of unification is as follows: **Instead** of adding spatial dimensions, which we consider a formal, even artificial, way of unification, we have explored the possibility that **all phenomena** have a common denominator. This common denominator is the **Geometrodynamics of spacetime**, since in the

GDM **space is all there is**. Thus, Riemannian geometry, applied to deformed spaces rather than to bent manifolds becomes our mathematical tool to explore the reality.

The GDM Goals

The GDM is a model of the physical reality, in which **space is   all there is.**

This expresses the drive to reductionism.

The GDM explains known, but currently unexplained,   phenomena.

This expresses the drive to understand.

The GDM predicts new phenomena that can be confirmed experimentally.

This is the requirement for specificity and falsifiability.

The GDM logically infers laws of physics.

No phenomenology and hence no need to ask where the laws come from.

The Constants of Nature

$c_T = c$ Velocity of transversal Space vibrations (EM waves) $[c_T]=LT^{-1}$

[c_L Velocity of longitudinal Space vibrations ($c_L > c_T$)] $[c_L]=LT^{-1}$

ħ Planck Constant $[ħ]=L^5T^{-1}$

G Gravitational Constant $[G]=T^{-2}$

α Fine Structure Constant $[α]=1$

Since $c_L/c = π/2·(1+ π α)$ we exclude c_L from the list and choose the known α instead. Longitudinal electromagnctic waves have recently been detected. In the GDM the elastic space vibrates transversely and/or longitudinally.

Note that in the current paradigm the number of constants is 20.

A Constant of Nature is a physical quantity that, measured locally by observers anywhere in space, and with any relative velocity with respect to each other and to space, results in the same value (invariance).

Note that a Constant of Nature is not necessarily regarded as a constant by an observer that observes other regions of space rather than his own. Our discussions on light velocity, both in SR and GR, will clarify this statement.

Motion and "Rest"

In the GDM **there is no rest** - only motion at the waves' velocities.

Elementary particles at **"rest"** are circularly rotating wavepackets. Their virtual geometric centers are at rest. When they move the wavepackets describe spirals.

The Units of the GDM

In the GDM all units are expressed by the unit of length L (**cm**) and the unit of time T (**sec**) only. A conversion from the **GDM system** of units to the **cgs system** enables calculations of known phenomena and of new, GDM-predicted, phenomena.

Einstein's vision

A. Einstein (1924)

In the present situation we are de facto forced to make a distinction between matter and fields, while we hope that later generations will be able to overcome this dualistic concept, and replace it with a unitary one, such as the field theory of today has sought in vain.

A. Einstein (1936)

$$R_{ik} - \frac{1}{2} g_{ik} R = \frac{8\pi G}{c^4} T_{ik}$$

..... is similar to a building, one wing of which is made of fine marble (left part of the equation), but the other wing of which is built of low-grade wood (right side of equation). The phenomenological representation of matter is, in fact, only a crude substitute for a representation which would do justice to all known properties of matter.

A. Einstein (1933)

…. the axiomatic basis of theoretical physics cannot be extracted from experience but must be freely invented…

The GDM realizes Einstein's vision.

A. This Book

We all have curiosity, but each to a different extent. We all want to understand reality, but everyone is interested in a different aspect of it. My curiosity, from childhood, was largely focused on the physical reality. I wanted to know why, for example, water flows in one pipe, while an electric current requires two "tubes" – a pair of metal wires. I expected to receive the answer from my father, who worked for the Electric Company, but he was not a technical man and could not give me the answer. I, a five-year-old boy, was amazed, a little annoyed, I asked him: you work for the Electric Company and you're not curious to know what is electricity?

In my youth (1950s), I built myself a laboratory for electrical experiments. I built radio receivers and audio amplifiers, and I also helped build the school's natural science laboratory.

Electricity "electrified" me, but what is electricity?

What is an electrical charge?

Why are there only two types of charge (+) and (-)?

What is attraction and repulsion between charges?

Why does charge appear in equal portions?

What gives charge its stability?

What is the field of a charge?

What is the radius of a charge?

I used to subscribe to journals like "Technology and Science for Youth", "The Young Technician" (I have them to this day). I sought advice from teachers and electrical engineers but did not get the answers I wanted. After graduating in mathematics and physics, I went on to gain a PhD in physics, but answers came there none! And today, in the year 2020, there are still no answers. But, with all due caution and modesty, I finally have them, and I want to share them with you.

While in high school, I was troubled by the question of infinity. Intuitively, there is only one infinity. Thus, there can be no large infinity and no small infinity.

While wandering through the bookstores in Ramat Gan (there were several) I came across a book by **Frankel**, at the time my teacher, on the **theory of Sets** (I still have the book), which was developed by **Cantor**. I was in shock that took some weeks to pass.

I learnt how to compare infinite Sets and to see that there are both large and small. In life, intuition can be helpful, but in science it might be a pitfall.

When I was an adult, and even before studying at the university, I learned that there are both true and false statements but there are also those which cannot be determined.

The language of physics is mathematics and geometry. Allegedly "on solid ground" but it is not, as was shown by **Kurt Gödel** in his **incompleteness theorems** (I have kept the book). We bring just a simple example of the mess that he created, **Goldbach**'s conjecture. Consider the following statement:

Any even number greater than 2 is the sum of two prime numbers.

This statement claims that it is possible that it is correct - **true** - and may not be correct – **false**, but it is also possible that **in principle** it cannot be determined if it is true or false.

It was another lesson in modesty.

And now in my third age I have decided to dedicate my time to the study of the physical reality. I was aware of the numerous unsolved problems in the study of the particles as in the study of the universe and the endeavors to build a theory titled:

Theory Of Everything - TOE of the physical reality.

All this seems to me a wonderful challenge for the Third Age, and especially now that nothing can, on the face of it, destroy my tranquility or harm my concentration.

We pause here to learn something about the history of science and the aspiration to build a **TOE**. We can only then see the size and scope of the mission I have taken on myself, see Chapter **D**.

B.   A Brief History of Physical Thought

First and foremost, to give you an idea of the difficulty of breaking a paradigm, which is what I am trying to do.

On the Ancients

Anaxagoras (500 – 428 BCE) was a Greek philosopher and astronomer. He believed that there is no absolute total formation and destruction **and no empty space**. Only later will we see that he was right.

Aristotle (322 – 384 BCE) developed many theories about nature and the way in which it works. Aristotle gave these theories the name, **physics**, although today many of these explanations would be included in the science of biology. Aristotle believed that nature is purposeful, meaning that a good explanation for an activity or event is one in terms of the purpose for which it was made.

Physics also describes activities and events by the means of the purpose for which they occur. But physics **mainly** explores the reasons for events. Aristotle adopted the theory of "the four elements", which also enables it to explain material changes in a purposeful manner.

The main principles of the Aristotelian physics are (there is no need to delve into them):

1. **Natural places**. Each element "aspires" to be in a different location relative to the center of the Earth, which is also the center of the Universe.

2. **Attraction/float**. An object moves in the direction of the location it aspires to reach.

3. **Straight line movement**. Movement in response to this force is in a straight line and at a fixed speed.

4. **Speed/density ratio**. Speed of movement is in inverse proportion to the density of the medium.

5. **Void is not possible**. Because, according to the previous rule, the speed of an object in emptiness is infinite.

6. **The Aether spreads in everything**. All points in space are filled with material.

7. **Infinite universe**. Space cannot have borders.

8. **Continuity theory**. Between atoms is emptiness, so material cannot be atomic.

9. **The fifth Essence or Aether**. Objects outside of the Earth are not made of earthly matter.

10. **The Eternal and Incorruptible Cosmos**. The sun and the planets are perfect spheres and do not change.

11. **Circular motion**. Planets move in a perfect circular motion.

These principles **are incorrect** and rely solely on observations and **logical thinking**. Aristotle **did not experiment**. Aristotle, for example, inadvertently stated that a heavy body falls to the ground faster than a light body. It was Galileo who conducted an experiment and proved that the **free fall** was identical for the two bodies. But Aristotle's physics became the dominant **paradigm** for about 1800 years, until Galileo's time.

What caused all those who dealt with science to be submissive to Aristotle's ideas for 1800 years? - God!

Today, too, physics has been under the influence of a paradigm for more than 100 years. This paradigm, which has promoted science in an astonishing way, is no longer able to answer my weighty questions.

I seek to change the paradigm and this transformation, as you will see, does indeed answer my questions.

Archimedes (287 – 212 BCE) was a Greek mathematician, **physicist**, and philosopher. His book **"The Sand Reckoner"**, concludes that the planets surround the sun. This was about 1750 years before **Copernicus** (1473-1543) (so where were they all?). Archimedes model was forgotten Fig. (B1).

Three hundred years later **Ptolemies** (Talmi) model appeared, Fig. (B2), that ruled till Copernicus.

It is important to emphasize: Neither the Sun revolving around the Earth – the **Geocentric** concept, nor the Earth revolving around the Sun – the **Heliocentric** concept, is correct.

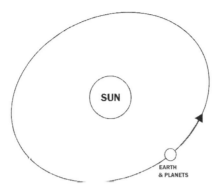

Fig. (B1) The Heliocentric System today and also according to

Archimedes and Copernicus

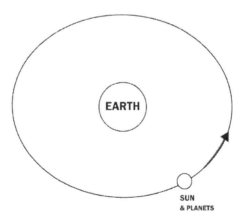

Fig. (B2) Ptolemies Geocentric System

As every physicist knows, two bodies moving around each other are actually moving around the common center of mass of both bodies, see Fig.(B3). The same applies to the Earth and the Sun. Because the Sun's mass is almost a million times larger than that of the Earth, the common center of mass is in the Sun. Thus, the heliocentric convention applies, although it is only an approximation.

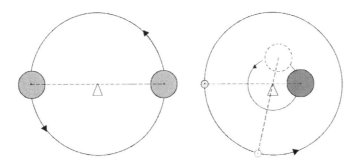

Fig. (B3) Common Center of Mass

Lucretius (55 – 99 BCE). His great work **on the nature of the universe** summarizes the main principle of the Epicurean school. The work is divided into six books: The second book, for example, discusses atomic theory and even raises the idea of worlds other than our own. This book is only a literary attempt to present an entire **Theory of Everything - TOE.**

The Three Philosophers

The Rambam, **Ibn Rushd**, **Thomas Aquinas** - In the twelfth and thirteenth centuries, these three philosophers emphasized the fact that there are two approaches to the physical truth: The serious approach to reality is the most complex and therefore difficult, if not impossible, to understand. The simplistic approach – accessible to most people, makes for easy understanding. The story of the world's creation in the Book of Genesis is an example of this (Rambam - Maimonides).

The Rambam, in his book, a Guide for the Perplexed instructs his disciple, an astronomer who is pretending to understand the composition of the heavens. Be satisfied, says the Rambam, with a model of the celestial movements and prove to us that this model is compatible with your observations.

New Physics

Galileo Galilei (1564 –1642**)** was not only the father of the new physics, and overthrower of the Aristotelian paradigm, which had been dominate for 1800 years, but he also initiated the first start-up company.

Galileo's father was a guitar player, part of a group that created the opera. Seeing his son reading Aristotle's book, he noted that Aristotle's theory of harmonies is wrong. As a proof of his claim, he demonstrated with his guitar. Galileo, noting Aristotle's argument that, in free fall, a heavy body falls faster than a light body wondered if Aristotle was also wrong on this.

Galileo decided that the real test for Aristotle's idea was an experiment. Dropping heavy and light bodies from the top of the tower in Pisa, he soon found than Aristotle was indeed wrong

This experiment demonstrated the importance of experimental physics. It established that the only test for the validity of a claim is an experiment or observation.

Galileo investigated movement and is known as the Father of Kinematics (the Theory of Motion). The Venetian Navy was interested in improving performance. Galileo's knowledge of kinematics gave birth to ballistics, the science of the flight behavior of projectiles. The funding of this research was a matter of some importance for Galileo.

In addition, the Navy contracted with Galileo for polishing lenses and building telescopes. This enabled the navy to discover approaching enemy ships, and Galileo to explore the heavens. The Venetian navy had made an investment in a scientist's venture.

Newton (1643 – 1727) Wrote the **Mathematical Principles of Natural Philosophy**, including his physical research in kinetics and the three laws of motion – **Dynamics**, and the force of **gravity** – **Gravitation**. He thus laid the foundations of classical mechanics. The mathematical model for the motion of celestial bodies was based on **Kepler laws** and other observations. Newton proved the laws of Kepler based on the gravitational central force. Assisted by the same principles he explained the cycles of Comets, the circulation of Tides, and other phenomena. His prediction that the shape of Earth was ellipsoidal was validated. Newton's determination that the universe is subject to mathematical principles has been a major influence on the Philosophy of Science.

In optics Newton invented and built the first reflecting telescope and developed a new theory of color. He worked on an atomic theory of light, whereby it consists of a flow of particles, now known as **photons**. He formulated the empirical law of cooling, and studied the first mathematical theory of sound.

Newton also developed calculus, thereby providing physics with a **language - mathematics**.

Boskovich

 - Croatian (1787 – 1711) in his book, **A Theory of Natural Philosophy,** presented for the first time a complete, unified, theory of the physical reality – a TOE. It was, of course, wrong.

Einstein (1879 – 1955) was known primarily for the **Theory of Special Relativity** and the **Theory of General Relativity**. This book takes a close look at these theories, and therefore, at this juncture, we concentrate on a limited number of fundamental matters relating to the teachings of this great man.

At the beginning of his scientific career, there was nothing known about the essence of space and Einstein considered it as a reference frame only. He thus kept with the view of Newton and others that speed is only relative and that there is no Special Reference System. This is of decisive importance in the development of the Theory of Special Relativity.

From this theory we see that the perception of space and time are **subjective**. Two observers, Reuven and Shimon, move in carriages relative to each other, at a fixed speed and on a straight line.

Each of our two observers carries an identical yardstick and clock and they look at each other.

Reuven will find that both Shimon's yardstick and his carriage are shorter than his, and Shimon's clock is slower than his.

Shimon, on the other hand, will see the exact same situation for Reuven.

This is a situation that can only be observed at speeds close to the speed of light.

Of necessarily, there is no real change — This is a completely symmetrical situation. The only change is the observers' perception of space and time which is completely subjective.

Today, this result is accepted by nearly all physicists. It is a major component of the current paradigm of physics.

However, since 1905, when the theory was presented, and Einstein's death in 1955, we have learned several new things about space.

With this new knowledge, me and others conclude that **space** is a **special reference system** and that there is a special meaning for **speed relative to space.**

My understanding is that all bodies, including yardsticks and carriages, in their motion relative to space, undergo a real contraction that increases with their speed.

Clocks in motion undergo a real retardation that increases with their speed.

Adopting this approach removes the subjectivism from the perception of space and time.

No, there is no need to throw out the Theory of Special Relativity. But it should be updated in the spirit of Einstein's teacher**, Lorenz**, who also explained that the **Aether** is a special reference system.

Today the role of the **Aether** is taken by **space**.

The General Theory of Relativity, accepted by all physicists, is the heart of our theory. However, in order to understand it, it is necessary to adopt my geometry of **Deformed Space** that I have created and which we will further discuss in Chapter **G**.

Wheeler (1911 – 2008), a disciple of Einstein, formulated the view that space is the only thing that exists and there is nothing else. Together with his students Misner and Thorne, Wheeler published this essentially intuitive view in a canonical book - Gravitation.

His view, which is actually a TOE, Wheeler called **The Geodynamics** of Space. I have adopted this expression, since my view is similar, and call my model of physical reality:

Spacetime **G**eometro**D**ynamic **M**odel of the physical reality – **GDM.**

Feynman (1918 – 1988) was a disciple of Wheeler. His contribution to science and the teaching of science compares favorably with that of the greatest of his predecessors. He constructed a calculation formalism for fields and, first and foremost, for the electromagnetic field named QUANTUM ELECTRO DYNAMICS - QED. This formalism yielded important results, but Feynman himself admitted that we don't really understand how it works (I recently published an article that explains both why and how).

Based on the success of this formalism came the perception that an elementary particle is an excitation of the field that is associated with it. That a particle is a sort of wave-packet. But on the other hand, it is point-like and structureless.

This determination, which is only a speculation, is an obstacle, since without finite size and structure, it is impossible to build models for particles nor to calculate their properties.

Einstein, Feynman and the Paradigm

Einstein's Special Theory of Relativity, Feynman's calculation formalism, and the accompanying concepts are the main components of the paradigm.

They were useful in building the paradigm and brought many benefits. Today, however, the paradigm must undergo a shift as it is unable to answer the questions shown in the next chapter, and many others that have remained unanswered for decades.

If we consider the Aether and Space (which is not a vacuum, but has properties) to be the same physical entity, then Einstein could have adopted my theory. Note his comments:

Einstein (1920) Ether and the Theory of Relativity

> *... the hypothesis of ether in itself is not in conflict with the special theory of relativity.*

> *... According to the general theory of relativity space without ether is unthinkable;*

C. Some Open Questions in the Paradigm and Why They Are Unresolved

Gravity

Particles and star masses bend space and other masses move according to the bending.

So, what is this bending?

How can a particle, if it is a point, bend space?

How does a particle, if it is a point, feel the bending and know which way to move?

What is attraction or perhaps repulsion between bodies?

Electromagnetism

What is an electrical charge?

Why are there only two types of charge?

What is the attraction and repulsion between chargers?

Why does charge appear in the same and equal portions?

What gives charge its stability?

What is the field of a charge?

And if charge does have size, what is it?

The Electron

What is its structure, if it has one?

Why does it have inertia, that implies mass?

What is the size of the mass?

Why does its mass increase in motion?

Why does it contract in motion, if this is indeed a real contraction?

The Universe

What is dark energy?

What is dark matter?

Why does the universe expand?

Why is the space Euclidian (flat)?

Where is anti-matter?

We will settle for this and mention that **we have all the answers**.

Physicists, who have been long aware of these questions, begin to understand that a new physics is required – a TOE.

Thus, the timing of the appearance of my articles and book is appropriate.

Why Are There No Answers?

There are three Pillars of Physics:

Einstein's   Special Theory of Relativity

Einstein's   General Theory of Relativity

Feynman's   Quantum Field Theory

These theories are the heart of the current Paradigm. They have yielded excellent results so far but are helpless in face of the above questions. We will explain why.

We also explain what to adopt, what should be changed and what needs to be completed to provide answers.

Special Relativity

Special relativity refers to speed (constant velocity) in a straight line as a relative variable (parameter). Reuven moves relative to Shimon as Shimon moves relative to Reuven. One, as if at rest, sees the other in motion.

Note that the speed in a straight line, with no acceleration, does not allow you to know if you are moving at all. In this theory, only relative motion has any meaning.

Such an approach, as we will explain, does not allow us to answer the questions in the above list that refer to an electron.

According to this theory, an observer in one system concludes that in the system of a second observer moving relative to the first observer, both the carriage and the yardstick inside contract and time is dilated. See Fig. (C1) for (Lorentz) **Length Contraction** and Fig. (C2) for (Larmor) **Time Dilation**, as the observer at "rest" observes.

However, the second observer will come to the same conclusions as the first observer. There is full symmetry here and therefore both the length contraction and the time dilation **are not real**. So, what is wrong?

About 25 years after the death of Einstein, it was discovered that space is filled with the noise of electromagnetic waves, with wavelengths of millimeters, a remnant of The Big Bang.

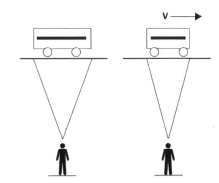

Fig. (C1) Length Contraction

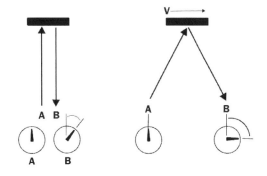

Fig. (C2) Time Dilation

This cosmic background noise is known as the **Cosmic Microwave Background (CMB)** or Thermal Radiation Bath.

The highest amplitude in this radiation has a wavelength of

2 millimeters. When moving relative to the radiation bath, that is, relative to space in which the radiation resides, a shortening of the 2 mm wavelength ensues, looking forward, as a result of the motion.

Looking In the opposite direction, a wavelength increase ensues. The greater the speed, the greater the shift in the wavelength.

From the size of the shift we get the speed relative to space.

This shift in wavelength due to speed is known as the **Doppler Shift.**

The conclusion is that space becomes a **Special Frame** (Universal) and everyone can measure their speed relative to space.

Unfortunately, the community of physicists did not take this fact on board.

With this new knowledge, the speed of the solar system in relation to space was measured. It was found to be about 371 kilometers per second from the cluster of galaxies Aquarius to the cluster of galaxies Leo and Virgo.

This fact that space is a universal framework opens a new approach to the conclusions arising from the Theory of Relativity. In this theory, the shortening of yardsticks and bodies as well as time dilation, which are seen by observers in frames other than their own, is only imaginary. But now, in light of the existence of a Universal system, it is possible to examine the possibility that the shortening of yardsticks and the change in the rhythm of clocks as a result of their speed relative to space is real, Fig. (C3).

This was the opinion of Lorenz, Einstein's mentor. But there was nothing, on which to base his suppositions, and they were rejected.

Today, with the detection of the cosmic background radiation we argue, as we expand below, that we should, in principle, return to Lorenz's approach.

This will open the way to solving the issues that we have raised. The formalism of Einstein's theory will be preserved, but the meaning of the theory, as we have explained, will change beyond all recognition.

Based on the new meaning, we can build a model of the electron and the other particles, and answer the questions that, so far, have had no answers.

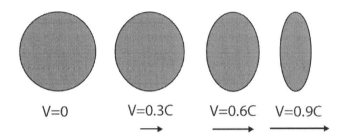

Fig. (C3) Real Contraction of Bodies (C the velocity of light 300,000 km/second)

General Relativity

Einstein himself believed, and said, that general relativity will always be at the heart of any future physics (he did not mention special relativity). Einstein did not know just how right he was and why. To understand his theory, we must learn about the process that preceded its creation. Galileo, is the father of **Kinematics** – the Theory of Motion. He knew how to describe the path of moving bodies, like the Venetian Navy's shells, but did not know why they moved the way they moved.

Newton was the first to add the 'Why' to Galileo's understanding of 'How' bodies moved in the way that Galileo described. Newton showed that the motion of bodies is determined by the forces that bodies apply on each other. This branch of physics is called **Dynamics.**

Tycho Brahe (1541-1601) conducted observations of the solar system's planets and created tables loaded with numbers. **Johannes Kepler (1594-1600)** examined these tables and concluded the kinematics of the planetary motion around the Sun in three laws known as **Kepler's laws**.

So now, a room full of tables has been reduced to just three laws. From Kepler's laws, Newton deduced that a central force applied by the Sun on the stars around dictates their paths. This force is known as Gravity. Newton, like all his contemporaries, thought that space, in which all the bodies move, is empty – vacuum – and without end. **Newton** proved, as a derivative of Kepler's laws, that the force between two bodies, such as the Sun and a planet, is proportional to their masses, and inversely proportional to the square of the distance between them.

This is the Law of **Universal Gravitation**. But how it is that two bodies can affect each other when they are in empty space. And how fast does the effect spread. What this force is and what is its origin was not clear then and is only partly clear today.

It was Einstein, in his Theory of General Relativity, who made a very significant step towards the understanding of gravity, thus allowing me to give the full answers. First of all, he realized that it would make sense to suppose that the bodies were in a real, **non-empty medium**, and that it was this medium that transferred the force of Gravity. Moreover, the speed of the spread of force in the medium is the same as the speed of waves in it. This medium, he determined, is **space**. This is a revolutionary determination. Instead of an empty space without any attributes, that serves as a reference frame only, we now have a non-empty space and can study its properties.

In order to learn about the features of space **Einstein** conducted a **thought experiment** (in the human brain rather than in practice) as described in Fig. (C4). This figure shows identical four carriages in which the following things occur:

In A, in a carriage positioned on the Earth's surface, a stone falls from a top shelf with the acceleration of free fall on to the floor of the carriage. At B the carriage accelerates upward with the same acceleration as free fall. A stone also falls from a top shelf, which is at the same height. The fall time must be the same (and it is indeed), since an observer, watching from inside has no way to know whether it is on the ground or someone is pulling it up with a rope. From this thought experiment, Einstein determined that the response of a mass to gravitation was equivalent to its response to acceleration (inertia). From here (historically I am not precise), we derive the **Equivalence Principle**, the **equivalence of gravitational and inertial mass.**

This law has been confirmed to a very high level of accuracy in many experiments. But it has not yet been proven theoretically, in spite of more than a century that has passed since its discovery. However, I have presented an article that proves that not only are gravitational and inertial mass equivalent, but they are **identical.**

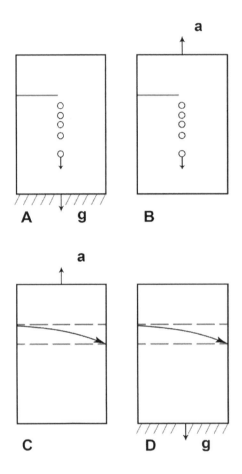

Fig. (C4) A Light Beam in a Gravitational Field

But let us continue.

In C, a light beam is sent from the shelf toward the right wall and parallel to the ceiling. If the carriage is at rest (or in constant motion in a straight line) the beam will hit the wall right in front of it. Both the beam's exit point and contact point are at the same height below the ceiling. If, however, the carriage is accelerated upwards, as the figure shows, the beam will hit the opposite side at a lower point. All this because of the final speed of the beam and the fact that while it is moving to the right the right wall moves upwards. In practice, this experiment is almost impossible because of the enormous speed of light.

From this thought experiment Einstein came in three steps to an amazing conclusion.

Cases A and B show that we cannot know what acceleration we are undergoing, that is, normal acceleration or the acceleration of free fall as the result of gravitation (Einstein, in his day, could not have thought otherwise. See Note at the end of this section). Therefore, of necessity, in case D where the carriage is not accelerated but is positioned on the Earth, it should get the same downward shift.

Eddington exploited a solar eclipse (1919) and demonstrated that a light beam from a distant star was bent as it passed the Sun.

Space is the medium in which a beam of light travels, ostensibly in a straight line. If it bends, it means that the Sun's mass is distorting space - bending it.

As a result of his thought experiment, Einstein concluded that gravity is nothing but bent space. This bending dictates the energy and motion of masses and light beams.

Here is Einstein's equation that expresses this idea:

$$R^{\mu\nu} - 1/2 R g^{\mu\nu} = 8\pi G/C^4 \cdot T_m^{\mu\nu}$$

The right-hand side of the equation represents energy and mass (which today is considered energy and nothing more), while the left-hand side represents bent space.

Einstein asked his friend **Marcel Grossman** to find a way to express the bending of space. His recommendation was the only suitable geometry at the time – **Riemannian geometry.**

Since then, many have tried to turn the equation into a general expression that applies to all the existing fields, not just the Gravitational field – the **Unified Field Formula** – as it is known.

The **first successful attempt**, by me, (note the addition of a new term in the right wing), is shown below:

$$R^{\mu\nu} - 1/2 R g^{\mu\nu} = 8\pi G/C^4 \cdot T_m{}^{\mu\nu} + 4\pi G^{1/2}/s^2 \cdot T_q{}^{\mu\nu}$$

Where S = 1 and [S] = LT^{-1}

So how did it come about, after more than a hundred years, that I now have a **Unified Equation** of gravity and electromagnetism?

The Theory of General Relativity relies on Riemannian Geometry which deals with bent (curved) surfaces (manifolds) and not with deformed spaces. The surface of a ball is, for example, a curved surface. A surface like this is two-dimensional, its curving is in the three-dimensional space, and its geometry is not Euclidean. On the other hand, my new geometry – **Barak Geometry** – deals with a deformed three-dimensional space. On the difference between bent manifolds and deformed spaces see Chapter **E** and **G**. In the Geometry Chapter **H** you will find the explanation of why Barak Geometry serves the General Theory of relativity better than Riemannian. It shows that a star does not bend space around it, as is believed today even though it is impossible to imagine it, but rather contracts space around it.

In addition, in Chapter **J**, I show that the electrical charge and its field are deformed space, and therefore electromagnetism and gravitation have a common denominator. From here the road to a Unified Field Formula (of gravitation and electricity) is long but paved.

By adopting the new geometry, whereas the Riemannian "formalism" remains the same as it was, our perception and understanding of general relativity has changed.

Referring to charge and its field as a spatial deformation creates a common denominator that enables the construction of the Unified Field Formula.

In other words, this provides proof that the gravitational and electromagnetic forces are expressions of a single force, the mechanical stretching and contracting (like a spring) of space.

Unification of all forces is **the proof that they are nothing but the tension of space**

So far, I have considered only the union between gravity and electromagnetism, but there are two more forces, the weak force and strong force. I will look at these forces, which appear to be nothing but electrical in nature, later. I will show that all four forces are expressions the elasticity of space. This reinforces our determination that there is nothing other than space and the only force is its elasticity.

Thus, the above extended equation becomes the equation of all forces, an equation of the macroscopic and microscopic worlds.

Time

Now we consider time as understood by Einstein:

Masses curve space and its curvature dictates the rate of clocks that are at different points in space (that is, dictates "the Flow of Time").

This is explained later on in Chapter **S**, but it is important to emphasize that the field formula refers to both space and time, or space-time. This is not simply a phrase.

Note (relates to previous Reservations) that Motion relative to a source of radiation can be determined, and the speed calculated, using the Doppler Effect. This is the effect in which motion towards a source encounters radiation with a shorter wavelength than at rest relative to the source. Moving from a source, radiation with a longer wavelength is encountered. Today, we know that the Universe is filled with microwave radiation, a relic of the Big Bang. This is called the **Cosmic Microwave Background, CMB**, and we will return to discuss it. The observer of a carriage can open a window and measure their motion relative to space and know that if there is no motion, gravity is working on it and if it is in motion it is accelerated.

For this matter to be fully understood, we suppose that space is filled not with microwave radiation (with a wavelength of millimeters), but with a uniform green radiation (with a wavelength of half a thousandth of a millimeter). If we move quickly relative to space, we will discover that space looks blue (shorter wavelength than green), behind us red (longer wavelength than green) and to the side (perpendicular to our motion) green. Further reservation, and this Einstein should have known, there is no parallel gravitational field to the parallel vertical walls of the carriage since a gravitational field is necessarily radial.

Quantum Field Theory (QFT)

This theory deals with all the elementary particles, but not only them. The first to be studied, were the electron and the photon, this study created **Quantum Electrodynamics - QED**. Today, this theory is part of **Quantum Field Theory- QFT**, and we concentrate on this. This theory was developed, following the contributions of many others, by **Feynman**.

The main idea of this theory is that the force between particles is a result of the exchange of certain force-carrying particles. This means that the force-carrying particle is alternately absorbed and emitted by the other particles.

As an example: between an electron, which carries a negative electrical charge, and a nearby electron, a photon moves back and forth which causes repulsion between them. We know from experience that two charges with the same sign (+) or (-) repel each other, and here we supposedly have an explanation.

To explain attraction between particles with opposite charges such as an electron and a positron (identical to an electron, except for its positive charge) we return to the photon. Of course, it is not reasonable to assume that the exchange can cause both attraction and repulsion, but not to worry, the mathematical formalism of the theory sets things straight.

Thanks to Feynman, this idea gave rise to a mathematical formalism that produced, with the help of Feynman Diagrams, see an example Fig. (C5), excellent results in various fields. In the title of this fig. Feynman expresses his wonder how come that the experimental number that expresses the amplitude of the interaction of a photon with an electron is the square root of the known **fine structure constant** α (**I have the answer**).

Feynman's formalism enabled the introduction of the known **Standard Model of Elementary Particles.**

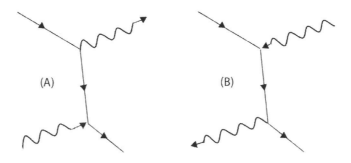

$$-\sqrt{\alpha} \sim -0.08542455\ldots$$

It's one of the greatest damn mysteries of physics: a magic number that comes to us with no understanding by man. you might say the "hand of god" wrote that number, and "we don't know how he pushed his pencil."

Fig. (C5) The Great Riddle

The Standard Model of Elementary Particles

This model has continued to produce results for decades, but some issues remain open. One example, out of many, is the question of the source of inertia of particles (the Higgs particle was supposed to explain inertia, but this explanation is problematic) and the ability to calculate their masses. Knowing how to calculate the masses of elementary particles is the **ultimate test** in physics. So here you are - My calculation, **the only one ever**, of the electron mass:

Electron/Positron Mass M$_e$

$$M_e = \frac{s^2 \sqrt{2}}{\pi(1+\pi\,\alpha)} \cdot \sqrt{G^{-1}\alpha\hbar c^{-3}} \qquad s=1 \; ([s^2] = L^2 T^{-2})$$

α, represents the **Fine Structure Constant.** G, h and c are the known constants. A dimensionality check: $[G^{-1}] = ML^{-3}T^2$ $[\alpha] = 1$

$[\hbar] = ML^2 T^{-1}$ $[C^{-3}] = L^{-3}t^3$ Thus: $M = [s^2 \sqrt{G^{-1}\alpha\hbar c^{-3}}\,] =$

$L^2 T^{-2}(ML^{-3}t^2 \cdot ML^2 T^{-1} \cdot L^{-3}t^3)^{1/2} = l^2t^2(M^2 L^4{}^t T^4)^{-1/2} = l^2t^2 ML^{-2t}T^2 = M$

M$_e$ (**calculated**) = 0.91036 · 10^{-27}gr

M$_e$ (**measured**) = 0.910938356 (11) · 10^{-27}gr

We have here 0.06% accuracy!

So why did the Standard Model stop from bringing results? The reason is simple: This model is based on **QFT**. In this model fields are imbedded in space one for each type of particle. In a given field, like that of the electron and the other particles, every excitation is a particle. Therefore, we have particles that are point-like and structureless. This is exactly **the drawback of the model.**

After all, how does a photon dancing create attraction or repulsion? How does an electron swallow or emit a dancing photon? How can you understand and calculate traits of a particle if it is a point? and more ….

And yet: The mathematical formalism of Feynman is excellent, and if you just ignore his perception of the reality and embrace my own, there are answers to the questions.

Examples of this are given below.

In summary, we have seen that Einstein and Feynman contributed much to the advancement of Physics, but they also raised obstacles. However, with my model - the GDM, their theories continue to be beneficial.

D. The Mission I Took on Myself –

To Build a TOE

In the middle of November 1993, at Palmahim Beach, I dove to "my" cave at 15 meters depth. This time not to go fishing, but to think. A nice fish that looked especially smart, approached me. I asked him what is your view of the world, what is your TOE? He said, "all is water". And what is your worldview? He asked, what is your TOE? "All is space." I replied.

This answer did not happen by chance.

In my second year at the university, I learned the theory of electricity – Maxwell's electromagnetism. I came back and thought about the essence of the elementary charge unit, carried by various particles like the electron. The units of charge are of two types, marked arbitrarily (+) and (−) and with no meaning, other than to distinguish between them. These charges have the property that those with the same symbols repel each other, while those with different symbols attract each other.

I asked myself: this bivalency, the (+) and (−), and this attraction and repulsion, how can we explain it? The following idea occurred to me:

If space is all that there is, then a concentrated contraction can, for example, be a positive charge while an expansion (dilution) be the negative charge. This is how you get the bivalency. As for the repulsion and attraction: A pair of charges with the same sign, whether they are two contractions or two expansions, create (the couple) tension in space that can only be weakened if they distance themselves from each other. And a pair of charges with different signs create tension in space that can only be reduced as they get closer together.

This explanation requires an extension, and our analogy in which space is a spring mattress can help. Let's say the mattress is soft, so the tensions are very low or zero. Note that a spring can be stretched or contracted, and in both cases, tension is created and this also occurs in space. A positive elementary charge is a microscopic contracted area that also contracts its surroundings, a contraction that decreases with distance, and this is the electric field of the charge.

When in space two positive charges are close to each other, the contraction is the sum of the contractions contributed by each charge. For the contraction, and hence the energy, to be reduced the charges must move away from each other – repulsion.

When in space two negative charges are close to each other, they include an expansion that is the sum of the expansions of each charge. For the expansion, and hence the energy, to be reduced the charges must move away from each other – repulsion.

When in space a positive and negative charge are close to each other space contraction by one is canceled by space expansion by the other. For the tensions and the energy of tensions to decline, the charges must come close to each other – hence attraction.

So far, this is a nice explanation by the way of analogy and nothing more. But imagine that I can summarize this story just by one mathematical definition of the **density of electrical charge.**

Moreover, from this definition alone I have derived and proved all of Maxwell's theory of electromagnetism.

Maxwell's theory is a phenomenological theory that rests entirely on experience, while I have constructed the entire theory on logical inferences, based on the above one definition only. This matter has been subject to peer scrutiny, published and is stimulating much interest.

So, I had an idea that space is everything, and I wanted to see if indeed it is. I was motivated and I had both time and means.

Therefore, I decided to devote 25 years (that's what it took), which was supposed to end on my Eightieth birthday, to build the Theory of Everything, the TOE. I declared my intentions to my spouse, sons and friends.

It was a crazy decision, because, after all, what could be my chance of success?

So why did I think I might be a person (a person and not the person) suitable for the task? I derived the confidence that I am the right person by looking back at my life. I completed a doctorate at the

Hebrew University of Jerusalem with a research thesis in Physics (on the essence of light). To the dismay of my tutor and mentor Prof. Yatsiv, I did not continue in academia. I had, from early childhood, already found a much more important task that concerned the security of the State of Israel. I was able to successfully complete this task.

From this success, I have derived the courage, technological knowledge, experience in leading people, and thinking out of the box, that is necessary to establish a start-up company.

And indeed, based on one of my inventions, I founded one of the first hi-tech companies in Israel. I turned it into a multinational company, that was eventually sold for billions of dollars. I went on to establish other companies.

So, what does all this have to do with physics? You may be surprised to learn that even scientific communities are influenced by the spirit of time – the **Zeitgeist**, and they have characteristic elements in sociology and the psychology of communities.

The variety of my life experiences has enabled me to understand these elements in the community of physicists, and to understand how they have shaped the paradigms of both the past and the present. And, in particular, to understand where the mines are laid.

An example is the dispute between Lorenz and his disciple Einstein that was resolved in favor of the latter. Was this dispute affected by the spirit of Logical Positivism, also called Logical Empiricism, that arose in Vienna at that time – I wonder.

There are, of course, more examples, but I will hold back.

The majority of scientists make use of the basic principles they have learned and read. These elements are considered to be almost impossible to appeal. But despite their training and talents, they are sometimes faced with a wall, problems that refuse to be resolved. Only a few scientists are able to breach this wall.

As an example, consider the orbit of the hot planet, Mercury, revolving around the Sun. Calculating its path using Newton's Law of Gravitation gives a result that deviates slightly from observations.

Only after many years, Einstein adopted an alternative theory to that of Newton, General Relativity, to show that calculation correlates to observation. Newton's theory, however, does not have to be discarded, it is an approximation, which follows General Relativity for the case of weak gravitation.

And another reason why I thought I might be suitable for the task.

I have never been an academic, anxious for his position, and afraid of exceeding the paradigm and hence being known as a crackpot.

While I am not an academic, over the years I have kept myself fit, not only physically but also professionally. Step by step, towards the 23rd year, since I started my project, I was able to calculate the masses of the elementary particles and found them to fit the experimental results.

In physics, this is the determining factor: Do you know how to calculate things, that so far no one has succeeded. Therefore, I believed that my project was proceeding successfully, and it was time to publish my work in a series of scientific articles. I have published

22 complex, professional scientific articles, which have received considerable attention.

This is nice, it proves there is interest, **but no more than that**. Real recognition is a long and painful matter when it comes to overcoming common perceptions.

Aristotle's Paradigm ruled for 1800 years before Galileo disproved it with the fall of bodies from the tower in Pisa.

Archimedes, in his book the Sand Reckoner, presented a model of the solar system, where the planets revolve around the Sun and not around the Earth.

This model was forgotten and only about 1800 years later the scientific world started to take an interest in the heliocentric model of Copernicus. In these matters, it seems, a lot of patience is required - something I have in abundance.

The day that marked 25 years since I began the project, was, as I had planned my 80th birthday. On the same day I published my eBook which is a collection of my articles that I had published till then, under the title:

A Spacetime GeometroDynamic Model (GDM) of the Physical Reality

In Hebrew, the name of my book begins with the word **Model**, so what is a model?

We have already used this word but in a more intuitive way.

A model is a collection of mathematical equations and geometric descriptions that refer to variables (parameters) and constants. Models are applicable in all sciences. In physics, variables and constants are physical quantities.

In our model we express all the physical quantities using just the density of space. We use only two units: a unit of length – for example a centimeter, and a unit of time – for example a second.

Some examples of a model

A model of the number of daily infections of the corona virus in a given city.

Constants: The city's area, the number of residents, their ages and background diseases, the number of apartments, their distribution by area and the number of rooms.

Variables: The distance between people.

Equations: Infection by the virus as a function of the distance between people. Infection by the virus as a function of age etc.

A model of the Solar system should predict the planetary trajectories.

Constants: The masses of the Sun and the planets and their locations in relation to the Sun.

Variables: Distances

Equations: Newton's Law of Universal Gravitation

The Objective of a model:

To create a concise language to describe the phenomena – **reductionism.**

Describe causal relationships – **Understanding.**

Predict phenomena that have not yet been observed - **specificity and test of validity.**

On Causality and Reductionism

From the dawn of humanity, we have sought to know the cause of the events that surround us, are with us and are inside us.

At the heart of this desire is the understanding that every result has a reason -**the principle of causality**.

In the event of an occurrence that consists of a complex of sub-occurrences, we seek to know if there is a primary reason.

This is the desire to reduce a multitude of things to a minimum-**reductionism**. We also want to know what objects around us, and we ourselves, are made of.

We recognize that these objects may consist of individual objects, which are themselves not complex. These objects are referred to as **elementary objects**.

This is the recognition that a complex object can be presented as a number of fundamental objects, once again - reductionism. It is the striving to reduce a multitude of things to the simplest possible object.

The ancient Greeks, for example, thought that there are four elementary things: Earth, air, water, and fire. The Greek **Democritus** later raised the explanation that materials are composed of basic particles, which are indivisible – **atoms.** Today, physicists believe that various atoms (more than a hundred) are built from a limited number of elementary particles. The number of elementary particles in atoms and others is 15 and with the anti-particles 29. We will see that some of them are not elementary at all.

The ancients also believed that the cause of reason was the will of the gods. But the aspiration to reductionism gave rise to faith in one God - **monotheism**. It was the **Akhenaten** the Egyptian, Judaism, Christianity, and Islam that preached this belief. Believers in monotheism are divided on many subjects, but we are interested in the dispute as to whether God (if there is one) is outside of the universe and dominates it – **transcendental**, or is the universe itself, as was the opinion of the philosopher Spinoza and others. This view is called **pantheism**.

In this book we present, simply and briefly, the possibility of extreme reductionism in recognition of physical reality. This option is also in favor for pantheism.

Science

Science is the subject of research that builds **models** that are meant to be compatible with reality. Psychology, sociology, chemistry, medicine, and of course, physics are examples of this.

Mathematics, on the other hand, is an art, the result of thoughts that can be completely detached from reality.

Truth

Physics does not deal with **truth**, which is the absolute determination that this is the way things are and there is no room for further investigation.

So, because for every reason there is a previous reason, the chain be infinite. Either way, all that physics does is the construction of models with temporary validity (**tentative**) that match reality in a one to one correspondence (**isomorphism**).

When a new phenomenon is discovered that does not support the model its validity expires.

Geometrodynamics is the second word in the name of my model and it refers to my main idea that there is nothing other than space. We expand on this issue in the next chapter.

E. Geometrodynamics and the Character and Purpose of this Book

When your research leans on the common and well-known Paradigm you do analytic work. When you want to explore the **unknown and outside the paradigm**, you must activate your imagination and make speculations that are not accepted so that you can build a new model of reality. A model whose validity is tested by applying it to reality. And the test of its benefits is its ability to predict new phenomena and to provide original insights.

In my model of reality, **there is nothing other than space**.

Meaning that every object in the universe whether a table, electron, we ourselves, the stars or the galaxies, are made from the elastic, cellular space which is made of cells that can resize themselves — See Fig. (E1) and Fig. (E2).

That's why I want to say that any material particle, for example, is a type of deformation, such as the contracting or the expanding of space – see Fig. (E3) and Fig. (E4). This disturbance is of a finite size in its expansion or contraction and **passes through space.** Meaning that what passes is the just shape of this particle, its geometry, and nothing else. Hence the expression Geometrodynamics.

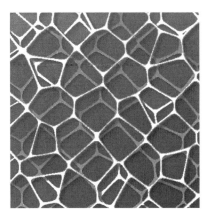

Fig. (E1) Cellular Space

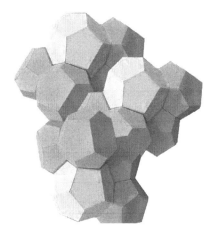

Fig. (E2) Kelvin's Cellular Space made of Octahedrons

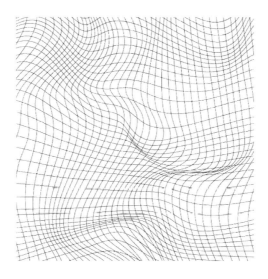

Fig. (E3) A Deformed Cellular Space

There is theoretical evidence that space is cellular and it has to do with space energy density calculations. The idea that space is elastic is a conclusion of General Relativity, and more so with my geometry.

Space as a Lattice

By attributing a cellular structure to space, we can explain its expansion, its elasticity and can introduce a cut-off in the wavelength of the vacuum state spectrum of its vibrations. Without this limitation on the wavelength, infinite energy densities arise. The need for a cut-off is addressed by **Sakharov**, **Misner** et al, and by **Zeldovich**. In addition, the **Bekenstein Bound** sets a limit to the information available about the other side of the horizon of a black hole. **Smolin** argues that:

There is no way to reconcile this with the view that space is continuous for that implies that each finite volume can contain an infinite amount of information.

I relate to space as a 3D elastic, deformable lattice, rather than a bent manifold. I have created a new geometry applicable for these 3D elastic, deformable lattices.

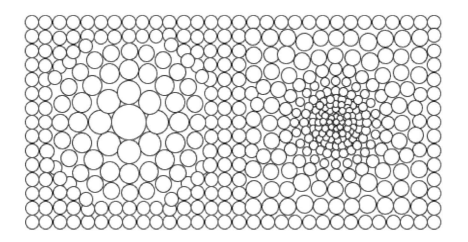

Fig. (E4) Electrical Charge: Left Negative - Right Positive

Fig. (E4) shows a two-dimensional representation of an elementary electrical charge that in reality is three-dimensional.

It is also possible to see the figure as the cross-section of the charge.

Let a sphere with a radius of several cells from the center represents the charge. The cells outside this circle are then considered the electric field of the charge. No sharp boundary between the charge and its field

A movement of the charge and its field to the right means that the cells remain in place and only the deformation moves to the right. This is Geometrodynamics.

This is undoubtedly not simple to take in – the idea that we ourselves are not matter but rather a moving geometry.

This model is the maximum possible reductionism.

This possibility, on the face of it, and especially for those who are not physicists, may be seen as deluded and unacceptable. Only physicists have the tools to examine the validity of the model. The general public can only be impressed by the fact that this is the maximum simplicity - **the Ultimate Beauty**.

From this determination that there is nothing foreign to space and there is nothing but space we want to create a new, concise and comprehensive description of the physical reality for the general public. This work is based on 25 years of research and has recently been published in 22 scientific articles and a book mainly in the journal HAL, see Chapter **W**. These publications can also be found on my web site,

https://cv.archives-ouvertes.fr/shlomo-barak.

The nature of the above kind of study is accepted by the community of theoretical physicists. I first asked myself, what is the most reductionist model of reality possible. I came to the conclusion that space is everything. Then I asked whether it was possible to invent the existing physics and beyond, while testing its compatibility with reality.

The invention of a model, using one's imagination, was **Einstein's** recommendation for the theoretical physicist.

In this matter, physics differs from other sciences. In medicine, the medical researcher recognizes the relevant biology. In biological research, the relevant chemistry, and in chemistry, the relevant physics.

But in physics where will you go?   It's endless. You're in the underworld. You already know (I think that I know) an elementary electric charge is a contraction or a dilation moving in space. You know that the space is cellular and elastic, but from what is it made, and what happens in a black hole. Can space rupture, what happened in the Big Bang? There are endless questions still open, still awaiting answers. That's what makes physics different, and that's what makes me so happy. It takes imagination and courage to fight for your opinion against the accepted one.

F. On Physical Reality

In this chapter, which you might find exhausting, we discuss the key concepts that will be required below.

The Essence of Space

In the past, space was considered a reference frame only — a frame for the objects in it. Take out the objects and space become meaningless. Today, most physicists are convinced that space is a kind of material entity, a cellular structure which has features similar to an elastic medium.

We know that our universe is expanding. We know that it is deformed (General Relativity). And this is, of course, tangible evidence of its being elastic. We know theoretically that it is cellular. We know a few more things, but nothing about its essence, from what is space made. And yet this limited knowledge is sufficient to justify our model of reality.

Dimensions of Space

There are just three dimensions of space. We have no need of multiple dimensions, as String Theory suggests.

Space Waves

An elastic space, of necessity, vibrates - that is it creates waves. Such waves are transverse waves and longitudinal waves, see below. All physicists agree, however, that gravitational waves, which have recently been discovered, are indeed transverse waves.

We claim that the electromagnetic waves – waves of Light, Radar, X-rays, Radio, etc. are also transvers waves of space. The transverse and longitudinal waves have different motion speeds.

Waves in General and the Transverse and Longitudinal Waves in Particular

Waves occur in a media. The media does not move. Waves are a disturbance in the media, which can be a local change in density or a local change, back and forth, of the media's components. It is this disturbance that is in motion.

In a pool of calm water, the surface of the water is flat. Dropping a stone in the center of the pool causes the water at the point of impact to move up and down relative to the calm waters. This is the disturbance that moves out towards the pool's banks.

The height and depth that the water rises above and below the level of the calm water is the **amplitude**, and the distance between two peaks of the wave is the **wavelength**. The time that elapses between one peak and the next is the **period time,** and the number of cycles that occur in a unit of time is the **frequency**. In this example, we use the dimensions of length, measured in inches or meters. In the case of an electric wave we use the dimensions of voltage, measured in Volts.

On a Transverse Wave

The example above is approximately that of a transvers wave.

In the case of a transverse space wave the up and down motion is due to the contraction and dilation of the space cells perpendicularly to the direction of propagation of the wave. The amplitude in this case is given in units of length.

On a Longitudinal Wave

A longitudinal wave is a contraction and expansion of the medium (a change of its density) along the direction of propagation and alternately this disturbance moves at a speed that exceeds that of a transverse wave moving in the same medium.

In this case, amplitude expresses the size of the change in density. A sound wave is a longitudinal wave in the air.

A spatial wave is the movement of local contractions and expansions of the medium's cells.

Wave Packages

Waves of different frequencies can form, in one small area, contractions or expansions of space, or swing between the two states. This disturbance in space necessarily moves at the speed of the waves. Such disturbance is called a **Wave Packet.**

Distorted Space and its Geometry (With a Hint of General Relativity)

Cellular space means a space consisting of cells. And elastic space means a distorted space that in part is expanding and in part is contracting. Expanding – the space cells are growing, contracting – the space cells are shrinking.

In such a space there is no use for the geometry of Euclid, which relates only to a uniform (**homogenous**) space, which is also the same in any direction (**isotropic**), see Fig. (F1). We need, therefore, a new geometry. In the new geometry, for example, the sum of the triangle's angles needs not necessarily be 180 degrees. The ratio between the circumference of the circle and the diameter need not necessarily be π =3.14

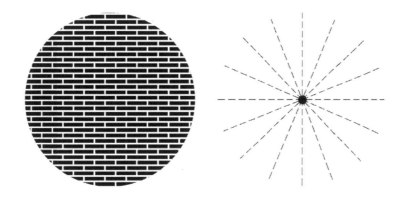

FIG. (F1) Left - Homogeneity   Right - Isotropy

Space Cells

Space cells are extremely small. They have never been seen and their lengths have not been measured. Theoretical estimates put their length – Plank's length – at trillions and trillions of times smaller than the length of the hydrogen atom.

Space Density

Space density is the number of space cells in a volume unit (e.g. cubic centimeters). The density of space is represented by the Greek letter:

ρ

The Elementary Particles

The material elementary particles, on which we expand later, incorporate an elementary charge, which is a longitudinal wave packet.

Longitudinal wave packets are characterized by being a contraction or expansion of space, or a swinging between the two modes (oscillation). Such particles are not strangers to space –they are wave packets that travel at the speed of a longitudinal wave.

In today's physics, the elementary particles are perceived as point-like and structureless. We, however, prove that they have a finite volume and a defined structure.

Rest and Motion

A material elementary particle, such as the electron, if it is in the state of "rest" relative to space, of necessity, it moves in a circle with the speed of a longitudinal wave. The center of the circle, which is a geometric point only, is at rest in relative to space.

A non-material particle, such as a photon, moves in a "straight" line (a geodesic), that curves with space, and the speed of a transverse wave.

Therefore, there is no rest – only movement relative to space at the speed of the waves. There are only two speeds, that of transverse waves and that of longitudinal waves.

Yardsticks and Distance

The distance between two points is measured using a yardstick.

We could, in theory, use a space cell as a yardstick.

In this case the distance between two points is the number of space cells between them on a straight line (or a geodesic).

If space is homogenous and isotropic – Euclidian as it is customary to call it - then between two points there is only one straight line, and therefore the distance is well defined.

If, however, space is deformed (not Euclidian) then it is possible to bridge the two points in different ways with different lengths. The shortest length, that is the smallest number of cells make up its length, is called the **Geodesic** line.

In a deformed space the size of the cells along the path is not necessarily uniform, but only their number is relevant.

There is also the possibility that a surface is curved, like that of a ball. In this case the cells are equal in size, and the geodesic line is that of the Arc of a Great Circle – the circle that is centered on the center of the ball and passes through the two points.

The Yardstick and the Distance as Seen by Different Observers

A uniform yardstick (standard) is a yardstick that has an equal number of space cells along its length. Observers in various places in space could, in principle, count cells to determine if the yardstick they are holding is standard or not. Note that in various places in space the sizes of space cells might differ, but the length of the yardstick is determined by their number only.

But a cell count is impossible. So how can these observers make measurements, and communicate between themselves, if they are at distant points in a deformed space, where its cells can have different sizes?

It is important to understand that not only space or the yardstick is deformed but so is the observer who is also made of cells.

An observer may not know anything from the study of their immediate surroundings, for example that they are themselves deformed, contracted, or expanded, relative to somewhere else in space. They may be able to know, if they investigate their larger environment that will reveal any deformation in space around them.

As an example, compare the measurements of an observer in a space station with those of an observer on a planet (Earth for example). The observer in the space station was equipped, before going into space, with the same yardstick as the observer on the planet.

We know, and will expand on this later, that a star deforms the space around it (gravitation). This deformation is reduced as the distance from the star increases.

Observing each other from a distance, they will both agree that, on the face of it, the observer in space has a longer yardstick than the observer on the planet as the cells in their expanded space are larger.

Such a view is not necessary today since the Theory of General Relativity enables the calculation of the phenomenon.

Barak's Geometry as Opposed to Riemannian Geometry

General relativity is based on Riemannian geometry, which deals with curved surfaces (manifolds) and not deformed spaces. The surface of a ball is, for example a curved surface. A surface like this is two-dimensional manifold, embedded in a three-dimensional space, and its geometry is not Euclidian.

On the other hand, our new geometry, Barak's Geometry, deals with deformed 3D spaces. Chapter **H** explains why Barak's serves the Theory of General Relativity more successfully than Riemann's. It shows that a star does not bend the space around it, as is believed today — but really cannot be imagined, but rather contracts space around it.

Clocks and Time

We don't know what is time, we only know what is motion, as the Greek philosopher Aristotle also believed. We can construct devices that are called clocks, in which the movement of the dials depict the "passage of time." Each cycle of the clock represents a unit of time. The measurement of the elapsed time between events is a measure of the number of time cycles that have elapsed between the events. We cannot attribute to time any meaning. We can only use the concept of time as a reference to the above.

Clocks and Time as Seen by Different Observers

We know, and there is experimental confirmation, that the rate of a clock is influenced by the spatial deformation. The same clock in a contracted space is slow, while in an expanded space – fast. That is, the same timepiece, in a space station, will be faster than if on the Earth. As a result, measuring time between events by different observers, one in space and the other on the Earth, will yield different results. The GPS system takes it into account; hence, it is so accurate.

Velocity and Acceleration

Distance and time are considered fundamental properties of reality. Therefore, the velocity that is the division of distance by time is considered to be resultant.

Since we hold that only movement has meaning, not time, we choose distance and speed as the fundamental properties of reality.

Acceleration is an increase of speed and deacceleration a reduction.

Velocity is relative. This was clear to Newton, and as such it is also considered by Einstein in his Theory of Special Relativity. I agree, but consider space to be a special reference system and that velocity relative to space affects bodies.

This velocity relative to space can be measured by the Doppler Shift of the Cosmic Microwave Background (CMB) radiation.

Speed of Light

The speed of light is the speed of an electromagnetic wave in space. This is also the speed of its particles – photons. I will further discuss electromagnetism and photons but for now, I only mention that I will show that electromagnetic waves are transverse waves of space.

Yardsticks and Clocks in Motion

I show that bodies, in their motion relative to space, contract as their spccd incrcascs and that clocks slow down.

These are real changes. In the Theory of Special Relativity, these are only imaginary changes.

Endless Space and its Universes

I assume that space is endless. In a tiny part of it is our universe, which we know is finite, with a well-known and well-defined radius and a measurable and well-known rate of expansion. Therefore, I assume that it is possible that there are many other universes in space.

Laws of Nature

A law of nature is a mathematical connection between physical quantities, which is always valid – at anytime and anywhere for all those who examine it. An example is the Laws of Electromagnetism.

I demonstrate that, given all we have shown so far, I can logically deduce all the laws of nature. This is contrary to the conventional understanding that these laws are **phenomenological** - deduced from experiment and observation only, and that they are laws whose source is unclear.

Constants of Nature

Constants of Nature are physical quantities, whose values when measured, are the same for anytime and anywhere. And for all who measure them. An example of a constant of nature is the speed of light.

It is customary to believe that there are some twenty constants of nature. We suggest that there are only four.

The Speed of Light as a Constant of Nature

We return to the observers on the space station and on the Earth. In space the yardstick is longer, and the clock is faster than on the Earth, where the yardstick is shorter and the clock slower. Although, originally both yardsticks and clocks were the same.

This is because on Earth space is denser than far away in space. The speed of light can be measured as follows: Let light pass along a yardstick from end to end and we measure its transition time. In space the light transverses a longer distance but the transition time is also longer because the clock is ticking faster. On Earth light transverses a shorter distance with a shorter transition time because the clock is ticking slower. In both cases, dividing the distance by the transit time gives the same result, the speed of light and therefore I refer to it as a constant of nature.

Note that the number of clock cycles, or beats, between two events determines the length of time between them. A fast rate indicates a long time while a slow rate indicates a short time. In the case of a non-deformed space, for two observers moving relative to space, one at a greater speed than the other, we get exactly the same situation and the same result as before. The fast observer is like an observer on Earth, while the slow observer is like an observer in space.

Symmetry in Nature and the Laws of Conservation

Emmy Noether proved the connection between symmetry in Nature and the Laws of Conservation.

We provide some examples:

Symmetry of displacement in time - the same occurrence (phenomenon) exactly repeats itself periodically (and remains fixed in time). In this case, the Law of **Energy Conservation** is held.

We compress a spring and tie it so that it does not open. Then it will remain so for a minute, an hour, a day, a year, and there is a **symmetry of displacement in time**. But the spring remains contracted, and so does the energy of contraction, and it is really the Conservation of Energy.

If a particular phenomenon exactly repeats itself, independent of its position in space, this is a **symmetry of displacement in space**, and in this case the Law of **Conservation of Linear Momentum** is held.

A body (particle) with a mass, is in rapid (uniform) motion on a straight line. In this case, the body has linear momentum which is the product of its mass and its speed.

If, in every place in space (symmetrical displacement), the mass (a scalar) is the same, and speed - its value and direction (a vector) is the same, then their multiplication that gives **the linear momentum** (a vector) is the same everywhere and **conservation of the linear momentum** is held.

If a particular phenomenon is preserved on rotation – **rotational symmetry** –then **circular momentum is conserved.**

It seems so simple - what is there to prove? It's hard for me to explain.

Please note, in the eyes of theoretical physicists, these are just words. Words do not convince them, the language of physics is mathematics, not English or Hebrew.

An additional symmetry that exists in nature relates to the laws of nature. Consider, for example, a particular occurrence, in a given frame, according to a certain Law of Nature. If the same occurrence occurs in a frame moving with fixed speed, in a straight line relative to the first frame, and obeys the same law, then there is a valid symmetry of the same law in both frames and in all of the frames that move relative to one another.

Such symmetry exists for Maxwell's laws of electromagnetism but not for Newton's laws, and therefore Einstein was forced to modify them.

Transition Law – **Transformation** – which determines how an occurrence in a given frame appears in a second frame, is called **Boost.**

An example of a Boost is a law according to which a particle at rest in a co-ordinate frame appears as a moving particle, at some speed along a straight direction, in another frame.

The Universe

Our universe (probably) has spherical symmetry and a known radius that is growing with time. This radius at the time of the big bang, which started the expansion, was almost a point. This universe contains ordinary material, radiation and mysterious Dark Matter, and Dark Energy. The quantitative ratio between them is measured and well known. But what is dark matter remains dark for almost 80 years and dark energy for 40 years.

The endless space, that includes our universe and others and all that happens in it, I call the Cosmos.

G. The New Geometry of the Deformed Space Lattice

Riemannian geometry is the mathematics of the Theory of General Relativity. This geometry deals with curved manifolds (explanation below).

The Theory of General Relativity focuses on our 3-D space and proves to us that it is a curved 3-D manifold in a 4-D hyperspace (this has nothing to do with the dimension of Time) and achieves excellent results. We **cannot imagine** this curving in 4-D, but we can make calculations.

Physicists have become accustomed to this situation. But this is precisely why they cannot solve various problems which we will discuss and solve.

Therefore, we present a **new geometry** with concepts such as those of the Riemannian geometry and with the same calculation formalism, but in contrast can be imagined and, hence, be useful in resolving the open issues.

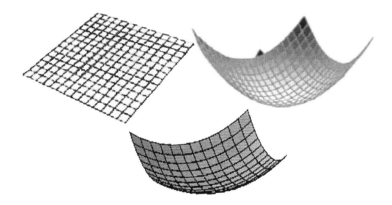

Fig. (G1) Manifolds: Plane (Euclidian) & Bent (Un Euclidian)

The new geometry assumes that space is cellular, that space consists of cells. There is no reason that space in Riemannian geometry should not be considered cellular as well, but it does not make any difference.

The difference between the two geometries is double:

In the new geometry, the infinite global space is Euclidian, three-dimensional and elastic. But this elasticity is manifested mainly locally.

Being an elastic, deformed space means a change in the size of its cells. Thus, this space is no longer Euclidian (see explanation below). Note that in infinite space a local volume is an electron, the Earth, and even our universe, which is finite.

In Riemannian geometry, the global space is also three dimensional, **but if it is cellular, then the cells retain their size.** Our three-dimensional space is an elastic three-dimensional manifold that can be curved within a four-dimensional hyperspace.

Here we are getting lost, our imagination just can't handle it. But the mathematical formalism is valid and working. There is something here that does not match with common sense: if the manifold is deformed how can the cell size be maintained?

After reading the material below, it is advised to reread this introduction from the beginning of the chapter.

Riemannian Geometry

A curved single-dimensional line in a

two - dimensional plane

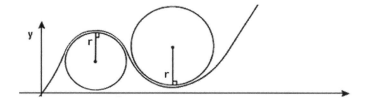

Fig. (G2) a Curved Line on a Plane

At a point, where the line is curved, a circle is tightly pressed to the curve – an **Osculatory circle**. The circle's radius at this point is called the **radius of curvature**. The smaller the radius the larger the curvature. The curvature of a line is termed positive if the osculatory circle is below the line and negative if above.

A Curved (2-D) Manifold in (3-D) Space

The two - dimensional manifold in Fig. (G3) is the surface of a ball. This manifold is curved, a positive curvature in a three-dimensional space. The radius of the osculatory circle, which is pushed to the point P is the radius R_0 of the ball

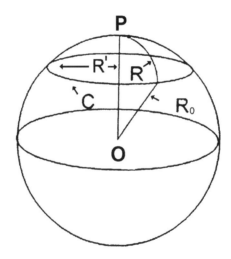

Fig. (G3) A Positively Curved manifold IN 3D SPACE

The smaller this radius, the greater is the curvature. If the manifold is not necessarily the surface of a ball, for example an ellipsoid, then take the largest osculatory radius, **R** and multiply it by smallest osculatory radius R. This product, **RR**, is the square of the average radius, while

K = 1/**RR** is the **Gaussian Curvature** of the manifold at point P. This curvature is considered positive since the two radii are from the same side of the manifold.

This is all valid for us, as observers outside the manifold, but within the 3-dimentional space around. A flat, two-dimensional observer on the surface of the ball, cannot see that this surface is curved. This observer will be able to realize that its manifold is curved only if they perform the following measurements on it:

Measure the distance from the point P to the circle whose circumference, C, is also measured.

The distance to the circle is its measured radius, R. Assuming that the manifold is flat, the radius that is calculated according to Euclidian geometry should be: R' = C/2π

If R = R'   the manifold is flat.

If R > R'   the observer on the manifold knows that the curvature is positive.

The **excess radius** is $\delta r = R - R' > 0$

There is a one-to-one mathematical correspondence between the excess radius and the Gaussian curvature. Therefore, an observer on the manifold and an outside observer will agree on the manifold's geometry.

Fig. (G4) Negative Bent Manifold Around Point P

In Fig. (G4) a negatively curved manifold appears around the point P. At this point, on the saddle appears a section of an osculatory circle (radius **R**), that faces upward and a similar section (radius R) that faces downward.

Since they are on either side of the manifold, the curvature is considered to be negative. The average of the radius squared, as in the previous case, is the product of the radii of these circles, and the Gaussian curvature is also the same as earlier but with a negative sign:

$K = -1/\mathbf{R}R$.

This is our conclusion as external observers. The inner observer, located on the manifold should again make measurements around P. They would see that the calculated R' the result of dividing the circumference of the circle around P by 2π, is greater than the measured R. Thus,

$\delta r = R - R' < 0$

and again, the observer residing on the manifold and exterior observer agree on the nature of the curvature of the manifold.

Everything is fine, but how can you imagine a 3-D curved manifold in a 4-D hyperspace? Well, we remind you, you can't.

The New Barak Geometry

Fig. (G5) shows a deformed plane in the sense that around the point P space cells are growing. Note, that each circle represents a spatial cell or a set of spatial cells.

For the two - dimensional observer on the plane, and even for us outside viewers, to learn about the geometry of this two-dimensional space, we must make measurements. We note that, in contrast to the case of the manifolds, here the two internal and external observers see and measure the same reality.

From the center, we move on a straight line and count the cells, in Fig. (G5) there are 8. This is the measured radius - 8 units of length. From the eighth cell we move along the circumference of the circle and count its cells – 36 longitudinal units.

The measured radius is R = 8 and the measured circumference is C = 36, but the calculated radius R' is:

$$R' = 36/2 \pi = 5.86$$

and therefore, the excess positive radius is:

$\delta R = R - R' > 0$

Thus, Fig. (**G**5) represents a positive deformed space around P.

It is also possible to say that in case of a positive deformation the ratio between the circumference and the measured radius is less than 2π, that is: C/R= 36/8 = 4.5 < 2π

$R_{measured} = 8$

$C_{measured} = 36$

$C/R = 36/8 = 4.5 < 2\pi$

$R_{measured} > R_{calculated}$

The Excess Radius

$\delta = R_{measured} - R_{calculated} > 0$

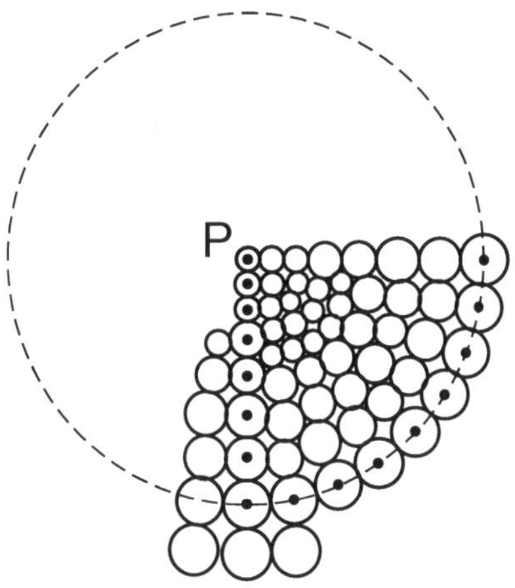

Fig. (G5) A Cellular Plane with Positive Deformation

Fig. (G6) shows a deformed plane in the sense that around the point P space cells are getting smaller. Note, that each circle represents a spatial cell or a set of spatial cells.

Here too we move from the center on a straight line and count the cells; in Fig. (G6) they number 8. This is the radius that we measured - eight units of length. From the eighth cell we move along the circumference of the circle and count the number of cells of which there are 64 - the number of longitudinal units.

$R_{MEAs} = 8$

$C_{meas} = 64$

$C/R = 10.2 > 2\pi$

$R_{MEAs} < R_{Cal}$

The Excess Radius

$\delta = R_{MEAs} - R_{Cal} < 0$

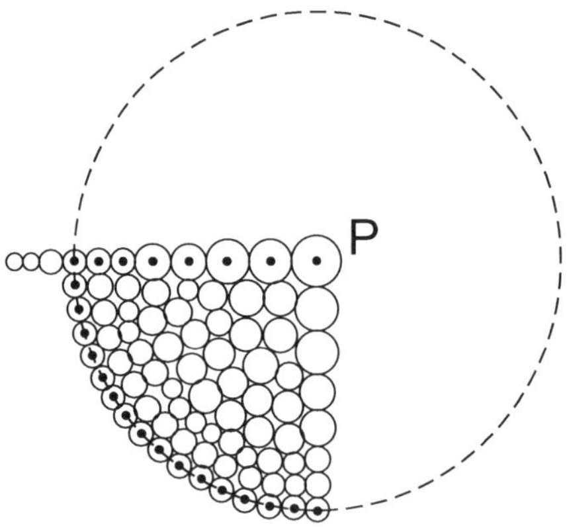

Fig. (G6) A Cellular Plane with Negative Deformation

The measured radius is R = 8 and measured circumference is:

C = 64, but the calculated radius R' is:

R' = 64/2 π = 10.2

and therefore, the excess radius is negative:

δr = R − R' < 0

Thus Fig. (G6) represents a negative deformed space around P.

It is also possible to say that, for a negative deformation the ratio between the circumference and the measured radius is greater than 2π, that is:

C/R = 64/8 = 8 >2π

Recall: in an **undeformed** space, cells are equal and Euclidian geometry is valid.

So far, we have looked at the concepts in the different geometries, and found that there is no need for any change in the Theory of General Relativity. It is, however, essential to understand its meaning, see the next Chapter.

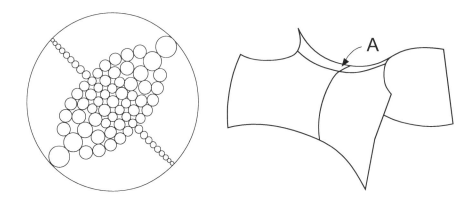

Fig. (G7) A Saddle as a 2D Manifold (Right) and as a 2D Deformed Space (Left)

Geodesic Line

On a warped (curved) manifold, the shortest distance between two points, A and B, is not, as we might think, a straight line. The shortest line is the **Geodesic line**. In the case of the surface of a ball, it is the arc of a great circle, whose center is that of the ball, and goes through points A and B.

For the case of a deformed 2-D space, Fig. (G8) shows, for an observer in this space, the shortest distance between A and B is not the dashed line, whose length is 7-cells plus two half cells, but rather the solid line whose length is 5-cells plus two half cells.

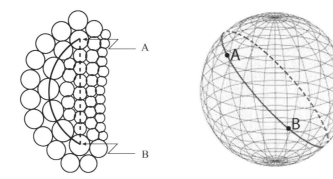

Fig. (G8) A Geodesic on a Spherical Surface (Right) and on a Deformed 2D Space (Left)

Parallel Transport of Vectors on A Curved Manifold and in A Deformed Space

Parallel Transport on a Manifold

This sub-Section is only for experts in geometry (taken from one of my books)

Fig. (7-5) shows the parallel transport of a vector on the surface of a sphere, where parallel transport means that both the tip and the back of the vector are equally displaced along the geodesic. We now transport a vector from O to P, and back through P'. The vector turns through an angle $\delta\vartheta$ so that $\mathbf{v}' = \mathbf{v} + \delta\mathbf{v}$. The curvature, k,

of the surface is defined in terms of δv as the vector, v, is moved

around an infinitesimal closed path with an infinitesimal area, σ.

(7-47) $\delta V = KV$

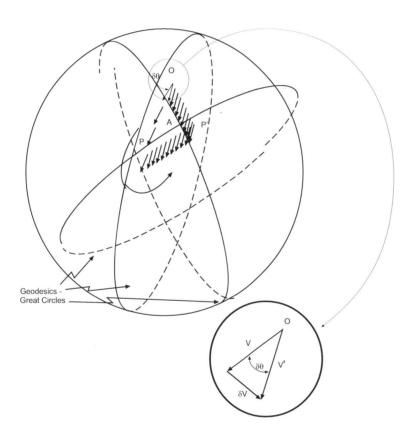

Fig. (7-5) Parallel Transport on a manifold

For a spherical surface with radius r, the curvature is $k = 1/r^2$.

Note that when a vector, v, is parallel transported along a geodesic,

116

the angle subtended by the vector and the geodesic (i.e., the tangent of the geodesic) is unchanged.

Parallel Transport in an Elastic Space

Fig. (7-6) shows a deformed two-dimensional space or a two-dimensional cross-section of a higher dimension elastic space. The transport from O to P directly, or via P', yields an angle $\delta\vartheta$, and

$$\delta V = Kv\sigma \qquad \text{the same as (7-47)}$$

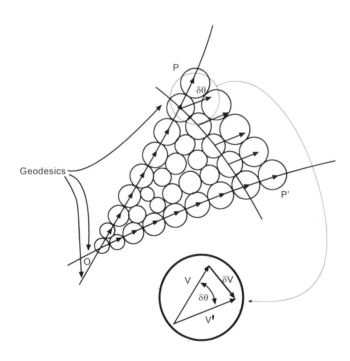

Fig. (7-6) Parallel Transport in a deformed space

117

On Another Difference Between the Two Geometries

On a curved manifold, it is possible that in the vicinity of a point there will be additional points with the same curvature.

On the surface of a ball, for example, there will be the same curvature around all the points on it. This characteristic is known as **global curvature.**

In a deformed space, if there is contraction or expansion around a point, then around adjacent points the deformation is, of necessity, different. This is known as a **local deformation.**

Adopting my geometry, with local deformations, enables the solving of a serious problem in cosmology.

The Flat Universe Problem

From observations and measurements cosmologists concluded that space in our universe is a three-dimensional manifold without curvature, **flat** in their language, that is **Euclidian**.

The problem of the cosmologists is that they do not understand how, from all possible curvatures, nature "chose", zero curvature – a flat universe as shown by the option on the right in Fig. (G9).

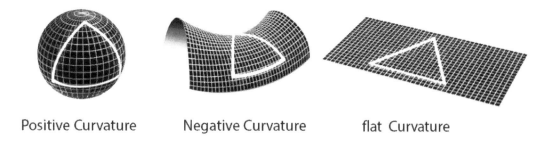

Positive Curvature   Negative Curvature   flat Curvature

Fig. (G9) Curvature of the Universe

My geometry provides a simple explanation. In the universe there is spatial contraction only around each galaxy and star, and this is local contraction. Therefore, space in the universe remains Euclidian. Of course, all the many equations that cosmologists have developed appear to say otherwise, but I will not look further at this.

How Do I Link the Two Geometries?

I have developed a rather simple formula, which gives the geodesic curvature, K, around a point according to (as a function of) the change in the density of space ρ around this point (appears in the article that I published on geometries).

$$K = \frac{4\pi}{45} \left(\frac{\nabla\rho}{\rho} \right)^2$$

In practical terms, there is no need to change the equations of General Relativity that use Riemannian geometry.

A positive deformation means space density increases toward a point. A negative deformation means space density decreases toward a point. Zero deformation means uniform density. All this affects our understanding of, for example, the behavior of light in space

H. The New Geometry and the New Physics

The New Meaning of Gravity in General Relativity

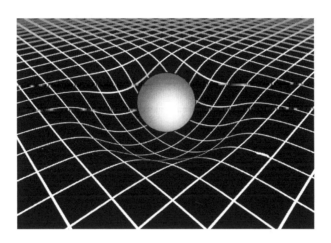

Fig. (H1) The Curving of Space by a Stellar Mass

Fig. (H1) is a typical illustration. This is how curvature by a mass is presented in all books. It is **meaningless** as we cannot imagine a curved three-dimensional space manifold bent in a four-dimensional hyperspace.

Fig. (H2) shows the true deformation of space by a mass, which is merely **space contraction**.

Fig. (H3) shows, again, the true deformation of space by a mass at point P - a deformation which is nothing but a contraction of space around P, the reduction in space cell's sizes - a positive "curvature".

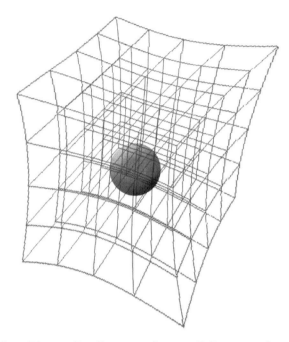

Fig. (H2) The True Deformation of Space by a Mass

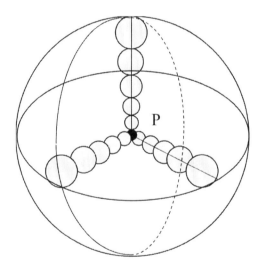

Fig. (H3) The True Deformation of Space by a Mass at

Point P

From the above, I conclude that gravity is a contraction of space!!!

This understanding finally allows us to answer (later in the book) questions in science that have been open for hundreds of years:

- Why does a ray of light curve when passing near a mass?
- How does mass contract space?
- How does another mass feel this contraction and move accordingly?
- How to build a Unified Field Formula (the Physicists' yearning)?

Why does a ray of light curve when passing near a mass?

The usual explanation is this:

Mass curves space. A ray of light should, therefore, move on a geodesic line, which means to curve. Although this is a valid explanation, it does not satisfy me.

My explanation:

A mass contracts space around it. In its vicinity, space is dense but its density, from the mass outwards, falls. Space is analogous to glass, in that its refractive index is large near the mass but decreases with the distance from it.

Space, close to a mass, is also analogous to compressed air, high density near the mass falls with increasing distance from it.

The study of optics tells us that a ray of light passing through a medium with a variable index of refraction is curved, see Fig. (H4).

These examples are a good analogy. The explanation is simpler. Space is the medium whose waves are light waves with their speed dependent on the density of space (as we explain, this does not contradict the fact that the speed of the light is a constant of nature).

When a ray of light passes through a media with a variable density the upper part of the ray (at a relatively large distance from the center of the mass) moves faster than the lower part (at a relatively smaller distance from the center of the mass). Of necessity the wave front is tilted, and the ray is curved.

This explanation is from our virtual point of view as observers out of the universe (**far observers**). For spectators in the media, in space, both their yardstick and their clock vary with the density of space and will, therefore, always give the same value for the speed of light.

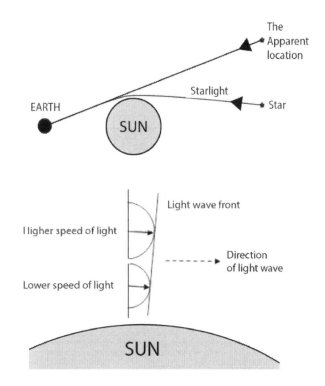

Fig. (H4) Deflection of a Light Beam

—

So, which explanation do you prefer? Tell me.

Black Hole - White Hole (Homage to Kusturica)

The needy, no matter what they receive from us: clothes, food, money, they want more and more. They swallow everything - like a **Black Hole**. In contrast, there are the needy that reject everything we offer them – like a **White Hole**.

But, let's be serious.

The solution to the equations of the Theory of General Relativity, for the case of the mass of a star is the **Schwarzschild Metric** for multi-dimensional, curved space.

This metric is kind of a Pythagorean theorem for a multi-dimensional curved space. More than this, we don't need to know, not now, not later. There are several terms in this metric. In the denominator of one of them, the following expression appears

$$r - \frac{2GM}{c^2}$$

Where

M – mass

G – Newton's Gravitational Constant

r – distance from the center of the mass

c – speed of light

If and when:

$$r = \frac{2GM}{c^2}$$

then, in the denominator of the same metric, a zero appears. It is understandable for it to tend to infinity. In this case the same star is considered a black hole. The radius for which the above equality holds, is called the **Schwarzschild radius** and is marked with a subscript S.

$$r_s = \frac{2GM}{c^2}$$

Now we know that if the ratio between mass M and its radius satisfies:

$$M/r > \frac{c^2}{2G}$$

then **we have a black hole** before us. The above ratio is about 10^{28}, a huge number. A black hole swallows light approaching it from the outside and prevents it exiting from the inside. Now we can know why. We have already learned that mass contracts the space around itself, but here it really compresses it. In such dense space, the speed of light falls sharply.

The space in a black hole, then, can be compared to a glass ball with a high refractive index in relation to the space around it. In this case, a beam of light that penetrates the ball is reflected around its walls and may be swallowed inside. A beam that originates inside will also be reflected and cannot escape.

A **white hole** is the opposite of a black hole. This is a space zone that is highly expanded relative to the space around it - in the same ratio as a black hole is compressed relative to the space surrounding it. In this zone, then, the speed of light is higher relative to its standard speed in space farther away outside. This time any light ray that reaches the white hole will be returned from it, while an inside ray will be held there. This is actually the interaction of a photon with an electron, as imagined by Feynman, because an electron, as we explain, is a white hole. It is clear that a mass cannot create a white hole, because it contracts the space around and inside it. Against this the process where a photon becomes an electron and positron (pair production) allows, as we show, to create a black hole which is the positive elementary charge and a white hole that is the negative elementary charge.

I. "Ironing" Space and the Ricci Flow

Topology is a branch of mathematics that deals with the study of the properties of space under continuous deformations (such as contraction, tension, and expansion).

Ricci Flow is a branch of topology. It appears here to explain the behavior of space - its dynamics under deformation (contraction, dilation). We have some evidence that space behaves as we describe but not assurance. However, this explanation does have value. It is included in the discussion of the essence of attraction and repulsion between charges that appears in Chapter **J** and completes the model.

By "ironing", we mean the process in which deformed zones of space gradually reduce the deformation, thanks to elasticity, so that the inner tension and the energy of tension decreases to a minimum.

We explain: a loose spring does not have internal tension. If we stretch it with an external force (with our muscles) it creates an internal force that opposes the force we apply. By stretching the spring, we do work. This increases the energy of the spring, the energy of tension. If we remove the force from the spring the internal tension will return the spring to its original relaxed state.

The tension and energy return to their initial values before the stretching. This situation applies to all systems in the universe including space. But physicists love brevity and generality, so they refer only to energy and determine that there is a tendency to minimum energy.

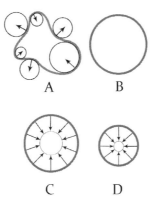

Fig. (I1) Ricci Flow in a Plane

Fig. (I2) Ricci Flow Transforms a Cube to a Sphere

Fig. (I1), shows a two-dimensional, deformed manifold. Its

demarcations are curved. The areas of the deformation are drawn

with their osculatory circuits that have radii which are the

corresponding radii of curvature. As you remember, the curvature K

is: K = 1/R.

The Ricci flow equation is:

$$\frac{\partial}{\partial t} g(t) = -2 \operatorname{Ric}(g(t))$$

It tells us that the speed of dissipation of the curving is according to

the amount of the curvature and in the direction of its radius.

And so, A goes to C. We get a circle where each of its points has the

same osculatory circle, and therefore it continues to contract, to a

point, see D. If, in this process it is required, that the area of the

manifold should be preserved, then the transition from A is to B.

Fig. (I 2) shows, on the left, a 3D cube, with the biggest deformation

at the corners. Therefore, the Ricci flow gradually transforms the cube

to a sphere, under the constraint that the volume is preserved.

J. Electric Charge and its Field as Deformed Space

Charge and the Field

An electrical charge is made up of elementary charges, all of which are exactly the same size, whether they are positive or negative. In my model, a positive elementary charge has spherical symmetry, and is a concentration, around a central point, of small space cells compared to the standard cell size far away in space. Far from this point, they grow to reach the standard cell size. This gradual change is continuous – there is no sharp boundary separating the concentration that is considered charge and the continuation of it, which is considered to be the electric field.

It was **Einstein's vision** that, one day, someone would create such a model. Fig. (J1) illustrates the description I have set out here. It shows the cross section of a three-dimensional spherical charge. At the bottom of the figure is a graph describing the density of space as a function of its position along the cross-section of the charge. ρ is the space density (the number of space cells per volume unit), while ρ_0 is the standard space density.

Since there is no sharp border between the charge and its field, care is required to choose the definition of the charge radius, r_0.

Every cell is analogous to a spring. A standard spatial cell, with no bodies around it, is analogous to a loose spring that has no tension, and therefore the energy of its tension is zero.

A cell that is small compared to a standard cell is analogous to a compressed spring, and hence it stores energy of compression.

A cell that is large compared to a standard cell is analogous to a stretched spring, and therefore it stores the energy of tension.

We choose (define) the radius of a charge as the radius for which the energy in the charge equals the energy in its field. This choice is arbitrary but allows us to calculate the radius and to show that it matches the measured radius.

This definition is related to a difficult issue, which till now remained unanswered. Feynman called this issue a major failure in our understanding of Electrical Theory. This is the issue of **where the energy is located - in the charge or in the field.**

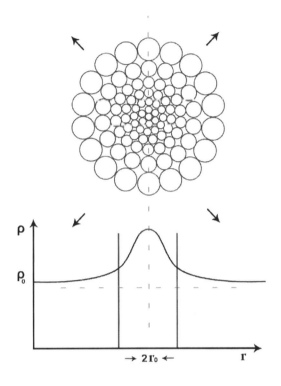

Fig. (J1) Positive Elementary Electric Charge

We explain this: calculating the energy of a charge (electrostatic), and of that the field, supposedly separately, gives the same result.

However, it is clear that there is no duplication of the energy, so the question is - where is it? Our model provides a clear answer: there is no separation between the charge and the field, so the calculated energy is the energy of both charge and field together.

According to the definition of the radius half of this energy is in the "charge" and half in the "field". This is an essential component in the calculation of the radius.

The ongoing discussion and the figures presented here may create a false impression that my theory is purely descriptive. This is not the case. My theory includes all the formalisms necessary for a physical theory.

As an example, I mention that from the definition of electrical charge density q, as a function of the density of space ρ, I derive all Maxwell's Electromagnetic Theory as a logical inference, while Maxwell's theory is phenomenological (based solely on experimental laws). This is an unprecedented achievement in physics based on visual imagination (confirmed by known physicists and published in a peer reviewed journal).

$$q = \frac{1}{4\pi} \frac{\rho - \rho_0}{\rho}$$

Many of the best physicists have proposed the intuitive suggestion that an electrical charge is a kind of **microscopic black hole**, which explains its stability. Since a positive elementary charge, according to my theory, is a positive curving of space, and since General Relativity deals with curved space, **I have shown** (proved rigorously) that it is indeed the case. I have proved that a positive elementary charge is really **a black hole,** and a negative charge is a **white hole** - there is such a thing and we discuss it below.

From all this I managed to calculate the radius of the elementary charge (the same for both types of charge) which is:

$$r_0 = \sqrt{2}/(2S^2) \cdot \sqrt{G\alpha\hbar C} \qquad \text{Where } S = 1, \ [S] = LT^{-1}$$

r_0 (calculated) $= 0.8774 \cdot 10^{13}$cm

Fortunately, **the radius of a positive elementary charge** found in the proton, (a particle that lies in atomic nuclei but can also be isolated outside them) was measured precisely and is:

r_P (measured) $= 0.8768(69) \cdot 10^{13}$ cm

and indeed, if we compare the calculated radius with the measured value we get:

r_0 (calculated) / r_p (measured) $= 0.8774 \cdot 10^{13} / 0.8768 \cdot 10^{-13} \sim 1.0007$

The accuracy of my calculation validates my model of the elementary charge, which I have discussed here.

I add that both black and white holes are very stable, which answers the question of the stability of the charges.

This is the place to point out that in my model of the electron and positron, the elementary charge revolves in a circle with radius R, and that this rotation gives it spin and as a result its magnetic moment. The calculation of R is much easier than that of r_0.

And, the ratio r_0/R is exactly the Fine Structure Constant α.

The character of the Fine Structure Constant has been, according to Feynman, one of the greatest riddles of Nature. We now have the answer.

Fig. (**J2**) presents a negative elementary electrical charge. This charge is a concentration of cells that are much larger than the standard cell size. This concentration decreases and tends to the standard size. It is, therefore, a negative deformation. The radius of the negative charge, r_0, is the same as that of the positive charge, as I proved.

The bottom of the figure shows a graph describing the density of space as a function of the position along the cross-section of the charge. ρ is the density of space (the number of space cells per unit volume) and ρ_0 the standard space density. In this case, the density of both the charge and its field is lower than the standard density.

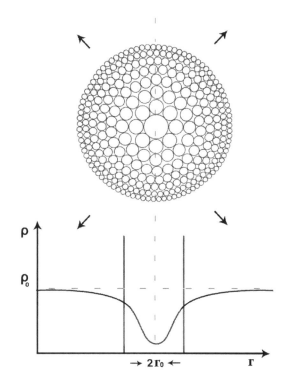

Fig. (J2) A Negative Elementary Electric Charge

We are now able to understand the meaning of attraction and repulsion. I hope you prefer my explanation over that of the "Dancing Photon".

Attraction and Repulsion

Fig. (J3) shows two positive charges and, enlarged, the area of the meeting of their fields. In this area we see the space cells (the drawing shows only the space cells that are on the line connecting the two charges). In this area and in the space between the two charges is the tension of contraction and therefore also the energy of contraction. A reduction in tension and energy is possible if the charges are separate one from the other and move away (just as a compressed spring return to its relaxed state).

Note that the meeting of the fields introduces deformation to space (Barak geometry) that Ricci flow requires to fade away. This deformation has cylindrical symmetry around the line that connects the two charges and therefore, of necessity, the deformation can fade only as the charges distance themselves from each other.

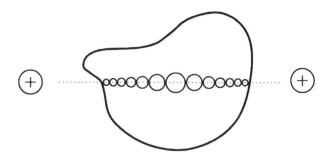

Fig. (J3) Repulsion

Fig. (J4) shows two negative charges and the enlarged area of the encounter between their fields. In this area we see the space cells (in the drawing only the space cells on the line connecting the two charges). In this area and in all the space between the charges there is stretching and therefore also stretching energy. Reducing tension and decreasing energy is possible if the charges move away from each other (as a tense spring returns to its relaxed state). Note that also here (Barak's geometry) Ricci flow explains the repulsion.

Figure (J5) shows two charges, one negative and one positive, and the area where their fields meet. This enlarged area shows the space cells (only the space cells on the line connecting the two charges).

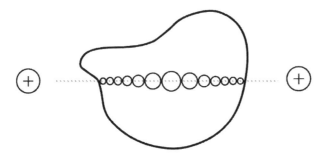

Fig. (J4) Repulsion

In this area, and in the space towards the center between the charges, on the right cells are contracted and on the left are expanded. Space energy can be reduced if the charges get close, so that the contraction and expansion cancel each other.

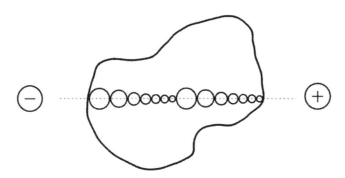

Fig. (J5) Attraction

If the charges come into contact, they annihilate each other and are replaced by two photons.

There is no naked elementary charge in nature, it is always integrated into a particle. An example of such a particle is the electron, built, as it appears, from a negative elementary charge that revolves in a circle that gives it angular momentum, which is referred to as the spin.

The reason for this kind of appearance lies in the source of the particle. Later I will explain that the electron and its companion the positron are created in a process where a photon (if energetic enough) revolves around an atom's nucleus. In tight circulation and with minimum energy, which is the couple's energy. This process is referred to as **pair production**. This is possible, as I explain, because the photon has all the necessary properties to become a couple. The photon, for example, has a single spin that is split between the couple – a single half for each.

Potential and Field (for Physicists)

The density of a charge, a scalar, is proportional to the electric potential. But the density of the charge is proportional to the density of space. It can be said that potential is an expression of spatial density. The electric field, a vector, is simply an expression of the gradient in the density of space.

On the Electric Field

Classical physics does not have an electric field that exists in its own right. If the charge disappears, so does the field. In the current physics, there is no elementary charge that exists in its own right. Elementary charge is a characteristic of charge-carrying particles. There are infinite fields, one for each type of particle, and the particle is nothing but an event in the field – an excitation. These fields are intertwined in space and adopt its topology.

As opposed to this I am satisfied with just one single "field" that is the infinite space. The electric field is nothing but a spatial deformation just like gravitation. The electron's charge, for example, deforms space, some 42 orders of magnitude more than its mass.

On a Magnetic Field

The ancients played with magnets and realized that a magnet has two poles – North and South. Any attempt to separate the poles failed. However, it was clear that there was a positive electrical charge separate from a negative electrical charge. Therefore, it was believed that magnetism and electricity were separate entities.

Maxwell (1862), after accumulating much experimental evidence, built the phenomenological electromagnetic theory. In this theory, magnetism and electricity are different expressions of the same phenomenon. I explain:

There is no magnetic field that stands by itself. The magnetic field has been invented purely for convenience, and do not let the appearance of such equations confuse you. When an electrical charge is in motion, its interaction with other charges is complex and contains the expression:

$$\frac{1}{c}\left(v' \times E\right)$$

where V is the speed of the charge, E its field strength and C the speed of light.

For convenience of using this expression in equations, we denote it by the letter **B** and call it the strength of the **magnetic field.** You are surprised, I know, but this is not my invention.

K.   Gravity and General Relativity

How Mass Contracts Space

Einstein proved to us that the presence of mass in space curves space but did not explain how the mass does it. I offer an explanation, the first of its kind, based on my replacement of curving with contraction.

Since each mass is composed of particles, the first question is how does the electron mass, for example, contract space.

The electron, as I explained, is a revolving negative elemental charge that gives it the spin (a chapter is dedicated to the detailed model). The charge deforms space – expands it – But also the spin of the charge, and thus of the mass (for which the charge is responsible because it is just the energy of the deformation) deforms space by causing it to contract. This contraction occurs because the charge, by revolving, "drags" space around it. This is the gravitational deformation, 42 orders of magnitude smaller than that of the charge.

This phenomenon of dragging space by a rotating mass is a prediction of General Relativity. This phenomenon is called **Frame Dragging.**

This phenomenon is confirmed by observational evidence. In a detailed discussion in one of my articles, I show that this is a possible explanation for the source of gravity. Contraction, whose source is spin, has no spherical symmetry and the reader rightly asks how this comply with spherical symmetry in macro, that is in a star. In a star the direction of spins is random and hence the symmetry. There is some questionable evidence that, for a body of material, in which there is a certain alignment of spins, spherical symmetry deviates from perfect. Such an experiment of confirmation or repudiation would be of considerable importance.

Now ask yourself what chance do physicists, dealing with QFT in the standard model of the particles, have to answer the question of how the mass curves space, if they think that a particle is point-like and structureless.

Please note that the current physics describes phenomena but finds it difficult to investigate them.

How a Mass Senses the Distortion of Space and Moves Accordingly – Free Fall

Again I, first and foremost, ask the question about the electron. The answer is complex and requires an understanding of the model of the electron. At this stage, I bring only the main points in my explanation that is given in detail below and also appear in several articles I have published.

Contracted space means that the density of space near a large mass is large and falls with distance from the mass. A density gradient is formed. But density determines the speed of light.

You may be surprised by this statement since you have been taught that the speed of light is a Constant of Nature. But you have forgotten, or may not know, what is a Constant of Nature. Please return to the definition that I have given.

I emphasize that the speed of waves in a medium depends inversely on its density. That is, near the mass, the speed of light is lower but increases as the distance increases. A gradient in the speed of light is formed.

At a distance where gravity is no longer noticeable, the speed of light is the standard speed in space.

An electron has spin that is its angular momentum.

This angular momentum, J, is dependent on the electron's mass, M, its speed of rotation, V, and the spin radius, R.

$J = MVR$

Conservation of Angular Momentum means that if V, in this case the speed of light, is getting smaller, then M and R must become larger.

M is larger only if R is smaller, and R is smaller if the electron is accelerated.

The result is that the electron falls in **free fall,** accelerated toward the mass where the light speed is lower. The electron can sense **the speed of light** only because it has a **finite size** so that its different parts are at different heights above the mass. The electron, having mass, creates also a gradient, and therefore the large mass falls free towards the electron. However, the ratio of the accelerations in this mutual fall is as the ratio of the masses.

This free and mutual fall is mistakenly perceived as an attraction between the masses. Let me remind you that I have explained attraction and repulsion in the chapter concerning charges.

Now comes a surprise: we have already studied that similar space deformations – positive in this case of gravitation – repel each other. Inevitable conclusion is that ...

Masses repel each other. Can this understanding explain the expansion of the universe? - We wonder.

The long-awaited union between electromagnetism and gravitation

From the day of the birth of general relativity, there have been many efforts, mostly by **Einstein** himself, to unite gravitation with electromagnetism. This effort was to yield an expansion of the field equation so that it would include the two types of phenomena. While these efforts failed, I have succeeded because I managed to create a common basis for both theories.

I have proven that charge and its field are nothing but spatial deformation. And I proved that mass also does not curve space but deforms it. This enables me to present the **Consolidated** field formula:

$$R^{\mu\nu} - 1/2 R g^{\mu\nu} = 8\pi G/C^4 \cdot T_m{}^{\mu\nu} + 4\pi G^{1/2}/s^2 \cdot T_q{}^{\mu\nu}$$

Where S = 1 and [S] = LT^{-1}

Note the added term on the right-hand side of the equation.

On gravitation and the possibility that it is quantized

General Relativity predicts the existence of gravitational waves. Recently they have been discovered in huge facilities in several places on Earth. So far there has not been found a theoretical way to present these waves as collections of particles - known by the name Gravitons. These hypothetic particles have not been found yet.

I present a model of the graviton that fits the attributes of the gravitational waves.

Note that the loss or addition of mass to a star can be by emission or absorption of small particles like elementary particles. This can weaken or strengthen the gravitational field possibly by emission or absorption of gravitons.

An example: The electrically neutral particle, with smallest mass, that a star can lose or gain is the positronium. This short-lived atom consists of an electron and a positron, which surround each other. Their spins can be oriented parallel or anti-parallel. This orientation is irrelevant to gravitation. Hence, this atom contributes to gravitation two whole units of gravitation, which the mass and its field can lose or gain. All this reminds us the graviton, Chapter O.

L.   The Standard Model of the "elementary" particles

Elementary particles are the particles whose different combinations comprise each and every material in the universe and they themselves are not made from others.

The **Standard Model** is based on **Quantum Field Theory – QFT-** and offers as a summary of experiments and theoretical work the table of particles that appear in Fig. (L1) **The Particle Table (Wikipedia).** In this table on the left column appears the word Quarks that relates to the family of six particles on the right. Under it appears the word Leptons that relates to another family of six particles on the right. Above you see Roman letters that indicate the column of particle's generations: First Second and Third. The first column to the left is the one of the first-generation particles, which are mostly common in nature. On the right-hand side appear the force carrying particles that dance between the material particles. A similar table of twelve Anti Quarks and Anti Leptons not presented here brings the total number of the elementary particles to 29.

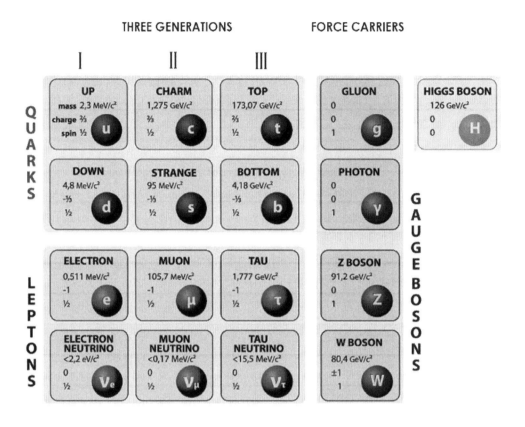

THREE GENERATIONS **FORCE CARRIERS**

Fig. (L1) Elementary Particles of the Standard Model

(Wikipedia)

The existence of Quarks was theorized by **Gell-Mann** and **Zweig** in 1964 and were discovered in SLAC lab. in 1968.

Problems that the standard model does not resolve

There is no understanding of the characteristics of the particles their origin and how to calculate their masses. And so, they relate to the masses as **Nature Constants** – along with the constants of classical physics they amount to 20.

It is unclear why there are three generations of particles (marked in the Table with Roman numerals from above).

Although the **Higgs boson** was presented as responsible for **inertia** but to say the least that is not serious.

It is worth noting that the atmosphere among physicists, these days, working on the standard model is that they should seek **physics beyond it**.

The Four Forces operating among the particles according to the standard Model:

Electromagnetism operates in short and long distances between electrical charges. The strength of the force is taken as a reference with the value 1.

The strong force, operates between quarks and protons and neutrons, is short-range and its strength relative to the electromagnetic force is about 100.

The weak force, operates in radioactive reactions, is short-range and its strength is 4 orders of magnitude smaller than the electromagnetic force.

Gravitation, operates between masses, is both short, and long-range with strength which is 42 orders of magnitude smaller than that of the electromagnetic force.

An order of magnitude is 10 times, whether smaller or larger, than a given quantity.

Two orders of magnitude is (10 times more than)^2=100 and so on.

 Glashow, Salam and Weinberg have shown that the weak force is an electromagnetic force.

The "unification" of forces

There is a wish among physicists to show that all the forces in nature are actually different aspects of a single force termed the **unifying force**.

My alternative model of the particles, is much simpler and in contrast to the Standard Model

In the next Chapter I show that quarks are made of Leptons and hence, they are not elementary.

I calculate the quarks masses. The results are within the error range of the experimental measurements.

I show why there are no single quarks in nature, but pairs and triples of them.

I show the structure of the Mesons and Baryons that are made of quarks.

I show the source of inertia.

I calculate the Leptons masses.

I unify all the four forces.

In Chapter **K** I show that gravitation and electromagnetism are actually the tension force in space. Later in Chapter **N** I show that the strong force is also electromagnetic. To sum it up: all the forces are actually one force, which is the tension in space.

I settle for the photon and add the Graviton from the particles that "carry" force. I show their structure and derive their attributes.

I reduce the number of Constants of Nature in my model from 20 in the standard model to only 4: The velocity of light c, the constant of gravitation G, Planck constant h and the Fine Structure Constant α.

Before I begin in an orderly manner with my model, I examine two of the most important issues that are related to each other, which have remained open for dozens of years. These issues are:

What is the essence of quarks?

Where is anti-matter?

Atoms are made of a nucleus that carry a number of elementary positive charges and the same number of electrons circulating around it. They are named atoms of **Matter**. In the Lab. it was possible to create short-lived atoms of hydrogen with a negative nucleus and circulating positrons. This kind of atoms are named **Anti-Matter**. But such atoms are not found in nature. Cosmologists and astrophysicists do not understand where is the anti-matter in our universe, and whether it was created in the first place.

In Chapter **M I resolve the issue by showing that the amount of matter equals exactly the amount of anti-matter in each and every atom in our universe.**

M. The Essence of Quarks- and the Question Where is the Anti-Matter?

The problems that require a solution

Wc have two first-generation quarks with their characteristics, that other than the size of the mass, appear also in a pair of second-generation quarks and in a third-generation pair. A total of 6 quarks. These couples carry the two types of electrical charge, and there are three other similar pairs with the opposite types of charge. And in total, 12 quarks.

Quarks are considered elementary, but they are always found in non-segregated threes or couples. This inexplicable trait in the current paradigm, termed **Confinement,** is explained later.

The quarks carry two types of electrical charge: 1/3 or 2/3 of the elementary charge, whether negative or positive. Such fractional charges were never discovered separately from the quarks. This phenomenon is inexplicable in the current paradigm, but it is explained here below.

The various Quarks masses have been measured. Since no one knows what their essence is, it is also not known how to calculate these masses. The calculation of these masses appears here in this Chapter.

In order to continue an introduction to the **Electron** and **Positron** is required, since I am going to show you that the **Quarks** are made of these particles

In 1897, **Thomson** discovered the **electron** that carries a negative electrical charge. It turned out that every negative, small or large electrical charge is made up of a number, of individual elementary charges that carry the same amount of charge. Hence, all the electrons have exactly the same charge unit.

A Positron is a fundamental particle similar to the electron, since its mass and spin are identical to those of the electron. In contrast, its electrical charge is equal to the electron charge but with the opposite type of charge, namely positive. Hence, the positron name.

The positron's existence was predicted by **the Dirac equation**, which was published in 1928 by **Dirac,** although Dirac himself did not come to this conclusion directly. The positron, termed **the anti-particle** of the electron, was first discovered   by **Anderson** in 1932.

The essence of Quarks as I understand Them

In my model, the quarks are nothing but electrons or positrons that move in winding tracks. A similar idea was expressed in the year 1982 by **Sakharov**.

Every sub-track in this model, is nothing but a quark. This idea explains: Why is it impossible to find single isolated quarks, why their electrical charge is supposedly a fraction of the elementary charge and many other things. In such a model we expel at once 12 elementary particles from the long list.

The couple of the first generation are according to the Standard Model:

The quark d (down) with a negative electric charge -1/3 of the elementary charge.

The quark u (up) with positive electric charge of +2/3 of the elementary charge.

 And their anti-particles:

The quark $\tilde{d}$ (anti-down) with a positive electric charge +1/3 of the elementary charge.

The quark $\tilde{u}$ (anti-up) with negative electric charge -2/3 of the elementary charge.

Note that the electron has a negative electrical charge (-), while its anti-particle positron is a positive charge (+). Here, the attributing of type of charge, + or -, to a particle or an anti -particle, is different (just a matter of denoting, but not something of fundamental nature).

In addition to the charge, Elementary particles also have angular momentum, **a spin,** given in units of $\hbar$. This spin appears in half integers 0, 1/2, 1, 3/2, 2, etc. of $\hbar$. This half integers are notated by the letter **s**.

The Quark d (down)

Fig. (**M**1) shows a trio of d quarks which are sub-tracks of a twisted electron at "rest". In a translational motion the trio becomes a trio of spirals.

In our model of quarks, we assign charge to each sub-track according to the time the electron (positron) spends on this sub-track. We, of course, assume that the tangential velocity is c.

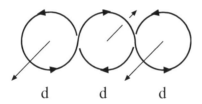

d   d   d

FIG. (M1) The Quark d

The electron spends one third of its full revolution time in each of the sub-tracks. We therefore assign it a charge of $1/3\ Q_0$. The resultant spin of this trio of quarks is $S = \frac{1}{2}$, due to the quarks individual spins, as Fig. (M1) shows. Each sub-track has the same spin as that of the electron. We refer to the sub-track of an electron as the quark, d, and to the sub-track of a positron as the anti-quark, $\tilde{d}$. It is still not fully

clear why the track is twisted.

It is thus clear that the quarks are **not** independent fundamental

particles, and therefore individual quarks do not exist.

Fig. (M2) shows again a trio of d quarks, but in this case with

S = 3/2:

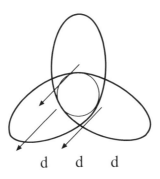

d   d   d

Fig. (M2) The Quark d

The Quark $\tilde{u}$ (anti-up)

If one twist in Fig. (M1) opens up; we get the structures shown in

Fig. (M3) and Fig. (M4), which represent **mesons**.

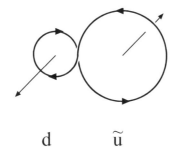

d ũ

Fig. (M3) Meson S = 0

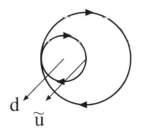

d ũ

Fig. (M4) Meson S = 1

An electron spends two thirds of its time in the sub-track with the double radius, therefore, we assign it a charge $2/3\ Q_0$ and refer to it as the quark ũ. For a positron, we refer to it as the quark u.

This simple model of quarks enables me to derive and accurately calculate their masses, for the first time in physics.

A Derivation and Calculation of the Quarks Masses

We know the electron mass M_e. From this mass, based on our quark model, we derive the masses $M_{\tilde{u}}$ and M_d of the first-generation quarks, which are also the masses M_u and $M_{\tilde{d}}$ of their anti-particles. The electron angular momentum $L = M_e R_e^2 \omega$ must be conserved. Hence it is the same L for each of the sub-tracks of the d quark, see Fig. (M1). For the ũ quark it is 2L, since the L of its companion d quark points in the opposite direction, see Fig. (M3). For the quarks, ω is the same, but R and M are different and conversely related. In a twisted track, which is a set of three quarks, ddd, the radius of each sub-track is $R = \frac{1}{3} R_e$.

The length of the electron wavepacket is conserved, hence:

$$2\pi R_e = 2\pi \frac{1}{3} R_e \times 3$$

The known relation $L = MR^2\omega$ gives:

$$M_d = \frac{L}{\omega R^2} = \frac{L}{\omega} \frac{1}{\left(\frac{1}{3}R_e\right)^2} = 9\frac{L}{\omega R_e^2} = 9M_e \qquad (m1)$$

For a twisted track of a pair of quarks, like $d\tilde{u}$, we get for $\tilde{u}$ a sub-track with $R = \dfrac{2}{3} R_e$, spin 2L and a mass:

$$M_{\tilde{u}} = 2\frac{9}{4} M_e = 4.5\, M_e \qquad\qquad \text{(m2)}$$

From (1) and (2) and $M_e = 0.51$ MeV we obtain the following results (3) and (4):

$$M_d = 4.5\ \text{MeV} \qquad\qquad \text{(m3)}$$

A recent experimental value is:

$M_d = 4.8 +/- 0.5$ MeV.

$$M_{\tilde{u}} = 2.\,25\ \text{MeV} \qquad\qquad \text{(m4)}$$

A recent experimental value is:

$M_{\tilde{u}} = 2.3 +/- 0.8$ MeV.

As you can see my results are within the error range of the measurements.

Let us now see if we can give a simple answer to the question **where is the anti-matter?**

In the Universe the Number of Electrons Equals the Number of Positrons

Atoms are built from a nucleus with a number of positive elementary electrical charges, and with the same number of negative electrons revolving around it. But the nucleus is built of quarks only, which according to our model are made of electrons and positrons. A Neutron is made of an equal number of electrons and positions (twisted topologically to become quarks). A Proton is made of electrons and positrons, as is the Neutron, but has one electron (three quarks) less. An atom is made of an equal number of protons and electrons. And hence:

In each and every atom in the entire Universe the Number of Electrons Equals the Number of Positrons.

This conclusion solves the long-standing issue of **where is the anti-matter? It is here all the time.**

So far, there is no evidence for the existence of stars and galaxies made of anti-matter (anti-hydrogen was first created in the laboratory in 1997).

The question: Why, at large, is the universe composed of matter only?

Now becomes: Why we do not see in nature atoms made of anti-protons and positrons?

In our GeometroDynamic Model of the Physical Reality (GDM) there is no **charge conjugation**. A negative charged nucleus curves space around it negatively. This might be the reason for instability in the orbital motion of a positron around it (hence anti-hydrogen created in the laboratory should have a limited lifetime.

The Mesons and Baryons

Fig (M3) and Fig. (M4) show mesons, which are a twisted electron or positron with only one twist. Fig. (M5) shows a meson composed of a twisted electron together with a twisted positron.

Overlapped dashed and solid circles represent the electromagnetic bond, of opposite charges, between the relevant quarks. These quarks that create a bond are **not numbered** as originating quarks of a particle, be it a meson, baryon or any other particle.

Note that in particle diagrams a **solid line** indicates an electron, and a **dashed line** a positron.

It seems that this electromagnetic bond, of opposite charges, between the relevant quarks is the known "strong force".

This subject is also discussed in Chapter **N**.

The π Family with Spin S=0

A single twisted track has a very short lifetime, as can be seen for the π$^+$ and π$^-$ mesons. For the π^0 meson, the lifetime is much shorter due to annihilation.

$$\pi^+ \to e^+ + \nu_e \quad 2.6 \cdot 10^{-8} \text{ sec}$$
$$\pi^0 \to 2\gamma \qquad 0.8 \cdot 10^{-16} \text{ sec}$$

A possible decay is:

$$\pi^0 \to \gamma + e^+ + e^- \qquad \text{and even} \qquad \pi^0 \to 2e^+ + 2e^-$$

The ρ Family with Spin S=1

From the reaction $\pi^+ \to e^+ + \nu_e$ and similar reactions, it seems as if a neutrino is incorporated in the π^+ construction.

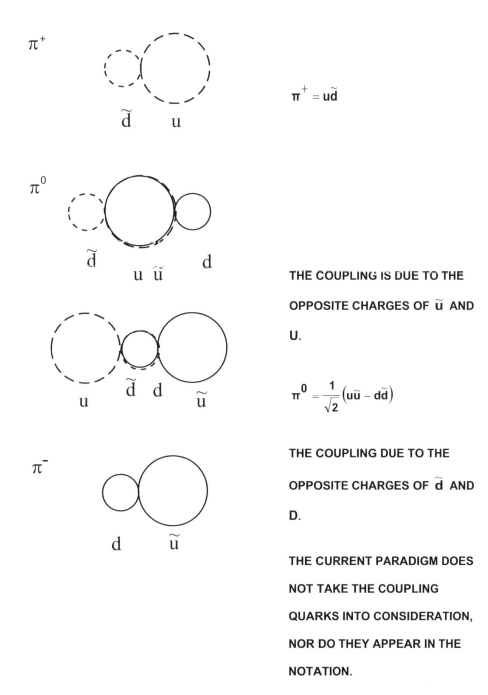

$$\pi^+ = u\tilde{d}$$

THE COUPLING IS DUE TO THE OPPOSITE CHARGES OF $\tilde{u}$ AND U.

$$\pi^0 = \frac{1}{\sqrt{2}}\left(u\tilde{u} - d\tilde{d}\right)$$

THE COUPLING DUE TO THE OPPOSITE CHARGES OF $\tilde{d}$ AND D.

THE CURRENT PARADIGM DOES NOT TAKE THE COUPLING QUARKS INTO CONSIDERATION, NOR DO THEY APPEAR IN THE NOTATION.

$$\pi^- = \tilde{u}d$$

Fig. (M5) The Π Mesons

$$\rho^+ = \widetilde{d}u$$

$$\rho^0 = \frac{1}{\sqrt{2}}\left(\widetilde{u}u - \widetilde{d}d\right)$$

$$\rho^- = \widetilde{u}d$$

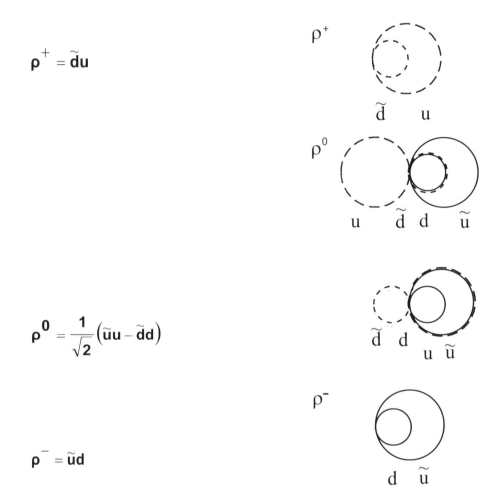

Fig. (M6) The P Mesons

Baryons

The **baryons** are composed of three quarks. As an example, consider the family, with the members: $\Delta^{++}\ \Delta^{+}\ \Delta^{0}\ \Delta^{-}$, that have the spin S = 3/2.

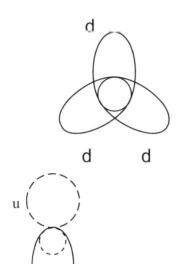

Q = -1

Δ⁻

S = 3/2

DDD

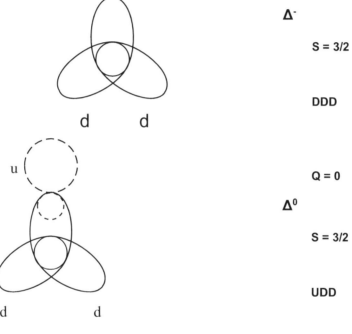

Q = 0

Δ⁰

S = 3/2

UDD

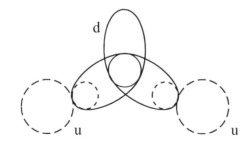

Q = +1

Δ⁺

S = 3/2

UUD

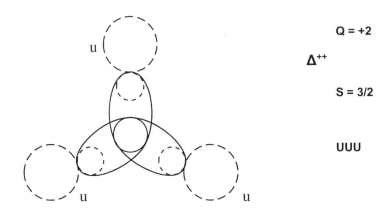

Q = +2

Δ⁺⁺

S = 3/2

UUU

FIG. (M7) The Δ Baryon

N. On the Neutron & Proton & Strong Force

I model the nucleon (proton or neutron) as kind of a motor with a neutral stator cage, which contains a large number of quarks, and a rotor, which contains only a few quarks termed: **valance quarks**. This rotor determines the charge and spin of the nucleon. My rotor models of the proton and neutron enable me to derive and calculate the **proton charge radius**. My result is well within the error range of the experimental result.

The Stator Model

The stator is composed of a number of twisted positrons and an identical number of twisted electrons. The total number of quarks, in the stator shown in Fig. (N1), is 3x3 + 3x3 = 18

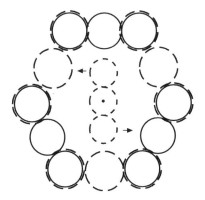

Fig. (N1) The Stator Structure and the Rotor

Note that the total number of quarks that construct a stator can also be much larger. The stator total charge is zero. The net charge of the nucleon (proton or neutron) comes from the rotor.

The spin contribution, of the stator type cage, to the total spin of the nucleon, might be zero, since in this case the magnetic interaction lowers the cage (structure of the stator) energy. The spin of the nucleon is thus, probably, the spin of its "rotor" which is $S = \frac{1}{2}$, as Fig. (N2) and Fig. (N4) show. This issue, of where the spin of the nucleon comes from, is known as the "proton spin crisis".

The Rotor Model

The **neutron** rotor, see the simplistic model in Fig. (N2), is composed of an electron and a positron in the form of three **valence quarks,** which are a pair of d quarks and one u quark. The mass of this rotor is $M_{neutron\ rotor} \sim 2M_d + 1M_u \sim 11.25 Mev$.

$Q_{charge\ unit} = 0$

Neutron

S = 1/2

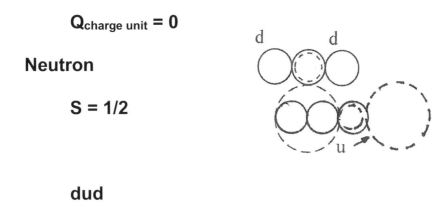

dud

Fig. (N2) The Neutron Rotor

Fig. (N3) shows the spatial charge distribution, known from scattering experiments. This is compatible with Fig. (N2), and with the fact that, despite having no charge, the neutron has a magnetic moment opposite to its spin direction.

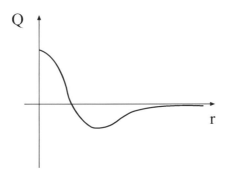

Fig. (N3) Neutron Charge Distribution

The **proton** rotor, see the simplistic model in Fig. (N4), is composed of one electron and two positrons in the form of three valence quarks, u, u, d. The charge distribution, shown in Fig. (N5), is compatible with the proposed model.

The mass of this rotor is:

$$M_{proton\ rotor} \sim 1M_d + 2M_u \sim 9\ Mev.$$

We, thus, arrive at a heavier neutron than the proton, which complies with experimental data.

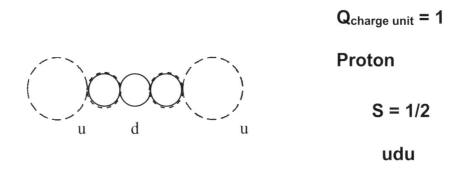

$Q_{charge\ unit} = 1$

Proton

S = 1/2

udu

Fig. (N4) The Proton Rotor

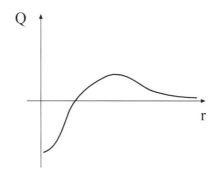

Fig. (N5) Proton Charge Distribution

The disintegration reaction of a free neutron, with a lifetime of ~10 minutes, is:

$$N \rightarrow P + e^- + \tilde{\nu}_e$$

And now we know **where the electron comes from**.

The mass difference between the Neutron and the Proton

The stators are identical hence, the difference in mass comes from the rotors. The masses of the rotors (in units of energy Mev):

$M_{neutron\ rotor} \sim 2M_d + 1M_u \sim 11.25Mev$

$M_{proton\ rotor} \sim 1M_d + 2M_u \sim 9\ Mev.$ Hence, the difference is:

$M_{neutron\ rotor} - M_{proton\ rotor} \sim 2.25\ Mev,$

And indeed, the mass of the neutron is larger than that of the proton. But my theoretical result should have matched the experimental measured difference which is:

$M_{neutron} - M_{proton} = 1.29\ Mev.$

I do not have an explanation for this discrepancy.

On the Strong Force

The Force between Quarks

Figures in Chapter **M**, which represent mesons and baryons, show couples of sub-tracks of an electron and a positron, which construct a bond. This indicates that the holding force of these structures, the force between quarks, is probably electromagnetic.

The Force between a Proton and a Neutron, and between Two Protons

On the possibility that the **strong force** is actually an electromagnetic force I learned from **Yukawa and Feynman.**

The **strong force** is short distance and about 100 times stronger than the electromagnetic force. This is **an attractive force only,** and **spin independent** (ignoring weak magnetic interactions).

Yukawa suggested that the source of this force is the exchange of a π^+ meson. And **Feynman** presented a prof that an exchange of a particle can generate an attractive force. He also was very explicit on the possibility that this idea shows that the strong force is electromagnetic.

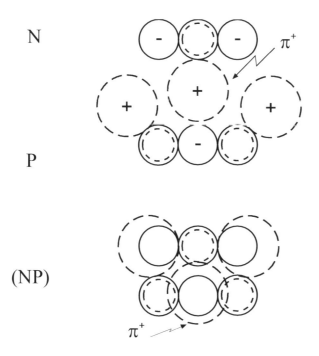

Fig. (N6) The (NP) Strong Force

Fig. (N6) shows how an electric field between three pairs of charges, of the neutron rotor and proton rotor, create an attracting force that binds them.

Note that when the neutron and proton are far apart, the inner distribution of charge is blurred and the effective field decays rapidly, which explains the short range. Note also that according to my GDM the radius of a particle is inversely proportional to its mass.

(PP)

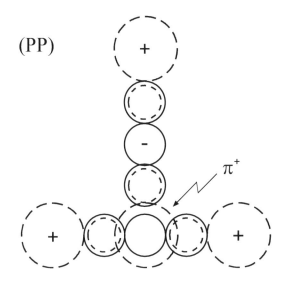

π^+

Fig. (N7) The (PP) Strong Force

The mass of a quark is about 10 times larger than that of an electron hence, its radius is 10 times smaller. The electric field is inversely proportional to the square of the radius hence its strength is 100 times larger and so is the force it applies on a nearby charge. We now consider the force between two protons, Fig. (N7). Here, as well, there is an attractive force at short range, but as the distance increases this force becomes repulsive since the particles have the same charge sign.

We consider the binding force, for both the neutron and proton, and proton and proton cases, to be the result of a π^+ meson exchange.

This meson is merely a twisted positron, and its movement back and forth, is the "exchange". This is the Yukawa theory of meson exchange, as the source of the Strong Force.

Feynman explains how an exchange of a particle can generate an attractive force. He describes the force between two protons of the ion H_2^+ as the result of the electron exchange between the protons. The reaction is:

$$(H, P) \overset{\rightarrow}{\underset{\leftarrow}{}} (P, H)$$

*The **attractive force** comes from the reduced energy of the system due to the possibility of the electron jumping from one proton to the other. In such a jump the system changes from the configuration (hydrogen atom, proton) to the configuration (proton, hydrogen atom), or switches back.*

Feynman further shows how the force between a proton and a neutron can be explained by the exchange of a Π^+ meson. Feynman concludes:

*Now we might ask the following question: could it be that forces between other kinds of particles have an analogous origin? What about, for example, **the nuclear force between a neutron and a proton, or between two protons?** In* *an attempt to explain the nature of nuclear forces, Yukawa proposed that the force between two nucleons is due to a similar exchange effect - only, in this case, due to the virtual exchange, not of an electron, but of a new particle, which he called a meson.*

The exchange in this case is:

$$P^+ \underset{\leftarrow}{\overset{\rightarrow}{}} N^0 + \Pi^+$$

The π⁺ meson is emitted from the proton to convert it into a neutron, and by combining with the other neutron to convert it into a proton, and vice versa.

The Standard Model, however, considers meson exchange as a complex effect of color interactions, and not a primary cause.

Based on the above and my GDM I am convinced that the Strong Force is an electromagnetic force. Hence, we have achieved the result that all the forces in nature are merely different manifestations of the same force of tension in space.

Note that this result emerged from my imagined quarks. It was Einstein how said that imagination is more important than knowledge.

O. My Model of Massless Elementary Particles

In this chapter I discuss massless particles (like the photon) and in the next massive particles (like the electron). Hence, we have to understand first and discuss the difference between energy and mass.

On Mass and Energy

In this chapter I discuss energetic particles, which move at the speed of light. They are massless particles. On the other hand, everybody is aware of the known relation:

U (Energy) = **M** (Mass) **x** **c²** (Square of light velocity),

as if energy is always mass. This notion is wrong. Mass is nothing but energy, but energy is not always mass. Energy is mass, depends on the way it is "packed". A package that attributes to the energy **inertia** (namely you have to apply force in order to accelerate the "package") is having a **mass**.

If no force is applied, a body is at rest or moves on a straight line with a constant velocity. This is Newton's first law. In order to change the velocity, one has to apply a force **F** on the body to accelerate it - an acceleration **a**. The ratio: **F/a = M defines M.**

This is Newton's second law.

The Elementary Particles in the GDM

The massless particles are:

ADAM and **EVE**

They construct the **Photon, Graviton,** and the **Neutrino.**

The massive particles are:

The **Electron** and the **Positron** of the first generation.

The **Muon** and the **Anti-Muon** of the second generation.

The **Tau** and the **Anti-Tau** of the third generation.

All of them are created in the process of pair production from a photon and also in other processes.

The Photoms

In my model there is only one pair of elementary particles – the Photoms.

In my scientific papers I called them photoms, since **they are actually the ground state vibrations of the electromagnetic field** (PHOTON AT THE BOTTOM IS A PHOTOM)

This pair construct all the other particles, as I show here and in the next chapter.

One photom is named **ADAM** (negative photom) and the other- **EVE** (positive photom).

Particles visualized as Springs

Let us assume that ADAM and EVE are two identical springs, see Fig. (O1). ADAM (C) is stretched periodically whereas EVE (B) is contracted periodically. (A) is the state of no tension. Both the amplitude and the frequency of these springs can take any value.

If they have the same frequency their energy of stretch equals that of contraction. If they are coupled, they will have the same frequency. Let the stretching and contracting be perpendicular to their motion through space and rotating. This rotation attributes to them the spin.

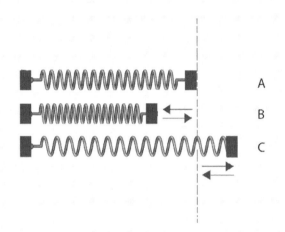

Fig. (O1) EVE and ADAM as "Springs"

Let me now present a particle which is composed of these elementary photoms.

A "photon", see Fig. (O2), is composed of two coupled springs – ADAM and EVE. They vibrate at the same frequency and with the same phase; when ADAM is stretched to the maximum EVE is contracted to the minimum. The energy of the photon is the energy of the springs and its frequency is their frequency. Since they rotate, after each half cycle they are in an upside-down position. This rotation is the photon's spin.

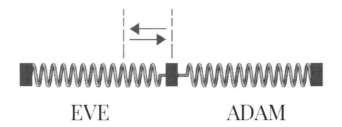

Fig. (O2) The Photon as Two "Springs"

Elementary Particles as the Vibrations of the Space Lattice

The lattice is composed of cells and to each of them we can relate as a spring. This spring can serve as an ADAM or an EVE, depending on the circumstances. But these cells are very friendly with their neighbors, they do not keep their vibrations to themselves, they transfer them to the next cell in line. This transfer is the particle's motion which is on a straight line (the geodesic actually), whereas the vibration is perpendicular to the line of motion. The cells themselves do not move; they stay where they are. The particle is not the spring from the previous sub-section it is the vibration that moves on. The velocity of its motion is the velocity of transvers waves in space – the velocity of light (300,000 kilometers per second). This velocity and the velocity of longitudinal waves are the only real velocities that exist.

Note that nothing is alien to space. The particles are merely the vibrations of space taking place in volumes of space that contain many space cells and move on continuously. **There is no rest only motion.** When a particle moves on a circle we can relate to the virtual center of the circle as if it is at **rest.** And of course, there is a possibility that this center moves slowly, much less than the light velocity. In this case the particle (the vibration) moves on a spiral, see Chapter **P**.

In Figs **O**3,4,6,9, and 10 we present in the following order the particles: ADAM, EVE, Photon, Graviton, Neutrino. I show how ADAM and EVE create all the other particles. In all these cases the particle, namely the vibration, enters from left and moves to the right (the vibration is always perpendicular to line of motion) circulating clockwise, as we look from behind and forwards. This circulation attributes to the particle its spin. This circulation is termed a circulation with **right helicity.**

In Figs **O**3,4,6,9, and 10, we see arrows towards the line of propagation or from it. The arrow's direction towards the line indicates the contraction of the space cells, and its direction from the line outwards it indicates the dilation (stretching) of these cells. The maximum contraction or dilation occurs close to the line of motion. These contractions and dilations change with time in a sinusoidal cycle. The arrows appear where the contraction and dilation are at the maximum. If the entrance from the left is at time "zero" then the arrows appear first after a quarter of a cycle and then again after three quarters of a cycle. The reader should try to create a clear picture of these motions in their mind.

Fig. (O3) represents the fundamental particle **EVE**

Fig. (O4) represents the fundamental particle **ADAM**

Recall that contracted space is positive charge whereas dilated space is negative charge.

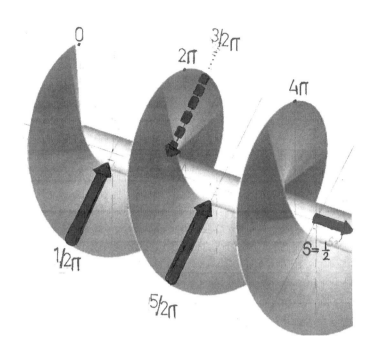

Fig. (O3) The Fundamental Particle EVE

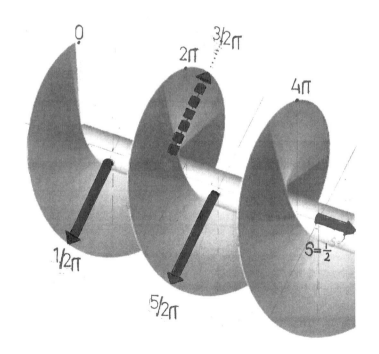

Fig. (O4) The Fundamental Particle ADAM

Photoms - the Ground State Photons

QED attributes to a photon in its ground state one half of the energy, half of the momentum, and half of the spin. To distinguish a photon from a ground state photon, we name it a **Photom** (a photon at the bottom is a photom). In the GDM, however, there are two types of photoms.

EVE The Positive Photom: This photom is an oscillating contraction of space (positive charge), close to the line of propagation. This oscillation is in a plane or in a rotating plane, around the line of propagation.

ADAM The Negative Photom: This photom is an oscillating dilation of space (negative charge) close to the line of propagation. This oscillation is in a plane or in a rotating plane, around the line of propagation.

I consider these photoms more fundamental than the photon – they construct the photon.

I show that EVE carries the oscillating positive elementary charge (that of the positron), whereas ADAM carries the oscillating elementary negative charge (that of the electron) Hence I consider them as the "positron" and "electron" of the **Dirac Sea**, and show that **vacuum polarization** is due to them. This way I dispel the need for a separate ground state (vacuum state) for the electromagnetic field and a separate ground state for the electron and positron field (Dirac sea).

The number of EVE and of ADAM photom particles in a volume unit of space

Here I use a calculation known as the counting of space vibrations in a given unit of volume – the reader should care only about the end result.

The spatial density of an ensemble of photoms of a given λ and a bandwidth $d\lambda$, is:

$n(v) = 8\pi v^2/c^3 \cdot dv$ but $v=c/\lambda$ and $dv=c/\lambda^2 \cdot d\lambda$

Hence: $n(\lambda)=8\pi/\lambda^4 \cdot d\lambda$

For photoms of $\lambda = 500nm$ and a bandwidth $d\lambda = 0.5nm$

the **spatial density** (which should interest the reader) is:

$n(\lambda) \sim 2\cdot 10^{11}$ **photoms per cubic centimeter.**

This huge number is of utmost importance in the understanding of the nature of light and the understanding of the essence of Quantum Phenomena.

Condensation and Dispersion – the Key to the Understanding of Quantum Phenomena

Fig. (O5), shows a symbolic space lattice, which is like a 3D fisherman's net. Imagine that each vertical plane, in Fig. (O5), going into the page, is a plane in which a photon or a photom is moving. If two adjacent photons or photoms of the same frequency oscillate in anti-phase side by side (**Left**) they stretch the lattice horizontally and move apart to ease the tension. The result is **dispersion** - a reduced spatial density of the photons or photoms. If, however, they oscillate in phase (**Right**), they move together to ease the tension and the result is **condensation** - higher density. A similar situation occurs if they move one below or above the other.

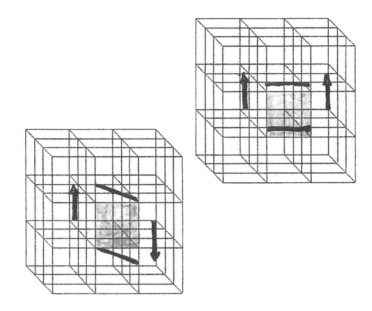

Fig. (O5) Dispersion and Condensation

Interference with Classical Waves – Ensembles of Photoms or Photons (See also Chapter T)

Photons or photoms, of the same wavelength, when they are in phase and closely packed, move as a classical wave. Let a wave front, of such a classical wave, hit the double slit; if the photons or photoms, which are coming from the two slits and hit the screen, are in phase (on the screen) they create maxima zones on the screen, and minima if out of phase. In other words; intensity is reduced in zones of **destructive** interference whereas in zones of **constructive** interference intensity is enhanced. Photons and photoms entering these zones, however, are **neither annihilated nor created** and the total energy is conserved. No annihilation or creation takes place, only **a spatial displacement of the particles,** as I have shown in the previous sub-section, that results in a reduction in their density (intensity) in one zone and an increase in their density (intensity) in the other.

The sun deflects the light of a far star by about a milliradian. The deflection that creates the above dispersion or condensation is much larger. We can only imagine the internal forces in the space lattice.

On Interference with Individual Photons and the quantum enigma, see Chapter T.

ADAM EVE and the Photon

On the photon we know the following:

Light is a stream of photons.

The energy of a photon U depends on its frequency υ times the Planck constant h, named after the physicist Planck:

$U = h \cdot \upsilon$

The photon lacks inertia, it does not own mass (despite the fact that energy and mass are equivalent) and it moves at the speed of light – after all this is light.

The photon has intrinsic angular momentum known as its **Spin.**

Spin, in general, comes in units **S**, which are half integers:

1/2, 1, 3/2, 2, 5/2, 3 ...... of $\hbar = h/2\pi$.

The photon's spin is S=1 and its intrinsic angular momentum is $\hbar$.

In quantum field theory - QFT - the photon is considered an excitation of the electromagnetic field. The lowest energy level of this field is embedded with excitations which have half of the photon's energy and half of its spin. We consider them to be our ADAM and EVE. These particles pack space separately with enormous densities. But sometimes ADAMs and EVEs adhere to create pairs and become photons, Fig. (O6), two pairs to become gravitons, and sometimes to become neutrinos.

Note again that EVE carries the oscillating positive elementary charge (that of the positron), whereas ADAM carries the oscillating elementary negative charge (that of the electron) Hence I consider them as the "positron" and "electron" of the **Dirac Sea**, and show that vacuum polarization is due to them.

All this means that the photon caries the two oscillating charges, but its net charge from a distance is zero since the charges cancel out the fields of each other. Physicists will understand that the **photon is an oscillating dipole that confines its oscillating field** (no transmission of energy**).

We know that an energetic enough photon can get close to the atomic nucleus and be converted in a process known **as pair production** to become a pair of electron and positron. Now it is clear from where the elementary charges of the electron and positron came. And since the elementary charges are of equal size, but of different signs, the charge of the photon is zero. Hence the oscillating charge of ADAM equals that of EVE. This fact strengthens my understanding that fractions of the elementary charges, like those supposedly in quarks do not exist.

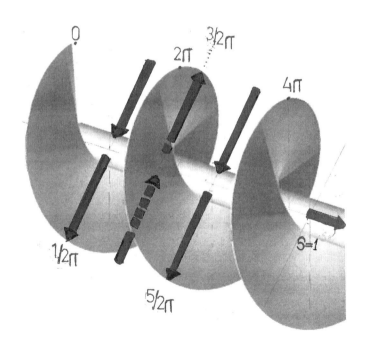

Fig. (O6) The Photon

More on the Photon

Photon Energy and the Nature of Planck Constant $\hbar$

The expression for the photon's energy is $U = K\,\lambda^2/2\pi^2$ where K is an attribute of space similar to the K of a spring. If the "Space Spring Constant K" is **a function of ω only** we guess that it can be:

$$K = M\omega^2 = (U/c^2)\omega^2 = \hbar\omega^3 / c^2$$

where $\hbar$, **not yet identified,** is a constant of proportionality.

Necessarily $U = \hbar\omega$ where $\hbar$ becomes the known quantum constant.

Thus, a classical functionality of $K(\omega) \propto \omega^3$ leads **to the basic quantum mechanical result for the energy and reveals the nature of the Planck constant.**

The Photon's Volume

My model of the photon enables me for the first time in physics to determine the volume of a photon as function of its wavelength λ.

$V_{Photon} = 6.75 \cdot 10^{-7} \cdot \lambda^3 cm^3$

The shorter is λ, the more compact is the photon.

For λ = 500nm Green light, we get:

$V_{Photon} = 6.75 \cdot 10^{-7} \cdot \lambda^3 \sim 8 \cdot 10^{-20} cm^3$.

Indeed, a point.

The Photon Spin $\hbar$

My model of the photon enables me to find out theoretically the photon spin L, for a circular polarized photon. Its linear momentum P = U/c times its radius of rotation $R_e = \lambda/2\pi$, gives $L = PR_e = U/c \cdot \lambda/2\pi$ but $U = \hbar\omega$. Hence, the known result:

$L = \hbar$

Space Polarizations - The Polarization of the Vacuum

A scattering experiment, conducted in the TRISTAN accelerator in Japan in 1997, found that the closer electrons get to each other, the field they sense is larger than expected. The explanation, given by **Koltick** (1997), was that in the immediate vicinity of the electron the creation and annihilation of pairs of electrons and positrons screen the charge of the electron by polarization, see Fig. (O7). This is the **Polarization of the Vacuum**. My explanation is somewhat different. Photoms can create space polarization. ADAM particles surround a positive charge and EVE particles adhere to their backs, see Fig. (O7), hence, space acts like a dielectric media and screens the positive charge.

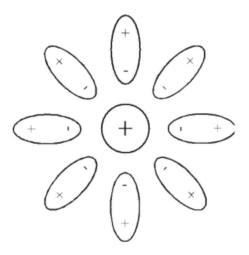

Fig. (O7) The "Net" Charge (Tristan Accelerator Japan 1997)

Thus, from a distance the charge will appear as carrying a smaller charge. If we approach the charge through the screen, the closer, we get the larger the charge will appear.

Based on this understanding we can dispel the need for virtual creation and annihilation of electron-positron pairs.

ADAM and EVE and the Graviton

Gravitational waves have recently been detected. These space waves are predicted by General Relativity. As of today, there is no theoretical proof, or observational evidence, for the existence of quanta of these waves. These quanta are considered by some to be the "force-carrying" mediators between masses - the Gravitons.

Here I suggest a model of the, as yet hypothetical, Graviton. We also relate to the effort to quantize gravitation, and raise arguments in support of the existence of Gravitons.

The Gravitational Wave

Fig. (O8) shows the effect of a linear polarized gravitational wave on a ring of particles, moving towards us perpendicularly to the page and through it, in different times. These times are the quarters of the cycle time T. This wave is a transversal wave of contracted and dilated space, where the contraction and dilation are perpendicular to each other and to the direction of propagation. Hence it moves at the light velocity c.

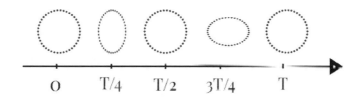

Fig. (O8) The Gravitational Wave

At T = 0 space is the standard normal space. After T/4 space is stretched (dilated) vertically and contracted horizontally. At T/2 space is the standard normal space, and at 3T/4 space is contracted vertically and stretched (dilated) horizontally.

Necessarily the Graviton description should comply with that of the gravitational wave.

The Graviton

The Graviton is composed of a pair of two ADAM particles back to back and a pair of two EVE particles back to back, Fig. (O9).

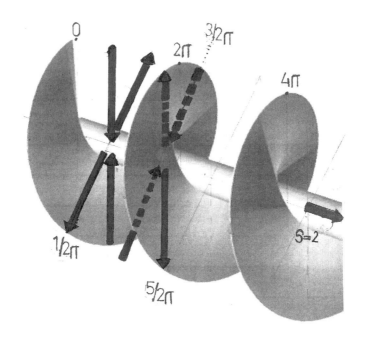

Fig. (O9) The Graviton

When the ADAMs stretch the EVEs contract. Each of the photoms

contributes spin s = 1/2 and together a total spin of

s = 2.

Note how this model complies with the gravitational wave Fig. (O8).

The Spin Energy and Size of the Graviton G

The G Spin

The spin of each photom is1/2 $\hbar$. Since the graviton is constructed

of 4 photoms its spin must be 2, hence:

$L_G = 2 \hbar$

We could also relate to the fact that in pair annihilation, in order to conserve angular momentum, two photons are created, and hence the above equation.

The Graviton Energy

The Graviton energy is simply the gain of gravitational energy lost in the annihilation of a pair of a particle and its anti-particle. Let a pair with mass M' be located on the surface of a mass M. The gravitational energy of the system M' and M due to the presence of M' is:

E_G = GMM'/R, R being the radius of M. The annihilation of the pair is a loss of energy to the system, since the photons created in the annihilation process leave the system. It is a long-standing issue as to where did the gravitational energy disappear. We contend that this energy is carried by a graviton, which also leaves the system. This understanding enables us to calculate typical graviton energies. Since the graviton is a transversal wavepacket it moves at the velocity c and its energy U is related to its angular frequency ω by: $U = \hbar\omega$

The Graviton Size

The size of a graviton seems to be like that of the photon, where λ is the wavelength of the graviton. Its volume is:

$$V_{Graviton} = 6.75 \cdot 10^{-7} \cdot \lambda^3 cm^3$$

The Quantization of Space Curvature and the Graviton

Einstein's Field Equation of General Relativity deals with spacetime curving by Energy/Momentum, which is due to angular momentum, as we have shown. By incorporating in this equation, the additional curving by Charge/Current, we have extended the equation to become relevant not only to the **macroscopic** world, of mainly neutral bodies, but also to the **microscopic** world of elementary particles. This equation expresses the idea that space curvature is quantized, since both angular momentum and charge are quantized.

The Quantized Space Curvature

The quantization of spacetime curvature is due to quantized angular momentum and charge. Thus, the creation of a pair of a particle and its anti-particle contributes twice to the curving by spin (and relevant energy). There is no contribution to curvature by a pair of bivalent elementary charges since the contributions of positive and negative curving cancel out. Note that in our theory - the GDM gravitation is space contraction. Thus, "quantizing gravitation" means that the amount of contraction jumps from one value to another by a quantum of contraction. The annihilation of a pair of a particle and its anti-particle subtracts twice the curving by spin (and relevant energy). This loss in curving (contraction), which is necessarily quantized, is a loss in space torsion and its relevant energy. This is more than a clue as to how the graviton is constructed.

ADAM EVE and the Neutrino

We know that the spin of the neutrino is $s = 1/2$, it moves at the speed of light c, and its mass is about one million times smaller than that of the electron. The neutrino appears mainly in interactions in which the weak force is involved. Hence, we are wondering whether the neutrino is incorporated in the structures of combinations of quarks as responsible for their twisted trucks.

In my model, Fig. (O10), the neutrino is EVE in one half cycle and ADAM in the other half.

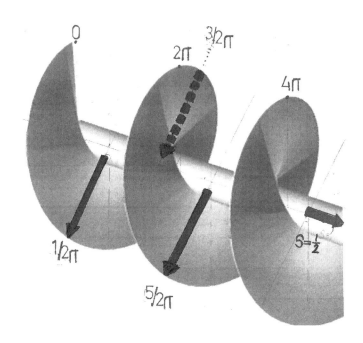

Fig. (O10), The Neutrino

We and the reality in which we live is a huge collection of vibrations moving at the speed of light, but the centers of their tracks are moving at slower speeds. Space is the 3D arena in which these patterns of vibrations move. It is their geometry of patterns that actually move, hence the name Geometrodynamics given to my model of the reality - GDM.

P. My Model of Massive Elementary Particles

It is worth noting that my model brings results that no-body, so far, has been able to provide, for example the calculations of the particles' masses. As of today, these masses are considered constants of nature, since nobody knows how to calculate them.

Each and every particle in this category contains an elementary electric charge. Further discussion on the nature of these elementary charges is our starting point.

The Bivalent Elementary Charges as Kind of Black and White Holes

Susskind (2004) wrote:

*One of the deepest lessons we have learned over the past decade is that **there is no fundamental difference between elementary particles and black holes**. As repeatedly emphasized by Gerard 't Hooft (1990), black holes are the natural extension of the* *elementary particle spectrum. This is especially clear in string theory where black holes are simply highly-excited string states. Does that mean that we should count every particle as a black hole?*

Relating just to the elementary charge, our answer to this question is **affirmative**.

This idea was first expressed by Salam and Strathdee (1977), Holzhey and Wilczek (1992), and also Sen (1995).

The intuition of these distinguished physicists is my inspiration.

My attribution of space deformation to an elementary charge, and the fact that charge is quantized, led me to pursue the possibility that positive and negative elementary charges are hitherto unrecognized kind of electrical black and white holes, respectively. This led me to the derivation and calculation, using cgs units, of the radii and masses presented in the following sub-Sections.

My Results for the Radii of the Elementary Charges

My calculated **radius r_p of the elementary positive charge,** based on general relativity, is:

r_p(calculated) = 0.8774 10^{-13} cm, (p1)

This is also the **radius r_p of the proton's elementary positive charge** (not the proton radius), which was measured by **Pohl** (2010) and is:

r_p(measured) = 0.8768(69) 10^{-13} cm.

My calculated result is well within the experimental error range with **an accuracy** of 0. 07%

This is also the **anti-proton** charge radius that can be and should be measured, and the **radii of the elementary negative and positive charges of the electron and positron**

Based on these radii I derive and calculate the **Mass M_e of the Electron/Positron**

On Pair Production

Pair production is the creation of an elementary particle and its antiparticle, by the interaction of an energetic photon with matter. The electron and positron pair is an example.

In the GDM, and also in **Loudon's** (2000) book, a photon is considered a transverse wavepacket, whereas I consider an elementary charge a longitudinal circulating wavepacket (of contracted or dilated space) A similar concept, suggested by Sakharov (1982) is titled: The Knot-Like Topological Structure of Elementary Charges. Pair production seems to be a **mode conversion** of the transverse wavepacket (the photon) into two longitudinal wavepackets rather than an extraction of an electron from Dirac's sea (the common conception). This conversion takes place during the circulation of an, energetic enough, photon around a positive nucleus. This circulation is possible, since the proton's charge is an electric black hole, which deforms space drastically. The photon spin 1 is divided equally between the particles (conservation of angular momentum) to attribute spin ½ for each particle of the pair.

Derivation and Calculation of the Longitudinal Wavepacket Velocity c_L and Feynman's Self Interactions

In the paradigm longitudinal electromagnetic waves do not exist theoretically and very few have been looking for them. In the GDM they exist theoretically and recently they have also been revealed. Here I present my way to calculate their velocity c_L.

QED uses the concept of virtual photons and Feynman Diagrams, to perform accurate calculations. The idea is that particles exchange virtual photons and can also **self-interact**. This section shows how **a classical approach to self-interaction** can yield a result for c_L. The buildup of a field around a suddenly created charge propagates, from the charge onwards, at velocity C. The sudden destruction of the charge causes the field around it to vanish at the same speed. Imagine, now, a circulating charge that moves with velocity c_L, where $c_L > C$.

In this case, if to move along half a circle takes less time than for the field to vanish along the diameter, **the charge will be affected by its own field** created when it passed the opposite point on the diameter, **as if** the charge, still existed on the other side of the diameter. We refer to this virtual charge as the **image** of the charge. **Self-interaction** is thus the interaction of a charge with its image, as we phrase it. Imagine the electron charge circulating with velocity c_L around a point. Self-interaction occurs if the time to circulate a half circle, $\pi r_e / c_L$, is shorter than, or equal to, the time for its propagating or retreating field to cross the diameter $2 r_e / c$. Thus, self-interaction takes place if at least:

$\pi\, r_e / c_L = 2\, r_e / c.$ The requirement for self-interaction is thus:

$c_L / c \geq \pi/2$ The minimal value of this ratio is:

$c_L / c = \pi/2$ By constructing a more accurate model of the electron I arrive at:

$c_L / c = \pi / 2\, (1 + \pi\, \alpha)$

$c_L / c = 1.6068$ (p2)

Based on the above I arrive at the next Section.

My Derivation and Calculation of the Electron Mass M_e

Here is my result, **the first of its kind in physics,** for the mass of the electron/positron M_e:

$$M_e = \frac{s^2\sqrt{2}}{\pi(1+\pi\,\alpha)} \cdot \sqrt{G^{-1}\alpha\hbar c^{-3}} \qquad s = 1\ ([s^2] = L^2T^{-2})$$

α is the fine structure constant, c the light velocity, G the gravitational constant and $\hbar$ Planck constant

Dimensionality test:

$$[G^{-1}] = ML^{-3}T^2 \quad [\alpha] = 1 \quad [\hbar] = ML^2T^{-1} \quad [c^{-3}] = L^{-3}T^3$$

$$M = [s^2\sqrt{G^{-1}\alpha\hbar c^{-3}}\,] = L^2T^{-2}(ML^{-3}T^2 \cdot ML^2T^{-1} \cdot L^{-3}T^3)^{1/2} =$$

$$L^2T^{-2}(M^2L^{-4}T^4)^{-1/2} = L^2T^{-2}ML^{-2}T^2 = M$$

M_e (calculated) $= 0.91036 \cdot 10^{-27}$gr

M_e (measured) $= 0.910938356(11) \cdot 10^{-27}$gr

The **accuracy** here is 0.06% !

I arrived at this result 23 years after starting my enterprise. I knew that my idea was good but I was not so sure if I could deliver. Only a few years ago I became convinced that I achieved my goal and started to publish my scientific papers.

The Stability of the Self-Circulation and the Anomalous Gyroscopic Moment

The self-circulation is kept stable by the **attractive** Lorentz force

$F = Q/c\ \mathbf{v_x B}$, towards the center of the circulation. The magnetic field $\mathbf{B}$, which the charge senses, is created by the circulation of its image. This force balances the **repulsive** force $F = Q{\cdot}Q/(2r_e)^2$ between the charge and its image. The magnetic field created by the circulating charge is $\mathbf{B} = 1/c\ \mathbf{v_x E}$. Hence:

$F=(Q/c)\mathbf{v_x B}=(Q/c)\mathbf{v_{x}}(1/c)\mathbf{v_x E}$ but $v = c$ and this equation becomes $F = Q\mathbf{E}$ or $F = Q{\cdot}Q/(2r_e)^2$ This centripetal force balances the repulsive force above. Note that this calculation is not dependent on whether we use c or c_L.

The **anomalous gyroscopic moment** is considered a quantum mechanical phenomenon that **cannot** be explained by classical physics.

Note, however, that the circulation of the self-interacting charge with its own "image" is a current of **"two"** charges that double **E** and hence double **B** = 1/c $\mathbf{v}_x\mathbf{E}$. These "two" charges are circulating along the larger circle of radius R_e related to the spin. We **wonder** if this is the cause for the factor 2 in the anomalous gyroscopic moment, as Dirac showed.

The Derivation and Calculations of the Muon and Tau Masses

The Muon

A photon that enters the pair-production process, by circulating the proton charge, might be converted into the heavy muon and anti-muon pair. This happens if the energy U_{photon} is high enough to retain the angular momentum of the particle/anti-particle $L = 1/2\hbar$, by circulation with radius r_e and velocity c_L, around the proton charge alone and with no need for an additional larger circulation with radius R_e. Hence:

$1/2\ \hbar = (U_\mu/c_L)\ r_e$ or:

$U_\mu = 1/2\ \hbar\ c_L\ /r_e$

Using (p2) for c_L and (p1) for r_e we get:

U_μ (calculated) = 180.15 10^{-6}erg =112.5 MeV   or:

$M_\mu = 112.5$ MeV/c^2

According to CODATA 2014:

U_μ(experimental) = 105.6583745(24) MeV

M_μ(experimental) = 105.6583745(24) MeV/c^2

The calculated result shows a deviation of ~ 6 % from the experimental CODATA value.

The Tau

According to the CODATA 2014:

U_τ/U_μ = 1776.84/105.66 = 16.82

$L = P{\cdot}R = (U_\tau/c')\ r$ and if L is retained then r/c' should be

$(1/16.82)\ r_\mu/c_L$ or:

$r/c' = (1/16.82)1.378 \ 10^{-13} / 1.5348 \ 310^{10} = 1.779 \ 10^{-25}$ sec.   This result occurs if $r < r_\mu$, which means that the elementary charge rotates around an inside point. But for rotation inside a black or white hole $c' < c_L$. Thus, r might be even smaller than $r_\mu/16.82$.

Note that the elementary charge of both the tau and the muon moves at the longitudinal velocity and there is no circulation that brings the overall average velocity down to that of the transverse velocity, c. In this case, the charge moves faster than the photons it radiates, which explains the short lifetime of these particles. In the case of the electron, the compound circulation of the charge brings down the average velocity to the light velocity, c. Hence, photons cannot be radiated (or radiated but re-absorbed). This explains the stability of the electron.

On the Three Generations of Quarks

It seems that these generations are the twisted circulations of the electron, muon and tau particles.

The Electron in Motion and Lorentz Transformation

"Rest" and Motion in the GDM

Every disturbance in space must move at the velocity of its elastic

waves, c_L or c_T.

A transverse disturbance in space moves at the speed of light

$c = c_T$, whereas a longitudinal disturbance moves at a higher

speed c_L

Note that a longitudinal wavepacket is necessarily a moving dilation,

contraction or an oscillation between the two.

As a consequence, **there is no state of rest**. "Rest" is defined,

therefore, as a situation in which a disturbance, although moving at

velocity c_L or c_T, is on a closed track. This orbital movement,

Dirac's Zitterbewegung, is the spin of elementary particles.

On constant translational velocity v, and accelerated motion, relative to space.

"Rest"

Fig. (P1) is a simple description of the electron (positron) at "Rest" and in Motion. The gray sphere (circle) represents the zone of drastically dilated (contracted) space, which is the electric charge. In this discussion we omit, for simplicity, the inner circulation of the charge, with radius r_e. We also do not show in Fig. (P1) that the circulation plane is **not** perpendicular to the velocity vector **v**.

"Rest" is described on the left of Fig. (P1). The zone of dilated space (charge) of our electron revolves, in the xy plane, around the origin with a radius R_0 (in the previous sections we notated this radius as R_e). In this case: $c = \omega R_o$. From now on, when we relate to the electron we also relate to the positron, unless otherwise is mentioned.

Motion

For simplicity we ignore in the following sections the inner circulation of the electric charge.

Fig. (P1), on the right, describes a translational motion. Motion is the situation in which the circle of revolution of the wavepacket becomes a spiral. On this spiral the **length of a revolution** is retained, since angular momentum is retained (explained below). Hence the spiral radius R is smaller than R_0. This is in analogy to a stretched spring. According to Fig. (P1):

$R = 1/\gamma \ R_0$

Note that R_0 is our R_e in the previous sections.

The resultant electron motion, however, is always at the wave velocity c. Thus, a translational motion at constant velocity, v, does not involve any exertion of force (a proof of Newton's first law). It is also obvious that necessarily v < c.

From this alone we derive similar **results** to that of the Theory of Special Relativity (SR), but without SR.

The **length of a revolution** is retained despite the reduction in R since angular momentum is retained. And the angular momentum is retained since the **energy is increasing.**

$$c_1^2 = c^2 - v^2 \quad \text{or:}$$

$$c_1 = c\left(1 - \beta^2\right)^{\frac{1}{2}} = \frac{1}{\gamma}c$$

where: $\quad \beta = \dfrac{v}{c}$

and: $\gamma = \left(1 - \beta^2\right)^{-\frac{1}{2}}$

Fig. (P1) Rest (left) and Motion (right)

Lorentz Transformation (LT)

Our model of the moving electron yields the LT. In a way, it is similar to the contracted particle in motion, used by **Lorentz** (1904) to derive his LT. Note that both models attribute the LT to the contraction of particles due to their motion. This contraction is also the reason for the slowing down of the rates of clocks. See Chapter **S, On Time.**

Newton's first law, and the **SR conclusion** that no particle or signal can move at a speed that exceeds the light/wave velocity c, are thus a natural result of our model. The helical motion, which is an electric current formally in the direction - z, is related to the magnetic field **B** and the vector potential **A**. The Circular Track is stable since the **centrifugal** force is balanced by an equal but opposite **centripetal** force. The Lorentz force, created by the magnetic field of the circulating charge acting on itself, is the required centripetal force.

The Electron Inertia

At rest, the energy of the electron is U_0, linear tangential momentum is

$P_o = U_0/c$ and the angular momentum is $L_0 = P_oR_o$.

In motion, energy, linear momentum and angular momentum are U, $P = U/c$ and $L = PR$ respectively.

The conservation of angular momentum $L = L_0$ (which is $1/2\hbar$ for the electron) implies that:

$PR = P_oR_o$ hence, $UR = U_0R_0$ but:

$$R = 1/\gamma \; R_0 \tag{p3}$$

Thus:

$$U = \gamma \, U_0 \tag{p4}$$

Considering the energy as purely electromagnetic, where the elementary charge Q is a sphere of radius r_0 , the relations

$U_0 = Q^2/2r_0$, $U = Q^2/2r$ and (p2) give:

$$r = 1/\gamma\ r_0 \tag{p5}$$

For $v \ll c$ (53) is:

$$r = (1 - v^2/2c^2)\ r_0 \tag{p6}$$

Acceleration is accompanied by an increase of energy U, and a reduction in the radii R and r. The applied force, needed to accelerate the particle, is doing work to curve space more strongly and thus to reduce r. This force is needed to increase stress and cause more strain in order to enlarge the curvature. Thus, we arrive at **Newton's Second Law** and understand **Inertia.**

Note that we have replaced Newton's axiomatic laws by our postulated model of an elementary particle. Some of the merits in this **replacement**, as we show here and elsewhere, are:

- It leads to the proof of the equivalence of gravitational mass and inertial mass. And, more than that, it shows that **gravitational mass is inertial mass**.

- It proves that **mass** is not a fundamental attribute of matter.

- It proves that **inertia** is an intrinsic attribute of matter, with no need for an additional field to induce it (**Higgs Field**).

Note that $L = 1/2\ \hbar$, $R = 1/2\ \hbar c/\ U$, $U_0 = Q^2/2r_0$ and $r = Q^2/2U$ give:

$\alpha = r/R = Q^2/\ \hbar c$ **Fine Structure Constant.**   (p7)

This result reveals the meaning of α.

Note also that at "rest" the angular momentum can point in any direction, whereas in motion it can point, in the direction of motion or opposite to it. This attribute is related to **Space Quantization.**

Relativistic Mass

Our "relativistic" relation (p2) gives:

$$U = \gamma U_0 = U_0 \left(1 - \frac{v^2}{c^2}\right)^{-\frac{1}{2}} \simeq U_0 + \frac{\frac{1}{2}U_0 v^2}{c^2} \qquad \text{The second term:}$$

$$\frac{\frac{1}{2} U_0 v^2}{c^2} = \frac{1}{2}(U_0/c^2)v^2 \ ,$$

is identified as the **kinetic energy** where:

$$M_0 = U_0 / c^2 \qquad\qquad\qquad (p8)$$

Thus, **inertial mass** becomes merely a **practical term.** We also get:

$$M = \gamma \, M_0 \qquad\qquad\qquad (p9)$$

The literature distinguishes between the **kinetic energy** $\frac{1}{2} M_0 v^2$, which a particle possesses by virtue of its motion, and its **internal energy** $M_0 c^2$. But here, the kinetic energy is also an internal energy of deformation (the reduction in size of r and R) that cannot be distinguished from the rest energy.

Note that our model for the moving electron, presented here, uses the simplified version of the much more detailed model of the electron at "rest" that appears elsewhere.

Q. The Cosmic Microwave Background (CMB)

At large, the CMB is isotropic and homogenous blackbody radiation, with a peak temperature of 2.7°k. The CMB was predicted theoretically by **Gamow** and discovered accidentally by **Penzias and Wilson**. In 1989 the CMB was again measured, this time by the Cosmic Background Explorer (COBE) satellite, see Fig. (Q1).

An observer's motion relative to the background radiation is accompanied by a Doppler shift, see Chapter **C**. This shift enables the measurement of the observer's velocity relative to the radiation bath (i.e., space's vibrations) "attached" to space.

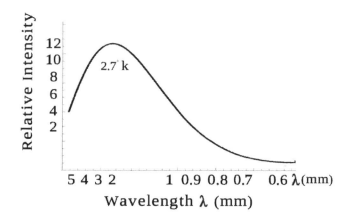

FIG. (Q1) The Cosmic Background

Velocity Relative to the Global Space

A CMB anisotropy was first observed by **Smoot** et al and interpreted as the result of the above Doppler shift.

Fig. (Q2) shows the vector of the velocity, in kilometers per second, of the solar system relative to space. Recently, the velocity of the Earth around the Sun and its rotational velocity have been derived from the Doppler shift.

The solar system velocity relative to space, see Fig. (Q2), is:

$v = 371.0 \pm 0.5$ km sec^{-1}.

This velocity is towards a point whose equatorial coordinates are:

$(\alpha, \delta) = (11.20^h \pm 0.01^h, -7.22^0 \pm 0.08^0)$.

This direction points, approximately, from the cluster of galaxies, Aquarius, towards the cluster Leo-Virgo.

Say the peak of the background radiation is green. An observer, seeing green in all directions, knows they are at rest relative to space. An observer, seeing blue in one direction, red in the opposite direction, and green on the sides, knows they are moving in the direction of the blue.

Similarly, we can also make a distinction regarding acceleration. An observer moving in a circle notices that tangentially to the circle there is no symmetry, the horizon in one direction looks red, and in the other, blue.

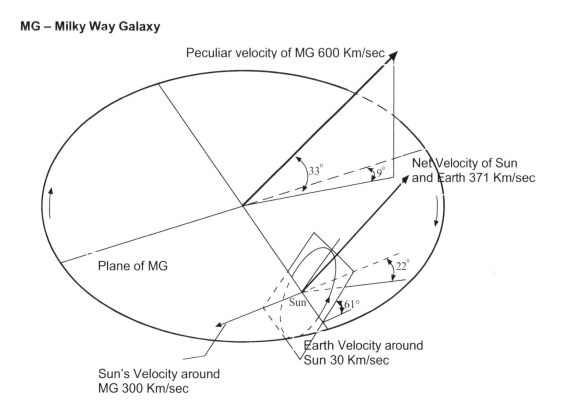

MG – Milky Way Galaxy

FIG. (Q2) Sun Velocity Relative to Space (Scientific American)

Coleman and Glashow, and myself adopted the idea that space is a **special frame**. Experiments to reveal the Earth Velocity Relative to the Global Space by measurements of light velocity in and opposite the Earth velocity vector direction failed. The full isotropy obtained is explained elsewhere.

Space Aether and the Theories of Relativity

In the past space was considered a frame of reference only. Absolute void (emptiness, vacuum) with no meaning without the embedded objects in it. Take out the objects and you have taken from space its meaning.

Later in the past physicists realized that waves accrue in media. Namely waves are the vibrations of a media, like sea waves in the sea or sound waves in the air. But then electromagnetic waves were discovered and the fact that light is an electromagnetic wave.

Immediately rose the question - what is the media of these waves. And since no evidence was found that could identify such a media the idea of the aether was invented. Necessarily it was assumed that this aether occupies the entire space. In this book I explain that the media of electromagnetic waves is space. Hence, we can relate to the terms space and aether as synonyms.

See what Einstein himself wrote about this subject:

Einstein (1920) Ether and the Theory of Relativity

> **… the hypothesis of ether in itself is not in conflict with the special theory of relativity.**

> **… According to the general theory of relativity space without ether is unthinkable;**

R. Updated Special Relativity

Special Relativity (SR) – A Reassessment

In SR, length contraction and time dilation are **not real**. In SR, neither space nor time is objective. Only **spacetime is objective and absolute**, since the interval ΔS^2 is invariant under Lorentz Transformation. In the GDM, physical objects get shorter in the direction of motion relative to space. Hence, the spatial distance between two disconnected objects, moving in the same direction and at the same velocity, is **retained.** SR considers these two objects to reside in **the same** inertial frame. Thus, an observer in another inertial frame concludes that **not only** the objects get shorter, but also the spatial distance between them.

I came across this situation reading Bell's book "Speakable and unspeakable in quantum mechanics".

Case Study

Consider two rockets in a frame **k**, a distance L_0 from each other and at **rest** relative to space. The rockets start to move till they both acquire velocity v, relative to the rest space frame **k**. We assume a

very slow and identical acceleration for both rockets until they reach

this velocity. The two rockets now reside in a new reference frame **k'**

moving at the velocity v relative to **k.**

In Fig. (R1) a beam of light travels from a source S, on the left rocket,

to a mirror M, on the right rocket, and back to a detector D.

According to the GDM, **for an observer at rest** in the space frame

k, L = L_0 regardless of the rockets motion, and the time taken for the

light to travel is:

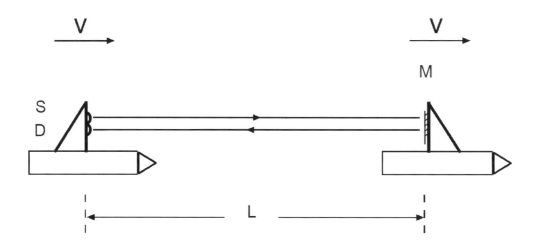

Fig. (R1) Two Rockets

$$\Delta T = \frac{L_0}{c+v} + \frac{L_0}{c-v} = \frac{2L_0}{c}\frac{1}{1-\frac{v^2}{c^2}} = \gamma^2 \Delta T_0 \qquad \text{(r1)}$$

where $\Delta T_0 = 2L_0/c$

For the observer on the left rocket

$$\Delta T = \gamma \, \Delta T_0 \qquad \text{(r2)}$$

since the unit of time of his clock is dilated.

In SR the two rockets reside in the same reference frame $\mathbf{k}'$,

moving relative to $\mathbf{k}$. Hence relative to $\mathbf{k}$ the distance $L = \dfrac{L_0}{\gamma}$ is

contracted and the travel time is:

$$\Delta T = \gamma \, \Delta T_0 \qquad \text{(r3)}$$

This difference, between (r3) and (r1), is the difference between the

predictions of the GDM and SR, **if** one considers $\mathbf{k}'$ a legitimate

frame in SR.

Simultaneity

From the previous Chapter **Q**, it is obvious that observers resting in space can determine whether certain events occurred simultaneously or at different times. The same goes for observers traveling at velocity, v, relative to space. They could also confirm within their system moving at velocity v relative to space whether certain events happened simultaneously or at different times. Events that occurred simultaneously for the observers within the resting system are also simultaneous for observers in motion – and vice versa.

Understandably, in SR, because of Einstein's synchronization procedures, what is simultaneous in one system is not simultaneous in another that is moving relative to the first.

In order to clarify this issue, consider again the moving carriage example Fig. (R2).

Let us suppose that the Earth is at rest relative to space. On earth there is a track that heads off in some direction, with an observer standing by its side. Let us suppose that a carriage travels on this track at velocity v relative to the track (and anyway relative to space) and within the carriage is an internal observer. The carriage has two doors A and B, see Fig. (R2). At the center is a multi-directional pulsating light source. When a pulse reaches detectors D_A, D_B, the doors open. The observer at the side of the track has two cameras, C_A and C_B, able to see a wide-angle view of doors A and B, respectively. These cameras are equipped with equal length cables, at whose ends lay monitors M_A and M_B, which the external observer watches.

If the carriage is at rest relative to the track, and sends a pulse of light, then the doors open simultaneously for both the internal observer and the external observer.

If the carriage is moving relative to the track, and a pulse of light is sent, then it reaches detector D_A after a period of time:

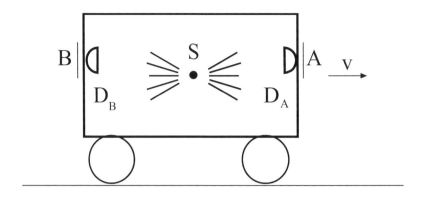

FIG. (R2) Simultaneity

$$\Delta T_A = \frac{L}{2} \frac{1}{c - v}$$

and to D$_B$ after:

$$\Delta T_B = \frac{L}{2} \frac{L}{c + v}$$

The external observer sees door B open

before door A, seeing that:

$$\Delta T_B < \Delta T_A$$

For the internal observer to determine what happened, they must

see the light returning from the doors to the center of the cabin – to

the observer.

The time of return from door A:

$$\Delta T_A' = \frac{L}{2} \frac{1}{c+v}$$

whereas from door B:

$$\Delta T_B' = \frac{L}{2} \frac{1}{c-v}$$

so, the total time it takes to

and from door A:

$$\Delta T_A'' = \Delta T_A + \Delta T_A' = \frac{L}{c} \frac{1}{1-\frac{v^2}{c^2}}$$

whereas from door B:

$$\Delta T_B'' = \Delta T_B + \Delta T_B' = \frac{L}{c} \frac{1}{1-\frac{v^2}{c^2}}$$

seeing that:

$$\Delta T_A'' = \Delta T_B''$$

for the internal observer, the doors appear to open simultaneously.

However, since the internal observer knows how to measure v, they can calculate and deduce that the doors did not open simultaneously. Therefore, there is no place for Einstein's SR argument about the relativity of simultaneity. There is no need, anyway, for a new perception of the causality principle.

Note

Einstein's SR gives no meaning to velocity v relative to the "stationary system", because it "can't be" measured.

Since $\Delta T_A'' = \Delta T_B''$ we can arbitrarily make the simplest assumption $\Delta T_A = \Delta T_A' = \Delta T_B = \Delta T_B'$. This is equivalent to stating that the speed of light in the carriage is c in every direction, or in every inertial system. From this Einstein derived the relativity of simultaneity and the relativity of the shortening of length and of the clock slowing down. And from this, the objective meaning is removed from time and space.

A Spherical Light Wave

Spherical wave fronts are emitted from the origin, O, of a co-ordinate system, **k**, starting at time, t_0. System **k** is at rest in space. **k'** is another co-ordinate system that happens to coincide with **k** at t_0 but moves at the speed v along x.

From Einstein's principle of constant light velocity, it is understood that in both **k** and **k'** an observer sees spherical wave fronts and, therefore:

$$x^2 + y^2 + z^2 - c^2t^2 = x'^2 + y'^2 + z'^2 - c^2t'^2$$

From this and the principle of relativily, Einstein 1905 (1923) obtained the **Lorentz Transformation** (LT).

We now consider the spherical wave fronts and try to understand what is really happening.

The observer in system **k**, obviously, sees a spherical wave. The observer in **k'** is, on the face of it, **supposed** to see contracted wave fronts in front of them and dilated wave fronts behind them, as shown in Fig. (R3), i.e., to see distorted wave fronts. But what does "to see" really mean? "To see" means to get back some scattered or reflected light, which is possible only if there are some scattering particles or mirrors in system **k'**. If there are such elements in **k'**, which are physically linked to it, the light that the observer sees has traveled back and forth and, since the lengths in **k'** are contracted, the observer in **k' does in fact see** spherical wave fronts.

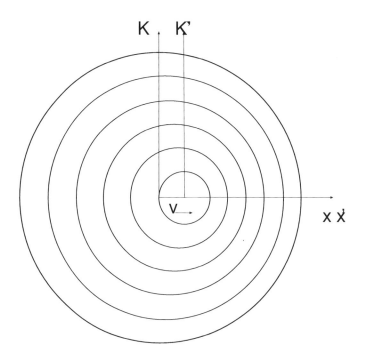

FIG. (R3) Spherical Light Wave

The Contraction of Macroscopic Bodies

Fitzgerald and **Lorentz** (1904) explained the then lack of ability to discover motion relative to the aether (**Michelson** and **Morley** 1887) assuming that the lengths of bodies are contracted in the direction of their motion:

$$L = L_0 \left(1 - \frac{v^2}{c^2}\right)^{\frac{1}{2}} = \frac{1}{\gamma} L_0 \qquad \textbf{Lorentz Length Contraction} \quad (r4)$$

The translational velocity v is with respect to space, as we see it. An observer moving in space would not notice any contraction, since not only the yardstick but also, they are contracted. However, they can always measure their velocity relative to space and calculate their own contraction. At this stage we can only speculate as to why and how a macroscopic body in motion is contracted.

We consider a possible explanation for macroscopic contraction.

According to Bell, and our exploration elsewhere the electric field of a moving charge is:

$$E' = \frac{HQ}{r'^2} \frac{1 - \beta^2}{\left(1 - \beta^2 \sin^2 \theta'\right)^{3/2}} \qquad (r5)$$

We denote the distance from the charge Q, momentarily at the origin, to the point (x',z') where the field is measured:

$r' = \left(x'^2 + z'^2\right)^{1/2}$. θ' denotes the angle between this radius vector and the velocity of the charge Q, which is moving in the positive x' direction in the frame k'. Then, since z' = r' sin θ', (4) is the magnitude of the field.

For low speeds the field reduces simply to $E' \approx HQ/r'^2$. But if β^2 is not negligible, at the same distance from the charge, the field is stronger at right angles to the motion than in the direction of the motion. Fig. (R4) shows a simple representation of the field indicating field lines in the x'z' plane. For the field in the x'y' plane we get an identical representation. Fig. (R4) shows that the field perpendicular to the direction of motion gets stronger whereas in the direction of motion - weaker. This phenomenon explains **macroscopic contraction**, since the orbits of electrons in atoms are distorted to become ellipses with their shorter axis in the direction of motion.

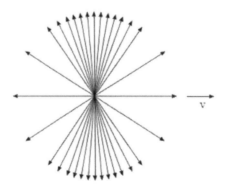

Fig. (R4) The Field of a Uniformly Moving Charge

The Direction of Emission from A Moving Radiator

A Macroscopic Radiator.

Fig. (R5) shows a projector. A point radiator is located at 0, the focal

point of parabolic mirror.

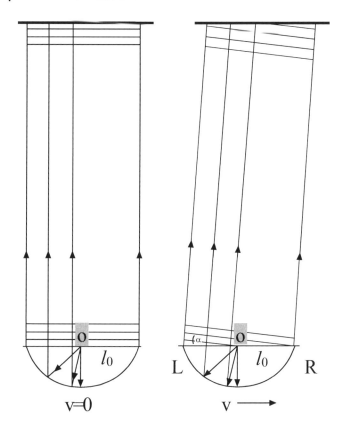

Fig. (R5) A Macroscopic Radiator

When the projector does not move, v = 0, the radiation reaches both

edges of the reflector at the same time, and the outgoing beam from

the reflector moves toward the ceiling with its wave front parallel to the ceiling. When the projector is on the move, v ≠ 0, the radiation from 0 reaches the left side of the parabolic mirror, before it reaches the right side, thus tilting the wave front and, actually, deflecting the beam.

This deflection accrues with any source of light whether macroscopic or microscopic. The conclusion is, thus, that **the motion of an emitter affects the synchrotron radiation.**

A source of light radiates isotropically when at rest relative to space, See Fig. (R6) left. When it moves the intensity in the direction of motion is stronger than behind, See Fig. (R6) right.

This effect, termed **synchrotron radiation,** complies with our understanding.

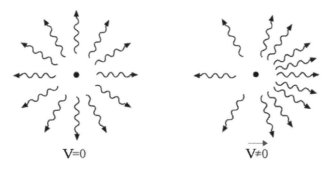

FIG. (R6) Synchrotron Radiation

S. On Time

Real motion is only that of the transvers or longitudinal waves. Space is a special frame and motion relative to space causes real contraction and deflection. These phenomena dispel the need for relating to time as a fundamental attribute of reality. The saying that "Time is Money", albeit with a different connotation, expresses our understanding that Time is indeed like Money.

Larmor Time Dilation

The Cell

Fig. (**S**1) and Fig. (**S**2) show a cell with sides L_0. The cell is equipped with a source S and detector D, on one side, and a mirror on the opposite side. If the cell is at rest relative to space, the time it takes for the light beam to reach the mirror from source S and back to detector D is ΔT_0:

$$\Delta T_0 = \frac{2L_0}{c} \qquad\qquad\qquad (s1)$$

A Moving Cell with a Beam Perpendicular to its Motion

Fig. (S1) shows the source S and detector D on the "floor", and the mirror on the "ceiling". If the cell moves in a direction perpendicular to the direction of the beam of light, the observer resting in space (outside the cell) sees a deflected beam:

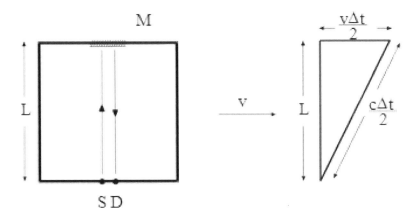

Fig. (S1) A Moving Cell

$$\left(\frac{c\Delta T}{2}\right)^2 = L^2 + \left(\frac{v\Delta T}{2}\right)^2$$

L = L₀ since there is **no contraction** in the direction perpendicular to the direction of motion.

Hence: $4L_0^2 = \left(c^2 - v^2\right)\Delta T^2$ and

$$\Delta T = \frac{2L_0}{c} \frac{1}{\left(1 - \dfrac{v^2}{c^2}\right)^{\frac{1}{2}}} \qquad \gamma = 1 / \left(1 - v^2/c^2\right)^{1/2} \quad \text{or}$$

$$\Delta T = \gamma \Delta T_0 \qquad \textbf{Larmor Time Dilation} \qquad \text{(s2)}$$

A Moving Cell with a Beam Parallel to its Motion

Fig. (S2) shows the source S and detector D on one side, and the mirror on the other side. When the cell and the light beam move at speed v relative to space:

$$\Delta T = \frac{L}{c + v} + \frac{L}{c - v} = \frac{2L}{c} \frac{1}{1 - \dfrac{v^2}{c^2}} = \frac{2L}{c} \gamma^2 \qquad \text{(s3)}$$

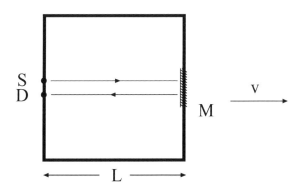

Fig. (S2) A Moving Cell

According to equation (s4):

$$L = \frac{L_0}{\gamma}$$ **Lorentz Length Contraction** (s4)

and again

$$\Delta T = \gamma \Delta T_0$$ **Larmor Time Dilation** (s5)

Based on (s2) and (s5) **we conclude time to be a scalar**.

On the Lifetime of the Muon

SR Interpretation

The muon particle decays via the weak interaction into an electron and a pair of neutrinos after 2.2 microseconds. In the late 1990s, scientists at Brookhaven National Laboratory, used the Alternative Gradient Synchrotron (AGS) to produce a beam of muons circulating around a 14m-diameter ring at a speed of 0.9994·c. Muons lifetime, at rest, is 2.2 microseconds.

If this is also the lifetime at this speed, they would manage no more than 15 turns of the ring before they disintegrate. But the muons managed around 433 turns, which means their lifetime was extended by a factor of 28.8 to just over 60 microseconds.

And indeed, for a speed of 0.9994·c the Lorentz factor of time-dilation is: γ = 28.87.

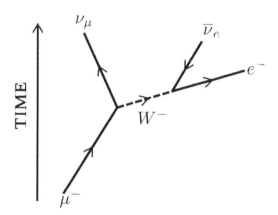

Fig. (S3) Feynman Diagram of the Muon Decay

SR predicts, as observed, that these speedy muons should live 28.87 times longer than at rest.

According to SR, we can also argue that space in the frame of the muon, which moves with a tangential velocity 0.9994·c relative to the Lab frame, is contracted, a Lorentz contraction, by the same

γ = 28.87. And as a result, the muon with its lifetime of 2.2 microseconds, moves 433 times around this contracted circumference. The fact that there are two alternate SR explanations is confusing.

GDM Interpretation

Fig. (S3) shows that the muon disintegrates via its interaction with the vibrating space around it. Hence the smaller it becomes the weaker is the interaction. The interaction dependence on γ is, therefore, reflected in the dependence of the particle's lifetime on γ:

$$T = \gamma T_0$$

Conclusion

We consider both length contraction, and light deflection to be real. Thus, we have dispelled the need to relate to time as a fundamental attribute of reality. Time appears as simply the division of Distance by Velocity. By virtue of motion, or deformed space, objects and light velocity change in a way that keeps light velocity constant, hence the term **constant of nature**, but time by itself has no meaning.

This conclusion has implications as to how we relate to the **first term** in the Schwarzschild metric:

$$ds^2 = -g_{00}c^2 dt^2 + 2g_{0r}dr\,dt + g_{rr}dr^2 + r^2\left(d\theta^2 + \sin^2\theta\,d\varphi^2\right).$$

Some physicists wrongly consider c to be **constant** whereas it is time that changes. We, in contrast, consider c to be a **variable**, but a **constant of nature**.

Note that a mass contracts space around it hence, accordingly light velocity c at the mass, is slower than that in inter-galactic space. Space is contracted, but so is the local observer close to the mass and their yardstick. Thus, the value for c, measured by the local observer, is the same as for the far-away observer. This is the reason for considering c a constant of nature, despite being a variable.

T.   THE PHOTON AND THE QUANTUM ENIGMA

In this chapter we dispel the need to attribute a **dualistic nature** to photons, namely that a photon is both a particle and a wave. The method used in resolving this case is applicable also to other issues of Quantum Mechanics.

Interference with Classical Waves – Ensembles of Photons

Photons or photoms, of the same wavelength, when they are in phase and closely packed, move as a classical wave. Let a wave front, of such a classical wave, hit the double slit, see Fig. (T1); if secondary waves, which are coming from the two slits and hit the screen, are in phase (on the screen) they create maxima zones of intensity on the screen, and minima if out of phase. In other words; intensity is reduced in zones of **destructive** interference whereas in zones of **constructive** interference intensity is enhanced. But these waves are ensembles of photons and photoms, see Fig. (T2) and (T3), entering these zones, and they are neither annihilated nor created and the total energy is conserved. No annihilation or creation takes place, only **a spatial displacement** of the particles that result in a reduction in their density (intensity) in one zone and an increase in their density (intensity) in the other.

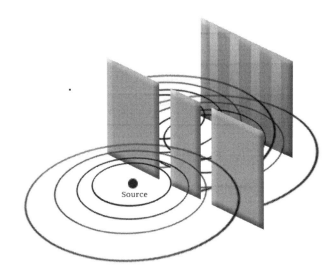

Fig.(T1) Interference with Classical EM Waves

The Table below gives some information about the slits.

WAVELENGTH	0.0005 mm (GREEN)
SLIT WIDTH	0.04 mm
SLIT SPACE	0.250 mm

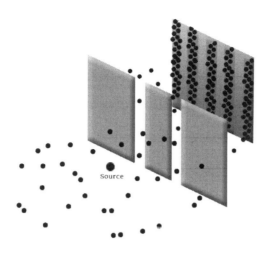

Fig.(T2) Interference with Photons

This displacement is due to the interaction of the photons with the space lattice, as we have already explained in Chapter **O**. This explanation is the first of its kind, and is applicable to other quantum issues. Hence, we can relate to the ensemble of photons in phase as a wave, see Fig. (T3). **But what about single photons?** What happens when we reduce the intensity of the source of light to the degree in which only single photons are delivered towards the slits. And at a rate that ensures that when one photon is on its way to the screen the next photon is not yet emitted. All this to ensure that no interaction takes place between the photons on their way to the screen.

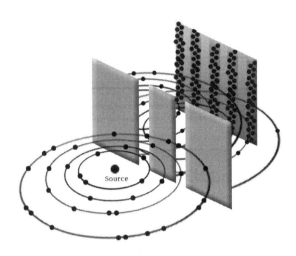

Fig. (T3) Interference of Waves and Particles

Note that when single photons reach the screen right after the experiment started, we see on the screen "snow" (no pattern), see Fig.(T4) up. Only with time the accumulation of photons reveals the interference pattern, see Fig.(T4) middle and down.

In the current paradigm this phenomenon is explained by attributing a dualistic nature to a single photon: the photon is both a particle and a wave. I beg to differ and suggest the following explanation, based on the understanding of "spontaneous" emission.

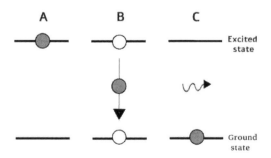

Fig. (T4) The Gradual Development of the Pattern

Stimulated and Spontaneous Emission

Fig. (T5) shows on the left an atom on a high energy level (upper line) above the lower energy level (bottom line-ground state). If a photon, with the same energy as that of the difference in the energy levels of the atom, arrives it can induce the emission of an identical photon by the atom, and its fall to the ground state. This process is termed **Stimulated Emission**.

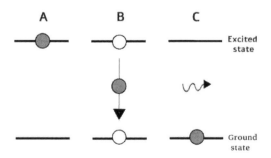

Fig. (T5) Stimulated and Spontaneous Emission

However, the atom can also emit a photon without an inducing photon from outside. This kind of emission is termed **Spontaneous Emission.** Some physicists, myself included, are convinced that in this case it is a photom (ground state photon) that induces the emission. Let me remind you that a photom is an ADAM or EVE. Below is evidence in support of my Spontaneous Emission idea. Fig. (T6) shows a beam of exited atoms running through a narrow tube. The rate of emission of photons from these atoms is reduced drastically compared to their rate outside the tube – more than ten times. The explanation is simple: In this tube modes of vibrations, namely photoms, perpendicular to the tube axis and with a wavelength twice the inner diameter of the tube cannot exist. Hence the number of photoms is drastically reduced and so is the spontaneous emission.

Fig. (T6) Damping Spontaneous Emission

In another experiment a mirror is placed close and parallel to a beam of exited atoms. This time the emission rate is doubled, since the mirror reflects incoming photoms back towards the beam, thus doubling their number per unit volume.

Interference with Individual Photons

There is a body of both experimental and theoretical work that shows how the vacuum state of the electromagnetic field (photoms) induces "spontaneous" emission, see the sub-section above. Thus, the basic state is that of a single photon plus a single photom. When one photom, out of the many that construct a wave front of photoms with a frequency that matches a transition in an excited atom (in the source), hits the exited atom it has a probability to induce emission in phase with a photon. The probability of the photon to hit a certain spot on the screen is thus the classical probability of the inducing photom to arrive at this same spot. But the photoms arrive as a classical wave and hence their unseen interference pattern on the screen. This explains the many, one at a time, photons accumulation effect that builds the interference pattern, see Fig. (T4).

This dispels the need to attribute a dualistic nature to photons and solves the collapse issue of the "wavefunction" (although there is no such thing for a photon). Note that the width and the height of the slits, as well as the distance between them, see the table above, comply with our understanding of the photon and photom nature, and the interference experiment.

In the year 2011 it was shown in a "Weak-Experiment" that a single photon, in the Double Slit experiment, goes all the way from the source to the screen through only one slit. The photon follows a trajectory known as the **D. Bohm trajectory**.

Our "mechanism" by which the photon is "guided" is also relevant to other elementary particles, atoms, molecules, and even microscopic bodies. The **statistical nature** of the process of single photons interference is clear, but inferentially it is **deterministic**.

This photoms wave is actually the **De Broglie guiding wave**.

As you can see there is no need for a new formalism in order to support my explanation. All it takes is imagination.

as **Einstein** said:

Imagination is more important than knowledge.

My explanation is even more convincing in the case of the following experiment.

PFLEEGOR & MANDEL's EXPERIMENT (1967)

Interference effects produced by the superposition of the light beams from two independent single-mode lasers have been investigated experimentally. It is found that interference takes place even under conditions in which the light intensities are so low, with high probability, one photon is absorbed before the next one is emitted by one or the other laser. Since the average number of registered photons per trial was only about 10, photon correlation techniques were required to demonstrate the interference. The interpretation of the experiment, and the question whether it demonstrates interference between two photons, are discussed.

The demonstration, a few years ago, that two light beams derived from two independent lasers can give rise to observable interference fringes led to a certain amount of debate. The discussion centered in part on the appropriate description of the state of a laser field, and on the question whether the experiment **disproved** a famous statement of Dirac (1958) that ...**each photon interferes only with itself. Interference between different photons never occurs.**

In this experiment, as shown in Fig. (T7) we get an interference pattern of laser beams delivered from two identical lasers. When one of the lasers is off, the pattern disappears (the result of all relevant theories). **However, if we reduce the intensity of the lasers to the extent that statistically the time of flight to the screen is shorter than the time between sequential deliveries of photons, we still get an interference pattern.**

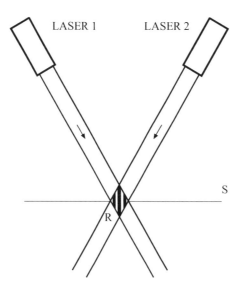

FIG. (T 7) Pfleeger and Mandel's Experiment

Suppose we adopt Dirac's argument that a photon interferes with itself, how do we get an interference pattern in the Pfleeger and Mandel experiment, without using two slits, or some similar device.

The guiding interference pattern, as I see it, is built by the "interference" of identical bunched photoms (waves) coming through the two lasers and the photons simply "ride" on them.

On EM Waves

Waves we encounter in nature are, most of the time, spherical waves rather than plane waves. However, far from a radiator, a spherical wave appears to be approximately a plane wave. Far from the radiator the electrical field of the wave $\mathbf{E}$ decreases as $1/r$ and hence its intensity, which is proportional to $\mathbf{E}^2$ decreases as $1/r^2$. Thus, the classical approach complies with the quantum approach. In this case, the intensity at a far distance r depends on the number of photons that are crossing a unit area and hence the dependence on $1/r^2$.

U.   The Universe

Fig. (U1) gives the distribution of energy/mass in the universe. We know a lot on 4.9 % of this content (white section), which relates, obviously, to the content of this book. We know to some extent on Dark Matter (gray section), but very little on Dark Energy (dark section).

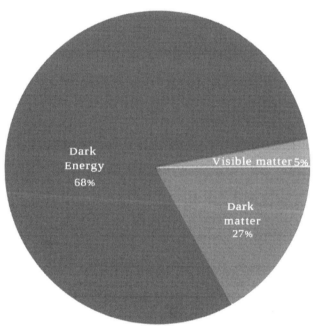

Fig. (U1) The Distribution of Energy/Mass in the

Universe

In this Chapter we discuss four of the cardinal issues in cosmology:

Why is the geometry of our universe Euclidian?

Chapter G covers the subject.

What is Dark Matter? this question has been open already

~ 85 years.

Why is the universe expanding? this question has been open

~ 90 years.

What is Dark Energy? this question has been open ~ 20 years.

Dark Matter

The measurement of the velocity of outlying stars revolving around galaxies is presented by the curve B in Fig. (U2). The expected curve according to the Newtonian theory of gravity was supposed to yield the curve A. This discrepancy is explained in three different ways:

Around galaxies there are halos of invisible mater – **dark matter**, that interact only gravitationally with visible matter. This opinion is held by the majority of physicists.

At a large distance from the centers of galaxies Newton's law of gravitation does not hold anymore and should be replaced by a new law. This law was found phenomenologically 30 years ago by Milgrom. No one so far has been able to prove this law theoretically.

My opinion, that differs from the above opinions, but complies with the Milgrom law, is presented below.

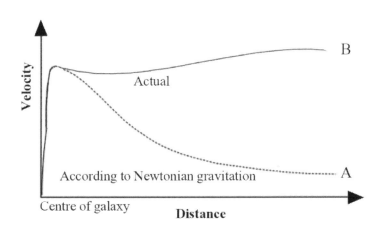

Fig. (U2) Rotation Curves in Galaxies

Dark Matter Resolution

I contend that Dark Matter is a Misinterpretation of Gradients in Space Density Around Galaxies.

General Relativity (GR) and its low field approximation - Newtonian gravitation - are nothing but deformed space. In Chapter G On bent (curved) manifolds and deformed spaces I show that the deformation of space is related to space density. Hence, gravitation is a gradient in space density. Inhomogeneous space expansion (gradients) around galaxies, due to the absence of Hubble space flow inside them, can thus create a central acceleration (gravitational field) that is wrongly interpreted as the result of the presence of Dark Matter.

Rotation Curves

The issue of Rotation Curves in galaxies led, in 1933, to the **Zwicky** hypothesis of Dark Matter (DM). Alternatively, it led, in 1983, to the suggestions by **Milgrom** to modify Newtonian Gravity (**MOND**) and by Bekenstein, in 2004, to modify General Relativity **with Tensor–Vector–Scalar gravity** (TeVeS).

I, however, dispel the need for both DM and a modification of GR. Based on the fact that space expansion in and around galaxies is inhomogeneous, I show that the phenomenological MOND equation indeed represents a new kind of central acceleration.

Again, on Light Velocity

The discussion here will clarify the fact that observers in all zones of space, regardless of their space densities, will claim to get the same result measuring light velocity with their standard yardsticks and clocks. Hence, we relate to Light Velocity as a **constant of nature.**

However, each and every faraway observer finds that according to his measurements and understanding light velocity elsewhere, where local observers reside, might vary according to space density in their locality. This is the result of light velocity dependence on the permittivity and permeability of space. But the permittivity and permeability of space depend on the density of space. Hence, we should not consider light velocity as a constant and should relate to the **coordinate speed of light** of GR as a real speed.

The Metric and Light Velocity

Schwarzschild, in 1916, was the first to find a solution to Einstein's field equation - a general spacetime metric - for the exterior of a spherically-symmetric star of radius R, i.e., for r > R:

$$ds^2 = -g_{00}c^2dt^2 + 2g_{0r}dr\,dt + g_{rr}dr^2 + r^2\left(d\theta^2 + \sin^2\theta\,d\varphi^2\right) \qquad \text{(u1)}$$

The metric's elements g_{00}, g_{0r} and g_{rr} are functions of r and t.

According to [13] the line element ds^2 is:

$$ds^2 = -e^{-\frac{2GM}{c^2 r}} c^2 dt^2 + e^{\frac{2GM}{c^2 r}} dr^2 + r^2 \left(d\theta^2 + \sin^2\theta \, d\varphi^2\right) \qquad \text{(u2)}$$

We denote a **gravitational scale factor**, a:

$$a = e^{-\frac{GM}{c^2 r}} \qquad \text{(u3)}$$

For the surface of the sun or the edge of our galaxy:

$GM/rc^2 \sim 10^{-6}$ and thus, $GM/rc^2 \ll 1$.

For $GM/rc^2 \ll 1$ equation (u3) is approximated as:

$a = (1 - GM/rc^2)$ $a < 1$ $r \to \infty$ $a \to 1$ (u4)

We rewrite equation (u2) to become:

$$ds^2 = -a^2 c^2 dt^2 + a^{-2} dr^2 + r^2 \left(d\theta^2 + \sin^2\theta \, d\varphi^2\right) \qquad \text{(u5)}$$

The metric in equation (u5) is derived by a faraway observer OB1 – far away from the center of a mass, M, that serves as the origin of their co-ordinates.

For OB1, a radial distance interval, dl, close to M, contains a smaller number of their yardstick units, dr, than dr_0, the number of the local observer OB2 yardstick units that dl contains. This is the result of the OB2 yardstick contraction (curving), which is the contraction of their local space. Hence:

$$dr_0 = a^{-1}dr \quad a < 1 \tag{u6}$$

From the **synchronization of clocks**, **Rindler** arrives (p. 184) at:

$$dt_0 = adt \quad a < 1 \tag{u7}$$

Thus, for OB1, a time interval, dτ, contains a larger number of time units, dt, than the number of time units, dt_0, for OB2.

The 4D **spacetime interval** between two events; the "emission" of a short pulse of light at point A and the "arrival" of this pulse at point B is:

$$ds^2 = 0.$$

Hence, using equation (u5):

$$-a^2c^2dt^2 + a^{-2}dr^2 = 0 \qquad \text{(u8)}$$

$$acdt = a^{-1}dr \qquad \text{(u9)}$$

$$dr/dt = a^2c \qquad \text{(u10)}$$

This, $dr/dt = c'$, for OB1, is the light velocity close to a mass M. Light velocity, for OB1, far away from M, is c (standard light velocity), whereas $dr/dt = c' < c$.

This, $dr/dt = c'$, is a local, real and slower, light velocity since, according to equation (u4), a < 1.

In the literature dr/dt in equation (u10) is called the **coordinate speed of light**. This is a misleading name, since dr/dt should be considered a **real speed**.

Substituting dr from equation (u6) and dt from equation (u7) in equation (u8) gives:

$$dr/dt = adr_0/a^{-1}dt_0 = a^2dr_0/dt_0 \qquad \text{(u11)}$$

Comparing equation (u11) to equation (u10), gives:

$$dr_0/dt_0 = c \qquad\qquad\qquad\qquad \text{(u12)}$$

And from (u11) again:

$$c' = a^2 c \qquad\qquad\qquad\qquad \text{(u13)}$$

The results here and my discussion elsewhere lead me to conclude that OB1 and OB2 measuring light velocity locally in their own zones of space arrive at the same result.

Due to this invariance, light velocity is considered **"a constant of nature"**, despite the fact that in different zones of space it behaves differently.

In conclusion:

$$dr_0 = a^{-1} dr \qquad\qquad\qquad\qquad \text{(u6)}$$

$$dt_0 = a dt \qquad\qquad\qquad\qquad \text{(u7)}$$

$$c' = a^2 c \qquad\qquad\qquad\qquad \text{(u13)}$$

The Gravitational Field as a Gradient in Light Velocity

Substituting a, equation (u4), in equation (u10), gives for the case $GM/rc^2 \ll 1$:

$dr/dt = a^2c = (1 - GM/rc^2)^2c \sim (1 - 2GM/rc^2)c = (1 + 2\varphi/c^2)c$ (u14)

From (u14) and $dr/dt = c'$ we get the gravitational potential φ:

$\varphi = \frac{1}{2} c (c' - c)$ (u15)

Note that $c' < c$, which complies with $\varphi < 0$. The field strength (central acceleration g) is thus:

$E_g = g = - d\varphi/dr = - \frac{1}{2} cdc'/dr$ (u16)

$\mathbf{E_g} = \mathbf{g} = - 1/2\, c\nabla\mathbf{c'}$ (u17)

Thus, the gravitational field (central acceleration) can be considered a gradient in light velocity.

Note that c' is not a scalar, it is a vector $\mathbf{c'}$, and $\nabla\mathbf{c'}$ is a gradient of a vector. This gradient involves Christoffel symbols which are involved in the GR field equation.

To check our derivation, we take (u14) and $c' = dr/dt$ and get:

$c' = (1 - 2GM/rc^2)c$ (u18)

$dc'/dr = 2GM/r^2c$ (u19)

Hence, according to equation (u16) the **central acceleration** is:

$g = \frac{1}{2} cdc'/dr = GM/r^2$ (u20)

$$\mathbf{g} = - (GM/r^3)\,\mathbf{r} \qquad\qquad\qquad\qquad \text{(u21)}$$

Note that M is a **gravitational mass**, since it comes from Einstein's GR field equation.

Note also that equations (u16) and (u17) are **general equations**, not necessarily limited to the Newtonian gravitational field.

This understanding leads to the understanding of free fall and yields the proof of the equivalence of inertial mass and gravitational mass.

The Overlooked Central Acceleration

The **Cosmological Scale Factor** (CSF), a, in the epoch of galaxies formation 500–700 Myr (Mega years)

($z = 8$–11) after the Big-Bang, is notated a_b. Taking $z = 9$ gives:

$a_b = 1/(z+1) = 0.1$, whereas the present CSF in the intergalactic space is $a_0 = 1$.

$$a_b = 0.1 \qquad a_0 = 1 \qquad\qquad\qquad\qquad \text{(u22)}$$

Note that the CSF, a, in this section **is not** the gravitational scale factor, a, although both relate to space density.

Space in the universe expands, but space within galaxies does not.

We, however, assume that at some point in the galaxy or on its

outskirts space starts to expand gradually to reach $a_0 = 1$.

A **toy function** for a variable CSF, in and around galaxies, is:

$$a = a_b + (a_0 - a_b)[1 - \exp(- r/(R/4))] \qquad (u23)$$

R is the Hubble sphere radius. For $r = 0$, $a = a_b$ and for $r \rightarrow R$,

$a = 0.98$, which is close to $a_0 = 1$.

Note that the radius of the universe is many times larger than the

Hubble sphere radius R. Taking R/4 is **arbitrary**, but based on the

size of "dark matter halos" it is **reasonable**; **it should**, however, be

supported by observations.

Substituting the values $a_b = 0.1$ and $a_0 = 1$, of equation (u22), in

equation (u23) gives:

$$a = 0.1 + 0.9[1 - \exp(- 4r/R)] \qquad (u24)$$

For $r << R$ equation (u24) becomes:

$$a = 0.1 + 3.6r/R \qquad (u25)$$

According to equations (u13) and (u25) and using the Hubble parameter $H = c/R$ (defined as $H = \dot{a}/a$) gives for $r \ll R$ the following value for dc'/dr:

$$dc'/dr = c \, d/dr \, (a^2) = c \, 2a \, da/dr = 2 \cdot a \cdot 3.6 \cdot c \, /R$$

Taking for a its average value $(a_b + a_0)/2 \sim 0.5$ gives:

$$dc'/dr = 0.36H \qquad\qquad\qquad (u26)$$

The H value as of today - the Hubble constant H_0, is:

$$H_0 = 2.26 \pm 0.25 \times 10^{-18} \text{ sec}^{-1}.$$

Substituting this value (without the error range, since we are using an artificial toy function) in equation (u26) gives:

$$dc'/dr = 0.36 \, H_0 = 0.81 \times 10^{-18} \text{sec}^{-1} \qquad\qquad (u27)$$

The value for the **central acceleration**, due to the inhomogeneous space density, as of today, is calculated using equations (u16) and (u27):

$$g = -\tfrac{1}{2} \, c \, dc'/dr = -1.22 \times 10^{-8} \text{ cm s}^{-2}. \qquad\qquad (u28)$$

This acceleration, notated g_0, is:

$$g_0 = -1.22 \times 10^{-8} \text{ cm s}^{-2} \qquad\qquad\qquad (u29)$$

The **geometric average (mean)** of the Newtonian **central acceleration** $g_N = -GM/r^2$, and g_0 gives:

$$g = -\frac{\sqrt{g_0 GM}}{r} \qquad\qquad (u30)$$

Equation (u30) **resembles** the **Milgrom MOND phenomenological** equation. According to MOND, for central accelerations smaller than g_0, the Newtonian central acceleration should be modified to become equation (u30). Our g_0, in contrast, is **a real** additional central acceleration. Thus, it is clear that our understanding is not related at all to MOND. We adhere to GR and its weak field Newtonian approximation and dispel the need to modify them.

Note the fit of our value for g_0, in equation (u29), to the observed MOND g_0, which is:

$$g_0 = -1.2 \pm 0.2 \times 10^{-8} \, \text{cm s}^{-2}. \qquad\qquad (u31)$$

Note, that the MOND theory uses the notation a_0 rather than g_0.

We take the **geometric average (mean)**, since central accelerations are related to radii of space curvatures. This subject, however, is beyond the scope of this paper.

Gravitation is the contraction of space, whereas space expansion is the dilation of space. g_N is the result of gravitational space contraction (curving) whereas g_0 is the result of space dilation (curving). Let r_0 denote the distance from the center of a galaxy at which space contraction was balanced by space dilation, in the epoch of the galaxy's creation. This balance at r_0, with the larger g_0 **of that time**, is expressed by the equality $g_N = g_0$, or:

$$GM/r_0^2 = g_0 \qquad\qquad (u32)$$

Thus:

$$r_0 = (GM/g_0)^{1/2} \qquad\qquad (u33)$$

Note the following:

With time H becomes smaller and so does the gradient in light velocity, see equation (u26). Thus, the zone of balance, at r_0, see (u33), moves forward, away from the center of the galaxy, as if "Dark Matter Halos" grow with time.

Our central acceleration, equation (u17), is based on a gradient in light velocity; hence we can explain lensing, including the lensing of empty zones of space with inhomogeneous space density.

Summary

The inhomogeneous expansion of space around galaxies creates a universal, so far overlooked, central acceleration, g_0 that explains Rotation Curves. Thus, I dispel the need for Dark Matter or a modification of the laws of physics. We simply have to understand them.

Space Expansion

Three are the options related to space expansion:

Galaxies move through space and drag with them the gravitational deformation, namely the contraction of space.

Galaxies hold space inside them and stretch space as they move apart due to large scale gravitational repulsion.

Galaxies partially move through space and partially drag space.

I have not come across a discussion nor new facts that could help me determine which is the case.

The first option does not comply with the fact that there is no expansion within galaxies.

The second option does not comply with the fact that there are cases in which a fast galaxy is getting detached from its Dark Matter halo.

Dark Energy

Some facts are worth mentioning:

Mass and dark matter density in the universe are getting smaller with space expansion

Radiation density in the universe is getting smaller with space expansion, which means that it is space that expands.

Dark energy density **is not** affected by space expansion.

Dark energy density is not related to space energy due to zero-point fluctuations density, which is many orders of magnitude larger than Dark Energy density.

Dark Energy density is close to twice the energy density of matter (including Dark Matter).

V. Summary

I have constructed a TOE of the physical reality, in which there is nothing but space. All the laws are derived as logical inferences. The unit of length and the unit of time are the only units needed in my model. All the particles are constructed from the photoms ADAM and EVE. And the only one force is the tension of space.

 If we and the infinite space are one and the same, then there is sense in Spinoza's notion that SPACE is GOD.

Halleluiah

*However, if we do discover a complete theory… then we shall take part in the discussion of the question of **why it is that we and the universe exist**.*

If we find the answer to that, it would be the ultimate triumph of human reason.

S. HAWKING (1987)

W. The Author HAL Web Site and Papers

DOMAINS
› List

AFFILIATIONS

- Taga Innovations 22

PRODUCTION YEAR

- 2020 2
- 2019 2
- 2018 5
- 2017 9
- 2016 4

Number of documents
22

Dr. Shlomo Barak

Dr. Barak was born and lives in Israel.

He holds a Ph.D. in Physics from the Hebrew University of Jerusalem.

He contributed to the defense of his country.

He contributed to technology and to the economy of his country.

His contribution to science is this collection of papers.

Taga Innovations   16 Beit Hillel St. Tel Aviv 67017 Israel

email: shlomo@tagapro.com

PREPRINTS, WORKING PAPERS, ...22 DOCUMENTS

Shlomo Barak. The Unification of Gravitation and Electromagnetism. 2020. ⟨hal-02616267⟩

Shlomo Barak. The QED Coupling Constant for an Electron to Emit or Absorb a Photon is Shown to be the Square Root of the Fine Structure Constant α. 2020. ⟨hal-02626064⟩

Shlomo Barak. On Bent Manifolds and Deformed Spaces. 2019. ⟨hal-01498435v3⟩

Shlomo Barak. On the Essence of Electric Charge: Part 2 How Charge Curves Space. 2019. ⟨hal-01402667v5⟩

Shlomo Barak. The Constancy of One-Way Light Velocity and the Possibility that Space is a Foamy Fluid. 2018. ⟨hal-01625000v2⟩

Shlomo Barak. The GeometroDynamic Model (CDM) of Reality in 80 THESES: A Realization of Einstein's Vision. 2018. ⟨hal-01524357v2⟩

Shlomo Barak. A GeometroDynamic Model (GDM) of Reality A Realization of Einstein's Vision. 2018. ⟨hal-01435685v4⟩

Shlomo Barak, Arie Zigler, Jenya Papeer. Isotropic One-Way Times of Flight of Laser Pulses and Einstein's "compressible fluid" Space. 2018. ⟨hal-01966893⟩

Shlomo Barak. A SPACETIME GEOMETRODYNAMIC MODEL (GDM) OF THE PHYSICAL REALITY. 2018. ⟨hal-01935260⟩

Shlomo Barak. Time is not Fundamental - unlike Distance and Velocity. 2017. ⟨hal-01502214⟩

Shlomo Barak. The GeometroDynamic Model (GDM) Versus String Theory (ST). 2017. ⟨hal-01524356⟩

Shlomo Barak. A Theoretical Derivation of the Milgrom MOND Equation. 2017. ⟨hal-01471151v4⟩

Shlomo Barak. On the Essence of Gravitation and Inertia Part 1: Inertia and Free Fall of an Elementary Particle. 2017. ⟨hal-01404143v7⟩

Shlomo Barak. Equations of Physics and Space Density. 2017. ⟨hal-01625004⟩

- Shlomo Barak. The Electron and the Quantum Enigma. 2017. ⟨hal-01631624⟩

- Shlomo Barak. Space as a Special Frame and Starlight Aberration. 2017. ⟨hal-01498454⟩

- Shlomo Barak. Electromagnetism as the Geometrodynamics of Space. 2017. ⟨hal-01498448⟩

- Shlomo Barak. The Graviton. 2017. ⟨hal-01524355⟩

- Shlomo Barak. On the Essence of Electric Charge Part 1: Charge as Deformed Space. 2016. ⟨hal-01401332⟩

- Shlomo Barak. On the Essence of Gravitation and Inertia Part 2: The Curving of Space by an Elementary Particle. 2016. ⟨hal-01405460⟩

- Shlomo Barak. Where is Anti-Matter?. 2016. ⟨hal-01423547⟩

- Shlomo Barak. The Photon and the Quantum Enigma. 2016. ⟨hal-0142

Printed in Germany
by Amazon Distribution
GmbH, Leipzig

21139271R00173